The Music of Harrison Birtwistle

Harrison Birtwistle has become the most eminent and acclaimed of contemporary British composers. This is the first book to provide a comprehensive view of his large and varied output. It contains descriptions of every published work, and also of a number of withdrawn and unpublished pieces. Revealing light is often cast on the more familiar pieces by considering these lesser-known areas of Birtwistle's œuvre.

The book is structured around a number of broad themes – themes of significance to Birtwistle, but also to much other music. These include theatre, song, time and texture. This approach emphasises the music's multifarious ways of meaning; now that even the academic world no longer takes the merits of 'difficult' contemporary music for granted, it is all the more important to assess what it represents beyond mere technical innovation. Dr Adlington thus avoids in-depth technical analysis, focusing instead upon the music's wider cultural significance.

Robert Adlington is a Lecturer in Music at the University of Nottingham.

Music in the Twentieth Century

GENERAL EDITOR Arnold Whittall

This series offers a wide perspective on music and musical life in the twentieth century.

Books included range from historical and biographical studies, concentrating particularly on the context and circumstances in which composers were writing, to analytical and critical studies concerned with the nature of musical language and questions of compositional process. The importance given to context will also be reflected in studies dealing with, for example, the patronage, publishing, and promotion of new music, and in accounts of the musical life of particular countries.

Some published titles

The Music of John Cage
James Pritchett
0 521 56544 8

The Music of Ruth Crawford Seeger
Joseph N. Straus
0 521 41646 9

The Music of Conlon Nancarrow
Kyle Gann
0 521 46534 6

The Stravinsky Legacy
Jonathan Cross
0 521 56365 8

Experimental Music: Cage and Beyond
Michael Nyman
0 521 65297 9 (hardback) 0 521 65383 5 (paperback)

The BBC and Ultra-Modern Music, 1922–1936
Jennifer Doctor
0 521 66117 x

Four Musical Minimalists: La Monte Young, Terry Riley, Steve Reich, Philip Glass
Keith Potter
0 521 48250 x

The Music of Harrison Birtwistle
Robert Adlington
0 521 63082 7

The Music of
Harrison Birtwistle

Robert Adlington

CAMBRIDGE
UNIVERSITY PRESS

PUBLISHED BY THE PRESS SYNDICATE OF THE UNIVERSITY OF CAMBRIDGE
The Pitt Building, Trumpington Street, Cambridge, United Kingdom

CAMBRIDGE UNIVERSITY PRESS
The Edinburgh Building, Cambridge CB2 2RU, UK   http://www.cup.cam.ac.uk
40 West 20th Street, New York, NY 10011–4211, USA   http://www.cup.org
10 Stamford Road, Oakleigh, Melbourne 3166, Australia

First published 2000

Printed in the United Kingdom at the University Press, Cambridge

Typeset in Adobe Minion 10.5/13.5 pt in QuarkXPress® [SE]

A catalogue record for this book is available from the British Library

Library of Congress cataloguing in publication data
Adlington, Robert.
The music of Harrison Birtwistle / Robert Adlington.
p.   cm. – (Music in the twentieth century)
Includes bibliographical references and index.
ISBN 0 521 63082 7 – (hardback)
1. Birtwistle, Harrison–Criticism and interpretation.   I. Title.
II. Series.
ML410.B605A35   2000
780′.92–DC21   00-22678   CIP

ISBN 0 521 63082 7 hardback

For Mum and Dad

Contents

Acknowledgements

This book has been improved and helped to completion by the assistance and suggestions of many people. Arnold Whittall has provided a number of insightful and constructive criticisms, for which I am very grateful. He will have saved me countless embarrassments (though maybe not as many as he would have wished). At Cambridge University Press Penny Souster has been a flexible and encouraging editor, and Jane Wheare identified numerous infelicities and inconsistencies in my text and offered elegant corrections. Rachel Woolley gave my draft text a degree of thorough attention I had no right to expect: the book is very much improved because of her meticulous, thoughtful and supportive advice. Elke Hockings and Miranda Jackson at Universal Edition (London) and David Allenby and Helen Bishop-Stephens at Boosey and Hawkes (London) have been unfailingly helpful in response to my numerous requests for scores, recordings and other materials. I would also like to extend my gratitude for advice and suggestions received from David Beard, David Bruce, Martin Butler; Matthew Greenall and all the staff at the British Music Information Centre in London; Tom Hall, Sam Hayden, Duncan Hunt, Julian Johnson, Alison Kay, Donna McKevitt, David Osmond-Smith; Jane Pritchard at the Rambert Dance Company in London; Brian Robison, Matthew Shorter, Phyllis Weliver and David York. I am particularly grateful to Tom Hall, who produced the music examples contained in this book. The School of Cultural and Community Studies at the University of Sussex generously provided funds for the production of these examples and for copyright costs. My thanks also to Harrison Birtwistle himself, for his permission to reproduce the first version of *Chorale from a Toy Shop* and part of the unpublished work *Signals*.

My work is indebted to two prominent published writers on Birtwistle's music, Michael Hall and Jonathan Cross – both of whom supervised earlier Birtwistle-related projects of mine. Each has recently published a further substantial work relating to Birtwistle. These volumes appeared at a very late stage in this book's development; I have endeavoured to incorporate some of their insights, but they have not received as much attention as they deserve.

Finally, I would like to acknowledge the influence that my students at the University of Sussex – particularly those in my seminar courses on

Birtwistle's *Secret Theatre*, and 'Classical Music and Society after 1945' – have had on my thinking about Birtwistle and contemporary music. Their preparedness to challenge my own certainties, and to offer plausible alternatives, remains a constant and invaluable source of stimulation.

I gratefully acknowledge the permission given by music publishers for the reproduction of extracts from Birtwistle's works, as follows:

Chorale from a Toy Shop: © Copyright 1972 by Universal Edition (London) Ltd., London. Reproduced by permission.

Deowa: © Copyright 1983 by Universal Edition (London) Ltd., London. Reproduced by permission.

Duets for Storab: © Copyright 1983 by Universal Edition (London) Ltd., London. Reproduced by permission.

Earth Dances: © Copyright Universal Edition (London) Ltd., 1985. Reproduced by permission.

Endless Parade: © Copyright 1987 by Universal Edition (London) Ltd., London. Reproduced by permission.

Entr'actes and Sappho Fragments: © Copyright 1965 by Universal Edition (London) Ltd., London. Reproduced by permission.

Epilogue: © Copyright 1979 by Universal Edition (London) Ltd., London. Reproduced by permission.

Four Poems by Jaan Kaplinski: © Copyright 1991 by Universal Edition (London) Ltd., London. Reproduced by permission.

The Mask of Orpheus: © Copyright 1986 by Universal Edition (London) Ltd., London. Reproduced by permission.

Monody for Corpus Christi: © Copyright 1961 by Universal Edition (London) Ltd., London. Reproduced by permission.

'Frieze 3' from Nine Movements for String Quartet: © Copyright 1996 by Boosey and Hawkes Music Publishers Ltd and Universal Edition (London) Ltd. Reprinted by permission of Boosey and Hawkes Music Publishers Ltd.

Panic: © Copyright 1995 by Boosey and Hawkes Music Publishers Ltd. Reprinted by permission of Boosey and Hawkes Music Publishers Ltd.

Pulse Sampler: © Copyright 1981 by Universal Edition (London) Ltd., London. Reproduced by permission.

Punch and Judy: © Copyright 1968 by Universal Edition (London) Ltd., London. Reproduced by permission.

Secret Theatre: © Copyright 1991 by Universal Edition (London) Ltd., London. Reproduced by permission.

Signals: © Copyright 1971 by Universal Edition (London) Ltd., London. Reproduced by permission.

Silbury Air: © Copyright 1979 by Universal Edition (London) Ltd., London. Reproduced by permission.

Slow Frieze: © Copyright 1996 by Boosey and Hawkes Music Publishers Ltd. Reprinted by permission of Boosey and Hawkes Music Publishers Ltd.

Songs by Myself: © Copyright 1986 by Universal Edition (London) Ltd., London. Reproduced by permission.

'Night' from Three Settings of Celan: © Copyright 1992 by Universal Edition (London) Ltd., London. Reproduced by permission.

Verses for Ensembles: © Copyright 1969 by Universal Edition (London) Ltd., London. Reproduced by permission.

White and Light: © Copyright 1989 by Universal Edition (London) Ltd., London. Reproduced by permission.

Words Overheard: © Copyright 1989 by Universal Edition (London) Ltd., London. Reproduced by permission.

The illustration from Paul Klee's *Notebooks: the Thinking Eye* (p. 179) is reproduced by kind permission of Schwabe & Co. AG, Verlag, Basel.

The original version of *Chorale from a Toy Shop* (p. 169), which originally appeared in *Tempo*, 81 (Summer 1967), is reproduced by kind permission of Malcolm McDonald.

Abbreviations and note on sources

The following abbreviations are used in this book:

HB   Michael Hall. *Harrison Birtwistle*. London: Robson Books, 1984.
HBRY   Michael Hall. *Harrison Birtwistle in Recent Years*. London: Robson
        Books, 1998.

Programme notes for which no date or other details are given are held by
Universal Edition, London.

Introduction

This book is intended to perform two functions. Firstly, it comprises a handbook to Birtwistle's music. It contains descriptions of every published work (as well as a number of withdrawn and unpublished ones), thereby giving a comprehensive view of Birtwistle's large output. Many of Birtwistle's works remain little known and little discussed. It is hoped that the student, concert-goer or record-buyer will be able to reach for this book, confident in the knowledge that it contains a succinct discussion of the piece they are interested in, however obscure. Of course, there are drawbacks to attempting such a comprehensive survey. Inevitably, particularly given the size of Birtwistle's œuvre (at the time of writing there are over ninety separate works), many works do not receive the detailed attention they deserve. Any number of Birtwistle's pieces would support lengthy studies in their own right – and in due course these more detailed studies will doubtless be written and published. However, the benefits of a complete survey are not simply felt by those seeking out the more unfamiliar corners of Birtwistle's music. A little-known work often casts revealing light on a better-known one, placing it in a fruitful context or emphasising aspects of it that have hitherto gone unremarked. In the following pages, shorter, less familiar works sometimes receive more attention than longer, better-known ones, precisely in order that such connections can be effectively established.

At the same time, this book reaches beyond the specifics of individual works. Its second main purpose is to adumbrate a number of broader themes – themes of significance to Birtwistle's music, and to contemporary classical music in general. These issues form the basis of the book's structure. Birtwistle's works are discussed not chronologically but according to a number of distinct topics (though within each chapter there remains a broad progress from early works to late). In part this approach is determined by the refusal of Birtwistle's output to follow a single, smooth evolutionary path: successive works often present the most disconcerting juxtapositions. But it is also intended to emphasise the music's multifarious ways of meaning – the ways in which it establishes a handle on things outside itself, negotiating a position for itself in a wider culture. In a sense, each of the following chapters comprises an essay in what is sometimes called 'hermeneutic criticism'. Nicholas Cook says about this type of writing on music that it 'consists of developing illuminating metaphors for particular compositions; such metaphors don't just represent something that you have already experienced, but lead you to experience the music differently. (In other words, they don't just reflect but change the way things are.)'[1]

In the case of the particular subject of this book, this sort of metaphorical, hermeneutic approach is more than simply an indulgence on the part of the author. It reflects an awareness that contemporary classical music guarantees itself increasing isolation and distrust so long as its discussion remains confined to questions of technique and internal structure. In an era where even the academic world, increasingly, no longer takes the merits of contemporary classical music for granted (recent influential scholarly writing blames musical modernism for everything from the perpetuation of sexual discrimination in musicology[2] to the death of classical music itself[3]), it becomes all the more important to assess what it represents beyond mere technical innovation; to assess how it communicates – or, not infrequently, resists communication. Sometimes this approach demands pointing up the disparity between what the music does and what the composer thinks it is doing: my discussion is mindful of Birtwistle's own views about his music, but it feels no overriding obligation to them.

My discussion also keeps in mind the controversy that has surrounded Birtwistle and his music in recent years. In the public sphere, the premiere of *Panic* at the 1995 Last Night of the Proms met with an unprecedentedly vehement public and press reception. It brought to a head the wider public notoriety that Birtwistle had gained during the revival of *Gawain* eighteen months earlier, when a posse of young, 'anti-modernist' composers mounted a campaign against the performances, and attracted a good deal of press attention in so doing. Such disapproval was not limited to enthusiasts of the Last Night and a handful of self-publicists, however, but increasingly extended into academia itself – one of the very arenas that was once accused of self-interestedly upholding the claims of avant-garde music. In recent years, academic music study has undergone a remarkable broadening to include a number of previously marginalised areas, including non-classical musics and cultural studies. This broadening has been accompanied by a growing suspicion of 'difficult' contemporary classical music, increasingly anomalous as its premises seem within the context of other contemporary musics and cultural traditions. The very public premiere of *Panic* ensured that, in Britain at least, Birtwistle came to be seen as the principal representative of musical modernism. In an introductory book about thinking about music, therefore, Nicholas Cook talked of Birtwistle's 'treatment of listeners with something bordering on contempt',[4] and Dai Griffiths asserted, in a long article in the journal *Music Analysis*, that it was time that music analysts 'at least toyed with the notion that, say, Beck's "Devil's Haircut" is in some ways a truer and more rounded thing than the last BBC "Prom" commission of Harrison Birtwistle'.[5] That such views are representative of wider trends in academia is evinced by the paragraph of recommendation that appears on the back of Cook's book, by the distinguished American musicologist Richard Taruskin: 'This book is bound to please Sir Elton more than it will Sir Harrison; but, love it or hate it, that is the direction academic music studies are taking.'[6]

The following account of Birtwistle's music does not enter into this debate directly, although some indication as to the direction a useful counter-argument might take is given in the final chapter, which looks more specifically at Birtwistle's relation to his audiences. Instead, the frame of reference for the larger discussions in this book is principally that of the 'high culture' within which Birtwistle's music largely positions itself. So, recognition is given both to the kinship that Birtwistle's music has with the music of other twentieth-century composers, including Stravinsky, Carter, Varèse, Webern and Messiaen, and to the sustenance it receives from the other fine arts – painting, poetry, literature and theatre. Greek theatre, for instance, figures largely in the first two chapters; Chapter 3 examines, amongst other things, the degree to which Birtwistle has adopted or eschewed the innovative text-setting methods of other contemporary classical composers; and the 'classic modernism' of Igor Stravinsky and Paul Klee provides the backdrop for large parts of Chapters 5 and 6 respectively. My discussion is underpinned, however, not so much by an unswerving confidence in the merits of Birtwistle's engagement with such artistic traditions, as by an awareness of the larger cultural context within which that engagement takes place. This perspective brings into the open some of the implications of Birtwistle's practices as they might be perceived from outside the culture within which he is largely working; it thus gives a measure of recognition to the partiality of that culture's values – the element of *contestability* – that motivates Birtwistle's critics. Instances where this perspective is particularly evident are my discussions of the violent and 'ritualistic' aspects of Birtwistle's theatre pieces, and of his treatment of the voice in his songs. Happily, this wider context also occasionally intervenes to suggest ways in which Birtwistle's music, for all its alleged 'exclusivity', fruitfully intersects with more widely appreciated cultural phenomena. For instance, as I suggest in Chapter 5, its verse structures provide a basis for a closer comparison with pop song than is usually recognised. A willingness to reach out beyond the usual frame of reference was an exemplary characteristic of Michael Nyman's critical writings on

Birtwistle in the late 1960s and early 1970s. His insistence upon, rather than avoidance of, the comparison between Birtwistle's modernism and contemporary developments in pop and American experimental music produced criticism of great trenchancy and balance. Such boldness has been too little evident in more recent writings on contemporary classical music.

A definite advantage of the thematic, 'hermeneutic' approach taken in this book is that it takes the emphasis off in-depth technical analysis. This is not to imply that such analysis is in itself a bad thing, but it does undoubtedly limit the wider usefulness of a discussion. The following chapters contain technical observations, of course, but anyone hoping for a comprehensive dissection of musical structure or Birtwistle's methods of working should look elsewhere (and increasingly there are places to look, a fact I have attempted to recognise in my notes). Score references, in the form of bar numbers or rehearsal numbers (the latter contained within square brackets), are included wherever they may be useful, but by and large access to scores is not essential to following the discussion. Additionally, my discussion traces an overall progression from topics requiring relatively little attention to structural detail ('Theatres', 'Roles') to those where it is much more germane ('Sections', 'Layers').

In order to make it easier to locate discussions of individual works, I have mostly restricted assessments of each piece to a single place in the book. This has necessitated difficult decisions about which aspects of each piece to bring into consideration, and which to leave unassessed. In the case of a small number of pieces (including *Refrains and Choruses*, *Verses for Ensembles* and *Secret Theatre*) this general rule has been relaxed in order to allow their full importance better to emerge. Needless to say, this procedure does not preclude passing references to pieces of relevance to an ongoing discussion. The 'Index of works' indicates the main discussion of each piece in bold print. Conversely, the reader who chooses to follow the discussion through the course of a whole chapter can get a more precise idea of the chronological picture from the numbers following the titles of each work at every sub-heading. These refer to the 'Chronological list of works' included at the back of the book.

1 Theatres

Nicholas Snowman has observed that, 'For some composers, creating opera or music-theatre somehow requires a different, separate compositional process from the rest of their output. Harrison Birtwistle, however, like Hector Berlioz and the young Stravinsky, is a composer whose work in whatever form is "theatrical".'[1] Snowman thus encapsulates a widely held view about Harrison Birtwistle's music: namely, that theatre is central to all of it, not just that of 'the stage'.[2] This interest in theatre is manifested in a compositional output that, alongside several large-scale operas and music theatre-pieces, includes numerous vocal and instrumental works whose titles and compositional premises allude to theatre and the theatrical. It is also reflected in positions of employment Birtwistle has held over the years. The best known of these is his period as musical director at London's National Theatre from 1975 to 1983, during which time he provided music for numerous stage productions (Michael Hall lists twelve in all[3]). He also worked at this time with the National Theatre Studio, an arena for experimental theatre and the development of the skills of the National Theatre company. Yet over a decade before he joined the National Theatre – even before his first opera *Punch and Judy* – Birtwistle was meeting the demand for theatre pieces for children, at the schools where he taught music.[4] The most visible products of this experience were two published works, *The Mark of the Goat* and *The Visions of Francesco Petrarca*, which anticipate the later, better-known stage works in intriguing ways. In the period between these posts of employment, Birtwistle also wrote the score to a film, Sidney Lumet's *The Offence*. The urge to engage with drama is clearly part of his compositional make-up.

The importance of theatre to Birtwistle's music is commonly recognised, but the connection is often made in a rather generalised way, which sometimes does little to elucidate the particular concerns of individual pieces. Of course, it is not hard to see how 'theatre' might become a rather indiscriminately applied interpretative tool. Birtwistle's music is often forbiddingly abstract and resistant to easy analysis, and the idea that it is all 'essentially theatrical' is likely to be gratefully accepted by critics struggling to find some way of making new works explicable. Additionally, Birtwistle's recurrent dramatic obsessions in the stage works suggest a reassuring consistency of approach across many years.[5] Myth and legend loom large, as do traditional or folk tales; and numerous more incidental narrative devices have acquired the status of persistent idées fixes: battles, decapitation, resurrection, nightmares, riddles, journeying, the seasons, numbers and counting, even colours, all recur in two or more of the stage works. This encourages the impression that a certain sort of theatricality is an intrinsic and unchanging feature of Birtwistle's musical idiom.

Such a view underestimates both the diversity of Birtwistle's 'theatres', and the sometimes troublesome implications, and contradictions with other aspects of Birtwistle's compositional preoccupations, to which they give rise. It is these things, as much as the consistent and familiar features, that the present chapter seeks to highlight. The first section focuses upon the violent subject-matters of Birtwistle's stage works, and the widespread impression that Birtwistle's music in general has a violent cast. The second section turns to myth, and the way in which different types of narration inflect the story being told. Birtwistle's fluctuating attitudes to the relationship of music and drama, and to their status as discrete categories, form the principal topic of the third section. And the competing tug and pull of 'narrative' and 'ritualistic' tendencies is examined at the end of the chapter. Successive sections each examine one or more of the stage works, progressing roughly chronologically through Birtwistle's output; the idea, though, is to explore themes that have resonances throughout Birtwistle's music, be it for theatre or concert hall, voice or instrument.

Violence

Punch and Judy (18)

A paradox presents itself when any composer working in an avant-garde idiom decides to combine music with some form of dramatic representation. On the one hand, post-war avant-garde musical idioms are defined in part by their refusal of conventionalised symbolic codes, a refusal that comes of the attempt to render music a purely formalist mode of articulation, expressing nothing beyond itself. On the other, it is precisely those symbolic codes that have traditionally governed the combination of music and drama, whereby certain musical configurations connote states of mind or characteristics of action or situation. The result, in the immediate post-war years, was that 'few young composers wanted to work in the theatre';[6] music and words were combined, if at all, in song rather than opera, where there was greater precedent for an indirect relationship between them.

Birtwistle's musical idiom was profoundly influenced by the European post-war avant-garde, and that he shares some of their ambivalence about the possibility of dramatic expression is clear from these comments in an interview with Paul Griffiths:

> [PG:] *You've said that when you're composing you're concerned with the structure and not with what it's . . .*
>
> [HB:] . . . saying. No, because I can't control that, can I? I don't see how one can.
>
> *But when you're writing incidental music it must be required that you know what it's saying?*
>
> Yes, that's a different activity.
>
> *But there must be something of that too in opera?*
>
> Yes, but I've got a feeling that my operatic efforts are in some degree on the side. They're occasional pieces.[7]

Birtwistle here appears to be suggesting that the need to admit an element of conventionalised musical signification in the stage works renders them marginal – tangential to his main compositional pursuits. It is not difficult to find such moments of conventional expressivity in Birtwistle's stage works: the exquisite lyricism of Judy's 'Passion Aria' in *Punch and Judy* or Lady de Hautdesert's 'Lullaby' in Act II of *Gawain*; the slapstick comedy of Madame Lena's sphinx in *The Second Mrs Kong*'s second act; the desolation of Orpheus' suicide at the end of Act II of *The Mask of Orpheus*. One is bound to balk at the idea that it is moments such as these, with their powerful dramatic impact, that render the operas 'occasional pieces' in Birtwistle's eyes. His comment was doubtless unpremeditated and perhaps should not be treated too literally. Nevertheless, his embarrassment must be taken on board too, for it is indicative of a paradox that touches all the stage works. The music appears to be charged with the conventional responsibility of reflecting the drama, yet elements of the musical idiom strongly resist a representational function.

This is not to say that avant-garde musical idioms are completely devoid of expressive potential. On the contrary, the very *refusal* to communicate by conventional means is itself highly expressive. Avant-garde music is widely perceived not in terms of abstract structure but as a hostile and aggressive statement. At least, that is the impression that tends to be given to anyone who has not made a special study of the music. Here, then, is a basis for reconciling avant-garde music and dramatic representation, and it is one that Birtwistle appears to have capitalised upon. Murder, infanticide, suicide and bodily violence feature prominently in the scenarios of the stage works, and they seem all too well suited to a musical idiom 'associated with violence rather than nuance', one that has been described as 'uncompromisingly aggressive'.[8] The predilection for violent subject-matters is evident as early as *The Visions of Francesco Petrarca*, a theatre piece for children written in 1965. This work sets a succession of Petrarch sonnets, each of which 'describes an incident in which something beautiful . . . is savagely destroyed'.[9] However, it is *Punch and Judy*, completed two years later, that has become the bench-mark for this aspect of Birtwistle's music. *Punch and Judy* establishes a pattern of ritualised violence that resurfaces both in later stage works and in the purely instrumental music.

Punch and Judy is unsparing in its aggression. It utilises a traditional children's entertainment renowned for its sadistic violence, reworked, in the words of the librettist Stephen Pruslin, 'to enable an audience of adults to re-experience the vividness of their childhood reactions'.[10] In addition, trappings of another historical dramatic form to privilege violent confrontation, namely ancient Greek tragedy, are grafted onto the traditional Punch story. The character of Choregos, for instance, who acts in *Punch and Judy* as a sort of master of ceremonies and 'one-man chorus',[11] takes his name from the trainer of the chorus in the ancient Greek theatre. And the overtly Greek-inspired *Tragoedia*, which is loosely based on Aristotle's description of classical tragedy, was, according to Birtwistle, written as 'a preliminary study' for the opera.[12] Its musical material and overall structure are both reflected in *Punch*.[13] The 'strong misogynistic strain'[14] of Greek tragedy also finds a resonance in Birtwistle's opera. Punch's first ceremonial victim is his wife, whose death is the most vicious and prolonged of the whole opera; Punch's murderous spree from this point becomes a specifically masculine adventure, motivated by his rampant desire to win Pretty Polly. It is not surprising, in the face of all this, that one writer was moved to describe *Punch and Judy* as, itself, essentially 'ancient Greek drama in the guise of popular puppetry'.[15]

Birtwistle's music after *Punch* retained many of the same qualities of great rhythmic trenchancy, formal abruptness and dynamic and registral extremes, and it was therefore perhaps inevitable that it would acquire a wider reputation for violence, even in the absence of subject-matter that makes it explicit. Commentators now routinely laud this quality as a quintessential feature of Birtwistle's style. But there is of course a danger that music that evokes violence ends up celebrating it. (This fear lay behind much of Adorno's criticism of Stravinsky, whose music 'does not identify with the victim, but rather with the destructive element'.[16]) *Punch and Judy* can only strengthen this suspicion. It depicts its brutalities voyeuristically, each of Punch's killings being ceremonially conducted on an 'Altar of Murder' – in sharp contrast, incidentally, to Greek tragedy where acts of violence never occur on stage.[17] Far from 'saying' nothing, then,

Birtwistle's music is vulnerable to charges that it is whole-heartedly expressive of brutal aggression.

Birtwistle has in the past appeared uncertain as to whether his music is intrinsically violent. In an interview with Norman Lebrecht, he contradicts himself:

> [NL:] *The roughness [of the sound] can come over as violence?*
> [HB:] In my music? No, I don't think it's violent. It's to do with the nature of the material. The music I write needs a physical presence. Something like Xenakis's music can only exist because it's loud. It speaks through four *ffff*s. With my material it might come over superficially as violent, but I don't feel I'm expressing anything. [*Pause*] I could contradict that. Maybe it is violent, I don't know.[18]

Birtwistle seems, here, to be reluctant entirely to distance his musical idiom from the expression of violence. His principal concern, however, appears to be with the nature of his material, rather than any expressive function. The painter Francis Bacon, for whose works and ideas Birtwistle has in recent years expressed great admiration,[19] provides an interesting parallel. Bacon similarly denied that the distorted imagery of his paintings was expressive of violence, claiming that, 'I don't even know what half of them mean. I'm not saying anything'.[20] However, he believed that the ordered imagery of his paintings could be understood to be violent in a less literal way:

> [Great art] comes out of a desire for ordering and for returning fact onto the nervous system in a more violent way . . . When talking about the violence of paint, it's nothing to do with the violence of war. It's to do with an attempt to remake the violence of reality itself. And the violence of reality is not only the simple violence meant when you say that a rose or something is violent, but it's the violence also of the suggestions within the image itself which can only be conveyed through paint.[21]

Bacon is interested, then, in a form of communication whose 'violence' lies not in some represented content but in its insistence upon a realignment of viewer and reality. This can only be achieved by forcefully asserting the specific qualities of the medium itself – in Bacon's case paint, in Birtwistle's sound – independently of the symbolic modes of comprehension that usually contain and restrict them. The viewer or listener needs to be shaken out of habitual forms of comprehension, rendered vulnerable to the raw sensuous stimuli of the artistic medium. This is possible only by extreme methods. Such an interpretation – acknowledging the possibility of a form of communication where coercion, far from representing an extolling of the virtues of physical violence, is intended to shake us from a restrictive and containing state – provides a possible counter-argument to more dogmatically literal readings of this aspect of Birtwistle's idiom.

It does not explain away the specific, troubling subject-matters of the stage works, however – least of all that of *Punch and Judy*. Nor does the justification that Aristotle provided for the violent cast of Greek tragedy; namely, that it arouses fear and pity which have the effect of an emotional 'catharsis' – that is to say, 'a powerful release of emotion which has a salutary effect on our emotional (and hence our ethical) disposition'.[22] That the unpleasantness of *Punch* cannot claim this specifically 'tragic' legitimation is indicated, firstly, by its ambivalent subtitle, which describes the work not as a tragedy, but as 'a tragical comedy or a comical tragedy'.[23] And the various elements that appear to align *Punch and Judy* with classical tragedy are, on closer acquaintance, used in a way that undermines a simple connection. The figure of Choregos, for instance, corresponds to no one element of Greek tragedy. In the dramatic festivals of ancient Greece, the *choregos* was 'a wealthy citizen who volunteered, or was co-opted, to pay for the Chorus and for most other features of the production'.[24] He had particular responsibility for management and training of the chorus, but there is no evidence that the *choregos* himself participated in the drama: his role was more analogous to that of the modern director.[25] In *Punch*, the character of Choregos reflects this original function in something of a dual role. He is treated partly as a chorus-substitute, reflecting aloud on the drama's events; but more strongly evident is the sense that he is in charge of the overall production. This latter function – Choregos as 'master of ceremonies' – makes reference not only to the Greek *choregos*, but also to diverse operatic forebears, ranging from the character of Music in the Prologue to Monteverdi's *Orfeo* (Choregos himself has been interpreted as 'representing music itself'[26]), to the Reader and Speaker in, respectively, Stravinsky's *Histoire du soldat* and *Oedipus Rex*. Unlike these antecedents, however, Choregos fails to maintain an appropriate dramatic distance, and in a surrealist twist the puppet-master himself becomes victim – twice – to Punch's murderous inclinations.

The relationship of *Tragœdia* to *Punch* is also not as direct as is sometimes thought. The loose correspondences between their overall formal shapes, and their shared, theatrical opposition of groups of instruments,[27] cannot be disputed. Birtwistle's own comment, however, that the music of *Tragœdia* 'appears practically note for note in my opera *Punch and Judy*'[28] is, at the very least, misleading. Gordon Crosse was nearer the mark when, reviewing the first performance, he found that 'very little of the earlier score has in fact been used in the opera: technical parallels are legion but the notes seem different'.[29] Moreover, the tone of the music seemed to have altered: 'It was fascinating to find that what one had naively felt as primitive, harsh "Greek tragedy" in *Tragœdia* becomes transmuted into comedy under the influence of the subject.'[30]

In his *Poetics* Aristotle drew a clear distinction between tragedy and comedy, asserting succinctly that 'comedy aims at representing men as worse than they are nowadays, tragedy as better'.[31] Under this definition the traditional Punch and Judy story, with all its unredeemed amorality, unquestionably comprises comedy. Birtwistle's music responds to this in important respects, resembling Greek comedy as much as Greek tragedy. Comic poets in ancient Greece were, according to Andrew Brown, 'much less concerned than tragedians with coherence and consistency of plot, and several of Aristophanes' plays degenerate by the end into a series of slapstick routines'.[32] Birtwistle's music, likewise, is exceedingly sectional and adopts a variety of guises. Michael Nyman identifies three alternating idioms, corresponding respectively to the violent, the lyrical and the banal.[33] The first expressive mode appears objective, purely descriptive of the violent proceedings. The second and third, on the other hand, go further in assessing the various characters. The lyrical moments – and there are many – attribute them with a degree of moral substance; crucially, though, they are as often given to the perpetrator (in Punch's lamenting 'Morals', for instance) as to the victims (Judy's beautiful 'Passion Aria II' being a prominent example). This is consistent with the morally neutral stance that prevails throughout the work.[34] The banal, nursery rhyme style has the opposite effect, stressing the characters' (and especially Punch's) mindless sadism. In addition to the alternation of these diverse idioms, Birtwistle fashions many of the opera's numbers into mini-exercises parodying historical styles or forms (a strategy that itself is ironically referential to Berg's *Wozzeck*[35]). *Punch and Judy* includes imitations of plainsong (b. 1068), Webern (b. 313), and Stravinsky (b. 383); and a carefully assembled canonic prelude (b. 925), sinfonia (b. 594), and gigue (b. 354). The resulting score comes close at times to a succession of comedy turns.

It is not just the stylistic diversity of the music of *Punch and Judy* that gives it its distinctive, 'comic' tone, but also its compulsive short-windedness. The opera comprises over a hundred short sections, clearly identified in the score and mostly separated by silence or a marked musical discontinuity. For all that *Punch and Judy* was conceived as 'an opera about opera . . . the collective generalization of known operas into a "source-opera" which, though written after them, would give the illusion of having been written before them',[36] the work remains innocent of the larger continuities central to operatic tragedy from the middle of the nineteenth century to well into the twentieth. It even forsakes earlier opera's principal agency of continuity: namely, recitative. Only a single, short section is actually called 'Recitative' (preceding Judy's Passion Aria at b. 187); all the other sections of the piece are more readily seen as arias, ensembles or choruses. So Michael Nyman's description of the work as 'the number opera *par excellence*'[37] is correct in the fullest sense: it comprises *nothing but* 'number'.

This denial of the musical continuity essential to operatic 'realism' is entirely in keeping with Pruslin's highly stylised text (although it is an element of the work undermined when productions fail to achieve a comparable artificiality, a failure that Birtwistle has commented upon on a number of occasions[38]). It also perhaps contributes to a certain undifferentiatedness of succession, in that the work's various numbers are never set in relief by the contrasting delivery of recitative.[39] Most significantly, though, the omission of recitative represents a further diminishing of the work's 'tragic' component, for it dismantles the conventional operatic parallel to classical tragedy's opposition of choral song (aria) and dramatic speech (recitative).[40] In Birtwistle's later stage works the contrasting functions of aria and recitative play a greater role, as will be seen in the next part of this chapter. In *Punch and Judy* the absence of recitative only emphasises the extent to which this is indeed a 'toy opera'.[41] The 'characters' – puppets, after all – in being denied recitative are thereby largely denied opportunities for character development or the exercising of volition. Instead they are deployed in a succession of static situations, just as a child deploys toys in play. The motivation for the deployment is not apparent to the toys, but exists only in the child's imagination. Their violent interactions, similarly, are best seen not as representative of some potentially cathartic, archetypal conflict, but as reflective of the more quotidian brutality of motiveless, childlike play.

Myth

The Mark of the Goat (16) • *The Visions of Francesco Petrarca* (17) •
Down by the Greenwood Side (27) • *The Mask of Orpheus* (60)

Puppets are again a prominent feature in *The Mask of Orpheus*. In the later work, though, actual puppets are used, rather than singers pretending to be puppets: their 'voices' are sung from a different part of the stage by singers not directly involved in the dramatic representation. And the puppets account for only one layer of the work's complex, multi-layered theatre, appearing alongside mimes and singing actors. In these as in many other respects, this massive 'lyric tragedy' (as the librettist Peter Zinovieff calls it) is considerably removed from the earlier work, with its relatively simple methods of representation and shrill high spirits.

Still, the title of *The Mask of Orpheus* hints at a broader, if more subtle, kinship. Masks were an important element of the original productions of Greek tragedy, worn by both actors and chorus. And such masked enactment gives all participants something of the depersonalised artificiality of the puppet. Zinovieff's libretto requests that all the singers should be masked, and the resulting stylisation is central to *The Mask of Orpheus* – as it was in a different way to *Punch and Judy*. As Birtwistle has commented, 'A mask allows you to be still . . . It's a move towards stillness, a move towards stylisation. As a piece, *The Mask of Orpheus* is totally non-naturalistic.'[42] Birtwistle's thinking may have been influenced in this respect by the experience of collaborating with the director Peter Hall and the playwright Tony Harrison on the National Theatre production of *The Oresteia*. For Harrison, masks are no mere historical convention but are intrinsic to tragedy:

> A Greek theatrical mask is part of the existential survival gear. It gives the bearing of survival to the actor wearing it. It represents a commitment to seeing everything through the eyes that never close. It represents a commitment to going on speaking when the always open eyes have witnessed something unspeakable. The masks must witness the unendurable. That is why they are created with their eyes open. The mouth must continue to speak in situations where the human being would be speechless or screaming and unable to articulate its agony.[43]

Masks act as a counterbalance to the size of the emotions expressed in tragedy; as Peter Hall says about these plays, 'They are so violent, hysterical, horrific, they could not be expressed without masks'.[44] The masks used in the *Oresteia* production, designed by Jocelyn Herbert, reflected these dramatic imperatives, and Herbert used similar designs for the first performances of *The Mask of Orpheus*. Where *Punch and Judy*'s puppets are oblivious to the atrocities to which they are submitted, the characters in *The Mask of Orpheus* must experience the full horror of their terrible fates.

For Birtwistle, however, the attraction of masks lies as much in their emphasis of the artificiality of theatre as in their reflection of the violence of tragedy. In this connection, the title of *The Mask of Orpheus* has a double meaning, referring not just to the facial visor of ancient Greek theatre but also to the more recent theatrical genre of masque.[45] Masque flourished in the courts of sixteenth- and early seventeenth-century Europe, and it put little emphasis on drama; instead, 'the main interest centred on the costumes, scenery, songs and dances . . . [The masque] has practically no story, no action, no crisis, and no inevitable ending'.[46] It is the *technique* of theatre that is brought to the fore in the masque; and it is this technique that is also foregrounded not just in *The Mask of Orpheus*, with its multi-layered story-telling and complex musical paraphernalia,[47] but in Birtwistle's stage works generally. In the earlier stage works, this focus on technique was manifested in the desire to dismantle any illusion of realism, to create a wholly artificial impression. This artificiality could be achieved by highly stylised costumes and acting styles, as in *Down by the Greenwood Side*, or by the almost total absence of prop, costume or any other form of stage-wizardry, as in the austere *Bow Down*. In either case, the aim was to adhere to a basic principle of post-war music theatre, namely 'the disintegration of the stage illusion'.[48] Accordingly, while the size and scale of *The Mask of Orpheus* are suggestive of grand opera, Birtwistle prefers to call it, too, 'a piece of music theatre'.[49] More recently, however, Birtwistle's interest has perceptibly shifted away from this focus on artificiality, back to the more traditional deployment of theatrical device in order to create and sustain believable stage illusions. *Gawain* presents fabulous challenges to any producer in this respect, requiring a stage horse for the Green Knight's appearance in Act I (clip-clops are written into the music), and setting such store by a realistic beheading that a large verbatim repeat is included in the score to allow it to be achieved. *The Second Mrs Kong* provides further evidence of the importance of theatrical presentation, for the director and designer Tom Cairns was closely involved in the work's very conception.[50] In this work, in the eyes of one commentator, 'the spectacle had been largely anticipated in the score'.[51]

The means of theatrical representation are not just an important element of *The Mask of Orpheus*, though: they are its central theme. As early as 1969, shortly after Birtwistle first received a commission from Peter Hall to write an opera for Covent Garden,[52] he was planning a work that, according to Michael Nyman, 'would play up the "discrepancy" between action and the description of action'.[53] In the work finally completed fourteen years later, it is indeed 'the telling rather than the tale which is the principal focus'.[54] Birtwistle's decision to draw upon Greek mythology for his subject-matter is, therefore, rather more than a naïve concession to an operatic tradition that stretches back through Stravinsky to Wagner and Monteverdi. In myth, tale and telling are inextricably inter-mingled, the existence of many distinct variants of mythic tales reminding us that none can be assumed faithful to the actual course of events. Birtwistle turns to myth, not, as in the case of both the Greek tragedians and many earlier composers, to invoke eternal certainties or verities – 'paradigms of human fortunes', as it were[55] – but rather to emphasise a fact about any form of narrative representation: namely, that the story can never be separated from the way it is told.

The Mask of Orpheus conducts a thorough exploration of this assertion. It incorporates a number of different versions of the Orpheus myth, and employs a variety of different ways of relating them. In so doing, it draws on elements of earlier works. In *Down by the Greenwood Side*, the traditional ballad of the Cruel Mother appears three times in slightly different forms, filmically interspersed between episodes of the traditional mummers' play. A similar examination of variants of a traditional ballad forms the basis for *Bow Down* (though this work was written well after the conception of *The Mask of Orpheus*). More unexpected, perhaps, are parallels with the two early theatre pieces for children, *The Mark of the Goat* and *The Visions of Francesco Petrarca*. Each of these anticipates *The Mask of Orpheus*' use of different modes of dramatic presentation – singing, mime, and puppetry – in its retelling of events. These early works raise the startling possibility that what appears as a highly sophisticated dramatic device in *The Mask of Orpheus* had its origins in the more pragmatic requirement to provide sufficiently varied roles for school children of different talents and abilities. In *The Mark of the Goat*, for instance, the story (a grim tale of individuals' defiance in the face of state oppression) 'is presented at two levels: first, the narrative which is told for the most part in rather stylised speech, and second, the actual drama, which is also stylised, and is enacted in both speech and music'.[56] *The Visions of Francesco Petrarca*, now withdrawn by the composer, similarly presents a 'polarity between a "musical-verbal" and a "dramatic" presentation of the same set of images . . . presenting [first] musical-verbal content and then actually embodying this content in mimed action'.[57] The final section of the work eventually combines sung and mimed versions of the story.

In effect, *The Mask of Orpheus* combines all these earlier devices. The various concurrent modes of presentation found in the pieces for children now relate not a single story line but, after the manner of *Down by the Greenwood Side*, different variants. The result is a multi-layered dramatic structure of great complexity where a number of different things may be going on at any one time. These are articulated on stage by multiple representations of the three main characters. Each of the principal roles of Orpheus, Euridice and Aristaeus appears as a singer, a mime and a puppet. These different impersonations sometimes inhabit separate acting areas on the stage. They may relate variants of the Orpheus myth in parallel, as in the second scene of Act I, where Euridice is shown both to reject Aristaeus' advances and to succumb to them (by Euridice Singer and Euridice Mime respectively). But they may also combine events drawn from *different parts* of the story. For instance, the start of Orpheus Singer's journey to the underworld is accompanied by a further representation of Euridice's death, this time by Euridice Puppet. 'Time Shifts' and 'Echoes' are introduced into the libretto to allow such juxtapositions, and freezes and interruptions further disrupt the narrative sequence. These complexities are introduced gradually during Act I: in the first scene, according to Zinovieff, 'the dissociation of words from the music and both from the action is established' and 'duality of roles is hinted at by the offstage voices of Orpheus Puppet and Euridice Puppet'; the second scene sees the introduction of 'simple synchrony: similar events happening at the same time' and 'duality of visible roles'; and Scene III 'introduces complex simultaneity (contrasted events seen at the same time)' and time distortion.[58]

The story-telling as a whole is rendered extremely artificial by formal structuring at both the local and large scales. As in *Punch and Judy* the action is partitioned into over a hundred tiny self-contained units, which Zinovieff describes as 'one long set of poems'.[59] The poems are organised into groups of three, reflecting the prevailing tripartitions of 'the Orphic symbological method',[60] although, in contrast to the literal symmetries of Pruslin's libretto to *Punch*, the connection between the three poems of a group is not always apparent. More prominent are the 'gross structures' of each Act.[61] These are based on the central events of the myth: in Act I, Euridice's wedding and funeral; in Act II, Orpheus' journey; in Act III, the sacrifice of Orpheus. The magnification of these events to span whole Acts gives the larger-scale narrative a stylised, statuesque quality.

An extra layer of complexity is provided by six brief, self-contained episodes depicting stories from Book X of Ovid's *Metamorphoses*. These interrupt the main drama at unexpected moments, occurring mid-scene rather than at the end or beginning. Zinovieff calls the three more violent episodes 'Passing Clouds of Abandon' and the three lyrical ones 'Allegorical Flowers of Reason', and they are inserted at moments of low and high tension respectively, so further emphasising their narrative incongruity. Once again, *Down by the Greenwood Side* represents something of a prototype for *The Mask of Orpheus* in this respect. This work, which is subtitled 'a dramatic pastoral', involves a soprano, four actors, a mime and a nine-instrument band based on that used for the Cornish Floral Dance.[62] It interleaves the pantomime of the traditional mummers' play, which tells of the death and restoration to life of St George as an allegory for the passing of the year, with the tragedy of the Cruel Mother, who felt compelled to kill her illegitimate children. Rather than emphasise their common concern with matters of death and rebirth the two stories are left to 'grate against each other in uneasy co-existence'.[63] Michael Nyman, the librettist for *Down by the Greenwood Side*, says that this brusque juxtaposition 'was suggested to me by a Rumanian peasant ikon I have in which Virgin and Child and St George and the Dragon are placed side by side, seemingly nonsensically, out of proportion with each other and in two different planes'.[64] The jolt between the two stories is heightened by the contrast between their musical settings, the Cruel Mother's ballads being entirely sung while the mummers' play is spoken to an instrumental accompaniment. A similarly contrasted treatment is given to the Clouds and Flowers in *The Mask of Orpheus*, their silent mime and wholly electronic music setting them apart from the vocal and instrumental storytelling that surrounds them. The narrative simplicity of the Clouds and Flowers also makes for a contrast with the multi-layered account of the Orpheus myth, just as the banal linearity of the mummers' play contrasts with the subtly altered perspectives of the different ballads of the Cruel Mother.

The fascination with variants – variants of stories, variants of ways of telling – may be understood as a manifestation of Birtwistle's obsession with complexity, and more specifically the idea of the complex multi-dimensional object, to be perceived from a number of different perspectives but never grasped in its totality. This obsession finds many forms of expression in Birtwistle's music, from the generation of material at the note-to-note level to issues of large-scale structure.[65] In *The Mask of Orpheus* it manifests itself most obviously in the fact that 'the audience is given the opportunity of witnessing the same event from a number of perspectives not only in sequence but also simultaneously'.[66] This aspect of the work led David Freeman to refer to it as 'cubist theatre'. But *The Mask of Orpheus* goes beyond the mere celebration of complexity. It not only places a number of different types of theatrical representation in juxtaposition but additionally sets out to analyse the different ways in which each of them signify. Song, mime or puppetry cannot be treated as equivalent forms of dramatic presentation, for each carries its own representational burden which unavoidably taints the 'content' it conveys. Zinovieff's libretto specifically identifies the singing personification of each of the three main characters with their human form, the mime with their heroic form and the puppet with their mythic or god-like form,[67] and these allocations are not a matter of accident. Of the three different personifications the singer is the only one to retain his or her *own* voice: song thus becomes representative of speech, thought and emotion, recognisably *human* qualities that are denied to the mime and the puppet. The mime is confined to the movement of the body. Such movement can be used to express feelings, but it is arguably more suited to the representation of action: a mime thus

aptly represents the somewhat depersonalised 'doer of deeds' that constitutes the archetypal hero. The puppet is more dehumanised still: it
acquires movement and speech only by virtue of some external agency.
Puppets have no thinking or doing existence independently of that which
is attributed to them from outside; accordingly, they are the ideal theatrical
form for conveying myth, whose reality is constructed rather than actual,
'recounted not seen'.[68] In *The Mask of Orpheus*, Birtwistle's customary
concern with the 'perspectival' nature of his material is thus transformed
into a more ambitious statement about the semiotic potential of different
forms of theatrical representation and, by extension, of the illusory neutrality of any form of telling.

The combination, in *The Mask of Orpheus*, of a number of different
modes of dramatic presentation is in many ways simply a continuation of
classical tragedy's disparate constituents, whose origins lie in the contrasting genres of spoken poetry and ceremonial choral song. According to
Andrew Brown, 'tragedy as we know it was born when these two traditions
were combined together, verse spoken by the poet (who was at first the sole
actor) being interspersed with songs sung by the Chorus'.[69] As we have
seen, recitative and aria have historically been viewed as the operatic
analogy to this particular combination of forms in tragedy, and (in sharp
contrast to *Punch and Judy*) this distinction remains prominent in
Zinovieff's libretto. Most of the 126 individual numbers in *The Mask of
Orpheus* are designated as either 'aria', 'recitative', 'music' (meaning no
song or speech) or 'mime'. These distinctions are used to structure the
internal progression of Zinovieff's poems in each scene. For instance, the
three danced 'Ceremonies' that form the basis of one of Zinovieff's 'gross
structures' are each preceded by a recitative and major aria. A similarly
systematic treatment of recitative and aria is found in Act II, where each of
the seventeen 'Arches' includes an aria and a recitative, representing fact
and fantasy respectively.[70]

Despite these provisions in the libretto, at the time of the first performances Birtwistle seemed more concerned to emphasise how the work
represented a *departure* from the concepts of aria and recitative:

> In writing the piece, I wanted to invent a formalism which does not rely on tra-
> dition . . . I wanted to create a formal world which was utterly new. The basic
> formal device of opera . . . is recitative and aria. Recitative concerns itself with
> the dramatic situation, aria with the poetics of the moment. In aria, there is a
> flowering of the moment as if time were standing still and you were singing
> around it. *The Mask of Orpheus* attempts to replace this formalism . . .[71]

Birtwistle goes on to argue that the tripartite representation of the three
main characters substitutes for the dramatic contrast that aria and recita-

tive usually provide. Birtwistle's setting does not completely ignore the distinction, however. On the whole, recitatives are delivered in speech or speech-song, while arias are sung more melismatically. The contrast is perceptible shortly after the start of the third scene of Act III, where the '3rd Recitative of Teaching' (erroneously labelled '3rd Sentence of Teaching' in both the score and the booklet to the 1997 recording) is followed by the '3rd Aria of Prophecy'. Birtwistle sets the first in a 'clipped' speech-song, each word separated by rests, while the second is tenuto and sustained, with a little melisma. Zinovieff's distinctions are not always so clearly projected, however, and are sometimes contradicted. Numbers described in the libretto as recitative may be thoroughly aria-like in character, as in Orpheus Singer's '3rd Scream of Passion' that closes the culminatory Fifteenth Arch in Act II; or, alternatively, speech may encroach into the arias, as in the '1st Duet of Love' in the first scene of Act I. The orchestra, meanwhile, appears not to acknowledge the distinction between recitative and aria at all.

As this suggests, in *The Mask of Orpheus* Birtwistle adheres only fitfully to the formal niceties of his libretto. Admittedly, rarely can a composer have been presented with such a prescriptive statement as Zinovieff's sixty-page text, down to split-second timings for the entire course of Act II. Nevertheless it would be difficult to infer much of Zinovieff's multi-dimensional, modular conception from the music alone, a fact that suggests intriguing limits to Birtwistle's oft-stated insistence on the mutual integration of music and drama (a subject to be considered further in the next section of this chapter). Birtwistle's justification for this state of affairs runs as follows:

> Throughout the piece, I've made a distinction between a series of closed forms which define the stage action, and a much more organic, through-composed substructure belonging exclusively to the orchestra. As in the Noh plays of Japan, the orchestra, even though it responds to the events on stage, has a life of its own. But the music it plays moves towards the most extreme representation of formalism: the moment in the last act when the principal characters appear only as puppets. At this point, the formal structure of the stage music and the organic structure of the orchestral music coincide.[72]

Birtwistle here acknowledges that the patterned modules of the libretto are only directly reflected in the music in Act III.

A more general correlation with the librettist's conception may nevertheless be discerned in the earlier acts. Zinovieff describes the piece as tracing Orpheus' 'transformation and transition from a man into a god', later adding that 'it is with this rather than with the plot itself, that the opera is most concerned'.[73] The three acts accordingly focus on, respectively,

Orpheus as man, hero, and god. In broad terms, Birtwistle's musical designs in each act map out this transition – indeed, they do so arguably more clearly than the libretto itself. In the context of the other two acts, Act I is an awkward, sprawling construction; at times its crude juxtapositions and mannered dramatic presentation can seem merely dated, a reflection of transient fads in music theatre. Whether intentionally or not, however, these qualities aptly symbolise the relative mundanity of Orpheus the man. Act II, in contrast, uses Orpheus' methodical description of the seventeen arches spanning the valley to the world of the dead as an opportunity for an unapologetically linear musical structure, unremittingly building in intensity. Such assured purposefulness is of course entirely suited for the representation of the heroic Orpheus. Likewise, as Orpheus is elevated to the status of mythic god in Act III the music assumes an appropriate tone of meditative reflectiveness – its short, clearly distinguishable formal elements almost ikon-like in their imperviousness to change and context.

By fighting shy of the extreme sectionality of the libretto, the music must also be seen as rather less *self-reflexive* than the libretto – rather less focused on the act of telling. Instead, it frequently takes a stake in the raw drama of the narrative, in just the manner that the rigorous formalism of Zinovieff's text denies. The music's very continuousness does much to maintain the unbroken theatrical spell – the tinge of realism – that was so consistently disrupted in *Punch and Judy*. This aspect of Birtwistle's music is symbolised by the electronic 'auras' (created, as was the rest of the work's electronic component, in collaboration with Barry Anderson) that underpin so much of the score. These ensure that moments of complete silence are unusual, the music instead setting about creating an uninterrupted, magical evocation of an alternative reality. Similarly, conventionalised forms of musical expressivity are more evident in the score than the composer's descriptions, with their emphasis upon ironic detachment, would lead one to believe. The languorous polyphony of Act I's love music, or the chorale-like religiosity of Act III's '3rd Song of Magic', in which Orpheus Singer acquires Apollo's language, are products of an unashamed focus on the tale rather than the telling.

Of all the acts, Act II best exemplifies these characteristics. Admittedly, here Birtwistle is helped by Zinovieff's libretto. Orpheus Singer's methodical description of the seventeen arches that he has to cross to reach the underworld stretches over most of the act, giving it a unity of purpose not apparent in the other two acts. This impression is enhanced by the process of gradual change that takes place with successive Arches. Each Arch comprises four subsections, two representing dream and two nightmare. The First Arch is weighted heavily towards the dream components, but each

Ex. 1.1. *The Mask of Orpheus*: perfect fifth dominating the end of Act II

successive Arch sees these diminish and the nightmare components grow, up to the Fifteenth Arch at the end of the second scene, which marks the climax of the act. The consequent, relentless darkening of mood traces a highly orthodox dramatic curve that helps mark out Orpheus Singer's aria as dramatic foreground – and that effectively relegates the other layers of mostly mimed activity taking place around him. Birtwistle's cumulative musical structure faithfully reflects this larger dramatic shape, while riding roughshod over the more incidental dramatic detail. Even Zinovieff's Orphic-inspired tripartite division of the act is largely ignored – acknowledged only by brief, tense electronic interludes, after which the music resumes its terrible course. The three scenes sound as a complete span. Integration is a particular feature of the act's close, the soft perfect fifth that forms the basis of the orchestral epilogue accompanying Orpheus' suicide having emerged subtly but decisively during the last verses of his aria (Ex. 1.1). This beautiful and moving concluding device is characteristic of an act that manages to amalgamate the pivotal moments of earlier Orphic operas – the graphic representation of hell, the lyrical urgency of Orpheus' song to win back Euridice, and his mournful lament at losing her – into a single statement of surprisingly conventional expressivity.

Music and drama

The Oresteia (59a) • Bow Down (52)

The previous discussion of *The Mask of Orpheus* noted a certain disparity between libretto and music. While the libretto appears artificial and excessively formalised, the music engages – at least in parts – in a powerful and straightforward narration. This is a simplistic reduction of a complex situation, but it was nevertheless striking at the work's 1996 revival how the dramatic sweep of Birtwistle's score came as something of a surprise to listeners whose knowledge of the work had hitherto been confined to the fastidious complexities of the libretto. Only the third act, with its clearly distinguishable and frequently recurring formal elements in both text and music, fully corresponds to the assertion in the libretto that 'all aspects are connected'.[74]

Whatever the divergences in practice, Birtwistle has made it clear on a number of occasions that the close co-operation of all elements of a music theatre piece is a matter of central concern. The music emerges as part of a wider theatrical conception, not separately from it; as Birtwistle says, 'when I write for the theatre I have very specific ideas about how they [the theatre pieces] should be done'.[75] This attitude was undoubtedly cemented during Birtwistle's period as music director at the National Theatre, an experience that, according to Michael Hall, convinced Birtwistle that 'music in the theatre was more effective when it was not incidental but integral'.[76] Two works written during this time exemplify this conviction. *Bow Down*, written in collaboration with Tony Harrison and first performed at the National Theatre, requires four musicians and five actors; but *all* the performers work together on stage, and all also contribute to its musical component. Andrew Clements describes the work as 'an unclassifiable fusion of music, text and gesture that was perhaps closer to the music-theatre ideal than anything produced during the movement's heyday ten years earlier'.[77] This attempt to blur distinctions between actor and musician is paralleled in the ballet piece *Pulse Field*, which, as the preface to the score puts it, 'is an attempt to reformulate and thereby to expand the relationships between music and the dance'. Again, the musicians appear on stage rather than playing from a pit, while conversely the movements of the dancers determine aspects of the music. Such 'reformulations' were not wholly new to Birtwistle's music, though no earlier piece went to the same extent of questioning the traditional roles of each individual performer. The music theatre of *Punch and Judy* and *Down by the Greenwood Side* is in part defined by the disintegration of the distinction between music and drama, a disintegration symbolised in both works by the placing of instrumentalists on stage. Numerous purely instrumental works, conversely, have involved an element of 'staging' and choreographed movement. Less novel, but equally indicative of Birtwistle's inclusive conception of theatre, are the important roles for mimes and dancers in *The Visions of Francesco Petrarca*, *Punch and Judy* and *The Mask of Orpheus*.

Jonathan Cross has described *The Mask of Orpheus* as 'a modern day *Gesamtkunstwerk*',[78] reflecting the shared interest of Wagner and Birtwistle in forging a novel art form from an amalgam of different theatrical practices. Like Birtwistle, Wagner was absorbed in the world of ancient Greek theatre. He conceived of his music dramas as modern recreations of the 'total art work' of Greek theatre, which for him represented a 'successful combination of the arts – poetry, drama, costumes, mime, instrumental music, dance, song – and as such had greater scope and expressive powers than any of the arts alone'.[79] The massive scale of Wagner's works could hardly seem more distant from the intimacies of *Bow Down* and *Pulse Field*. Yet a specific connection does exist, in the form of Aeschylus' *The Oresteia*. Birtwistle claims that he joined the National Theatre in 1975 specifically because of Peter Hall's intention to mount Aeschylus' trilogy in new translations by Tony Harrison,[80] but in taking six years to reach the stage, the project became a rather protracted obsession whose influence may be felt on the smaller theatre pieces written in the meantime. A letter written by Tony Harrison indicates that Wagner was a specific model for the eventual form of the Aeschylus production, and thus, indirectly, for *Bow Down* and *Pulse Field* as well:

> I'm convinced that the *leitmotiv* notion which Wagner is said to have come upon through his reading of the *Oresteia* is one we can press further I mean musically, poetically, spatially, visually, so that we are hooked by eye, ear, and mind at the same time.[81]

In order to achieve this integrated effect, composer, writer, director and designer (Jocelyn Herbert) each took comparably important roles, forming what Harrison called 'a "dramatic collaborative"'.[82] No aspect of the production was to be treated as self-contained or independent of any other aspect.

Harrison's translations of the three plays that make up *The Oresteia* themselves reflect this. His concern was as much with the text's musical qualities – specifically, its rhythmic profile – as with its strictly semantic meaning. The metric form of Aeschylus' verse was far more than a mere matter of poetic convention: 'We must never in the whole piece be let off the rhythmical hook, *never* . . . Regular rhythm, form in poetry is like the mask[:] it enables you to go beyond the scream as a reaction to events that in the normal course of life would make you do just that.'[83] The rhythm of the text, according to Harrison, both maintains the momentum and tension of the drama and stylises the dramatic representation, thus making bearable the terrible acts portrayed therein. Birtwistle's simple rhythmic setting of the choruses respects this priority: regular metric patterns are played by three percussionists, whose function is to 'govern the way in which the drama is paced, and . . . to keep the rhythm going'.[84] Changes of speed and metre help vary the delivery of Aeschylus' exceptionally long choruses. Aside from this percussive rhythmic underpinning, Birtwistle provides a harp and clarinettists: according to Birtwistle, 'the harp has another punctuating role, which is to span the silences, while the wind instruments have sustained notes, and they play in unison in the bursts of incidental music that cover entrances and exits'.[85] Selected verses of the choruses are additionally given simple diatonic settings.

At the time of the production most critical attention was focused upon Harrison's translation, with its relentless neologisms and flat northern English vowels. It was generally felt that both music and stage direction 'faultlessly subordinated themselves to [Harrison's] text. Nothing in the performance directed attention away from the words.'[86] If the non-verbal elements of the production did take an essentially supporting role, it was nevertheless a thoroughly integrated one. This is true in a pragmatic as well as a poetic sense. While masks were important to Hall's and Harrison's initial conceptions, they became indispensable once the importance of rhythm had been decided upon. Built into each mask was a metronome, heard only by the actor, intended to provide rhythmic stability and the possibility of precise tempo changes.[87] The masks were thus *made necessary* by the 'music' of the words. In turn, the masks dictated a certain approach to movement, for, as Jocelyn Herbert has commented, the effect of a mask is to throw emphasis onto a performer's body: 'Through the concentration on the text demanded by the mask and the power of the simplest movement when wearing a mask, [actors] could learn to work with their bodies instead of just their faces.'[88] In this way, a musical conception of the text enforced a costume design which then implied a certain acting style and use of the stage.

The complex, dense richness of Aeschylus' language as rendered by Harrison perhaps meant that, despite this unusual integration of different aspects of the production, a privileging of the text was inevitable. *Bow Down*, Birtwistle's first collaboration with Tony Harrison, by comparison renders musical and verbal theatre in a state of mutually responsive equilibrium – more so than in any other of Birtwistle's stage works.[89] The work is based on numerous different versions of the traditional ballad of the 'Two Sisters'. This tells the story of how one sister drowns the other in order to take her lover. The murdered sister's body is discovered and plundered by a rapacious miller, but later a blind musician uses her bones and hair to build a harp. This is brought to her sister's wedding, where, of its own accord, it denounces the murderess, who is then put to death. The piece juxtaposes sung and spoken versions of the ballad with purely instrumental music, and, as mentioned above, all the performers contribute to both the acting and the music. This integration of dramatic elements was in part the result of the work's origin in a workshop process that involved the original performers working alongside composer and poet; the published score was assembled only retrospectively.

In important respects *Bow Down* goes considerably beyond the Greek's limited combination of the arts. For instance, while it does appear that the actors of the ancient Greek theatre chanted their verse rhythmically, reflecting the strong metric profile of the poetic verses,[90] in other respects the 'musical' aspect of tragedy was kept distinct. The chorus and actors remained separate on the stage and never interchanged their roles, and the musicians (unlike the other participants) were not masked.[91] Instrumental accompaniment was in all likelihood the sole responsibility of the 'aulete' (a musician, named after his reed instrument, the aulos), who sat aside from the action and accompanied lyric monodies and exchanges between actor and chorus; the actors themselves did not play instruments.[92] The interchangeability of roles that is such an important feature of *Bow Down* also distinguishes it from an alternative model that has been proposed for the work: the Japanese theatre.[93] In the ancient Nō drama, different dramatic practices (music, movement and dance, words, costume) certainly contribute on roughly equal terms, musicians sharing the stage with actors. Sets and stage props are also reduced to a minimum, as in *Bow Down*. But while both kabuki and Nō feature a stylised vocalisation that approaches song, and give an important role to the chorus (to the extent of giving the chorus passages that supplant lines that would normally be spoken by the actors), clear distinctions are maintained between instrumental musicians and actors, and between actors and chorus.

There is much to be said for approaching *Bow Down* less in terms of ancient or exotic theatrical traditions than as an exploration of the very idea of *performance*. In particular, the kind of theatre presented by *Bow Down* points to the constraints of the distinct categories – music, speech, dance and so on – that we traditionally impose upon acts of performance. As in *The Oresteia*, the detailed rhythmicisation and precisely specified vocal contours of the word-setting in *Bow Down* emphasise the impossibility and artificiality of absolute distinctions between speech and music. Words are rarely present in the piece without their rhythmic qualities or articulatory sensuousness being strongly emphasised. Similarly, by having all the performers alternate between acting and playing instruments, *Bow Down* highlights the importance of physical movement to all human production of musical sound: musical performance, Birtwistle seems to be suggesting, does not exist in a neat opposition to mime or dance. In place of the conventional categories, *Bow Down* posits a wider, inclusive category that emphasises the common basis of all acts of performance in the human body. It proposes a conception of performance that is about the exploration of the body's physical potential and constraints.

Specific aspects of the piece underline this. Firstly, timings are regularly determined by the 'breathing cycle' of the Chorus, so that it is the length of individual performers' inhalation and exhalation that measures out events rather than an abstract duration or metre. Secondly, the fable of the Two

Sisters, with its speaking harp fashioned out of a human body, itself presents a rich network of connections between music, speech and body: it can hardly be fortuitous that it should come to be aligned with a similarly integrative theatrical presentation.

The conception of performance presented in *Bow Down* may be detected in lesser degrees in much of Birtwistle's music – in the element of staging present in so many of the instrumental works, or the negotiations of language and sound in some of the vocal music. These receive further discussion in Chapters 2 and 3 respectively. Birtwistle and Harrison's third collaboration, however, represents a move away from the sort of integrative theatre presented in *Bow Down* and *The Oresteia*. *Yan Tan Tethera* is in many regards a conventional chamber opera, and it acts as a reminder that the sort of integration that Birtwistle usually seeks between the various elements of his music theatre pieces continues to acknowledge the governing role of the music: 'the way the theatre speaks has to match the way the music speaks',[94] not the other way round. Librettists have correspondingly striven to fashion texts that correspond to Birtwistle's own musico-formal predilections. They have met with varying degrees of success. As we shall see in the final section of this chapter, in the recent operas Birtwistle has frequently ignored the cyclical and repetitive elements dutifully supplied by his librettists, as his priorities increasingly shift towards faithfulness to the ongoing dramatic thrust of the narrative.

Narratives and rituals

Yan Tan Tethera (63) • *Gawain* (81) • *Fanfare for Will* (72) • *The Second Mrs Kong* (90)

By comparison with the complexities of *Bow Down* or *The Mask of Orpheus*, *Yan Tan Tethera* makes for a striking contrast. The scenario takes the form of a simple narrative (concerning a northern shepherd who has travelled south with his flock), and contains no other plots, no double-level action and no narrative variants. The narration proceeds largely in concordance with the sequence of events in the story. Tony Harrison's libretto does contain a number of prominent textual repetitions, however.[95] Presumably Harrison believed that these not only served to stylise an otherwise largely conventional drama, but that they also gave scope for the 'ritualistic' repetitions characteristic of some of Birtwistle's music. Yet Birtwistle's response to these repeated verbal motives is unpredictable: only two (Alan's 'I know there's a piper but don't know where . . .' and 'Stuff my ears with earth and clay . . .') are consistently set to identical music in voice and orchestra; some (for example, 'I think of the North . . .' and 'Thirteen, thirteen . . .') reappear with the same vocal line but an altered orchestral accompaniment; and others (such as 'I wave, he never waves back . . .' and 'Yan Tan Tethera') receive different settings on each occasion, ranging from the closely similar to the wholly different.

In the context of *Punch and Judy*, where the repetitious structure of the text was so closely matched by near-identical repetitions in the music, such inconsistencies may seem peculiar. They are a reflection of what Birtwistle saw at the time as a decisive shift in compositional priorities, one that necessitated a degree of unfaithfulness to Harrison's libretto. This new compositional stance centres upon a renewed sense of responsibility to the recent musical past – a determination to respect 'the sanctity of the context'[96] over the dictates of any pre-compositional structure or scheme: 'I don't want to pick something up I've dropped some time back and slot it into a new context willy-nilly. The context of the moment is unique and must exert an influence, a strong influence.'[97] In *Yan Tan Tethera* the influence of the immediate musical context moderates Harrison's repetitive scheme, and the resulting subtle balance between contrived repetition and organic continuity is perhaps reflected in the work's somewhat contradictory subtitle, 'a mechanical pastoral'. The idea of the 'sanctity of the context' has remained a mantra for Birtwistle ever since *Yan Tan Tethera*. It has contributed to the impression that the later operas take a more 'realistic', narrative form than did the earlier stage works, 'music and drama tending to reinforce each other rather than follow contradictory paths'.[98]

The formal conceits and harsher discontinuities of the earlier stage works, by comparison, have been interpreted as primarily anti-narrative in function, answering to the imperatives of Birtwistle's musical forms rather than the demands of a linear narrative. Just as the contemporary instrumental works feature cyclic repetition, verse and refrain structures and other forms of abrupt juxtaposition, so the early stage works take on a similarly formalised quality – less realistic than 'ritualistic'. The association of disruptive and repetitive musical forms with ritual has been common in twentieth-century music, Stravinsky's *Le sacre du printemps* serving as a blueprint for successive generations of composers keen to escape more 'naturalistic' modes of musical expression.[99] In Birtwistle's earlier stage works, the ritualistic character of the formal designs is reinforced by other features. Firstly, characters tend to be relatively anonymous – types, rather than individuals with whom we might feel drawn to empathise. This is especially true of *Punch and Judy* and *Down by the Greenwood Side*; as Paul Griffiths remarks in relation to the former, 'like Stravinsky in *Renard*,

Birtwistle here takes up a form of popular theatre having more to do with ritual than with psychological drama'.[100] Peter Zinovieff argues that the situation in *The Mask of Orpheus* is rather different, for it is 'concerned over and over again with the state of mind of Orpheus and, to a lesser degree, of Euridice'.[101] Yet this ostensible focus on character psychology is diffused rather than intensified by the piece's multiple presentation of each mythic figure, making it hard to identify with any of the dramatis personae as real individuals. A second consideration in the creation of the impression of a 'ritualistic theatre' is the prominent part played by various types of ritual in the actual scenarios of the stage works. Instances include the ceremonial murders in *Punch and Judy*, and the three 'Ceremonies' (The Wedding, The Funeral and The Sacrifice) that punctuate *The Mask of Orpheus*. *Down by the Greenwood Side*, in incorporating the seasonal mummers' play, may also be said to be 'about' ritual.

Despite the shift in Birtwistle's compositional outlook that occurred at the time of *Yan Tan Tethera*, this interest in ritual is by no means completely absent from later works. *Gawain* is marked by similar 'ritualistic' features to those just described. Although its simpler approach to storytelling makes its characters more realistic than is the case in *The Mask of Orpheus*, a degree of character anonymity remains. This is partly due to the libretto's basis in the famous late fourteenth-century romance *Sir Gawain and the Green Knight*. The story tells of a challenge laid down at King Arthur's court by a mysterious Green Knight: he will receive an axe-blow on the understanding that whoever delivers it will in turn accept a blow from him in a year's time. Gawain accepts the challenge willingly, but the Green Knight survives and Gawain is then obliged to meet his side of the bargain. True to its genre, this long narrative poem evokes an idealised world, in which Gawain is a stylised representation of chivalric gallantry and courtesy, rather than a character in the modern sense. Something of this psychological two-dimensionality is carried through into the opera.[102] The romance's concern with various types of social ritual is also reflected in the opera. The ritual dressing of Gawain as he prepares to leave on his journey at the end of Act I and the ritual courting of Gawain and Lady de Hautdesert in Act II are not just incidental events but comprise important scenes in their own right. In a number of ways, then, *Gawain* takes on a ritualistic cast.

Each of the two ritual scenes just mentioned is the occasion for an extended musical verse scheme, whose static, cyclical qualities seem wholly appropriate to the 'timelessness' of ritual. However, this sort of musical formalisation, familiar from *Punch and Judy* and the last act of

The Mask of Orpheus, sits less easily in *Gawain*, where it chafes with the contrary, narrativistic impulse to observe 'the sanctity of the context'. If anything the music to *Gawain* places a higher premium on moment-to-moment continuity than that of *Yan Tan Tethera*, its urgent sweep incorporating some frankly illustrative moments (notably the Green Knight's horse in Act I and the hunting horns in Act II) yet at the same time making little concession to the network of textual repetitions and allusions that permeates David Harsent's libretto. Several important recurring lines of text (including 'Night after night, the same dream . . .', 'Now at the year's dead end . . .', 'You carry it closer than your shadow . . .', and 'Cross of Christ . . .') pass largely unnoticed because they are set to wholly different music on each occasion. This apparent disregard for the structure of the text could conceivably be explained in terms of one of the opera's principal themes: the unreined natural world that Harsent depicts as a persistent threat to human certainties is symbolised by a 'wild' music that fails to respect the text's cosy repetitiousness. But the refusal of the composer to be pinned down by the contrived formal patterning of the libretto seems at odds with the imposing verse schemes that appear elsewhere in the work.

This tug and pull, between 'narrative' and 'ritualist' tendencies, is most keenly felt in connection with 'The Turning of the Seasons', the masque sequence that closes the first act. In the work's original form, this scene lasted a full half hour. It was in many respects a second attempt at an idea initially intended for the scene changes in *Yan Tan Tethera*: a theatrical version of a giant astrological clock, whose rotations move not only characters but also, symbolically, seasons and time, sometimes at different rates simultaneously. In the original production of *Gawain*, multiple stage revolves allowed the depiction of three different temporal levels: the seasons, passing from winter through to winter again, each season represented by one of the masque's five sections; the daily cycle, whose progress from night through full day and back to night is superimposed upon each season; and Gawain's preparations for his journey, to which the other temporal levels form a backdrop. Gawain's anticipation, as he is stripped, washed and armed, of his re-encounter with the Green Knight is interspersed with Guinevere's reflections upon his heroism, Marian motets from the choir and interjections from Morgan and Lady de Hautdesert on the inevitability of time and the seasons.

This ambitious 'ritual' structure undoubtedly represented a challenge to *Gawain*'s longer-term narrative, as was recognised in reviews of the first performance:

> Birtwistle has always been obsessed by ritual repetitions in his stage-works, and repetition is indeed an essential element in musical composition. But dramatic repetition, the same text or the same action, is another matter . . . The essence of theatre is timing. Birtwistle is as repetitively literal as the oath-taking rituals of a coronation or church service.[103]

Birtwistle's decision to remove the masque for *Gawain*'s revival in 1994 dramatically confirmed its incongruity. He explained his decision in an interview with Mark Pappenheim: 'It's a sort of mistake . . . *Gawain* is about story-telling and, in some aspects, it's quite naive . . . The main thrust of the narrative was, to a degree, held up too much . . . [The new version] is better, that's all – simpler, clearer, tells the story.'[104] In place of the old masque Birtwistle inserted a hugely accelerated scene, setting a drastically shorter text and using identical music for each season; the scene is effectively transformed from being the opera's central statement into little more than a footnote to the first act. In the same interview Birtwistle suggested that these changes were advantageous to the shape of the whole work, allowing a clearer presentation of (in the words of Pappenheim) 'the dualities that underpin the piece – between inside and outside, man and nature, Christian and pagan'.[105] Nevertheless, the fate of the original Seasons masque, which in advance of *Gawain*'s first performance Birtwistle described as a central 'musical flowering' of prime importance,[106] is symbolic of a conflict of compositional interests that continues to pervade the revised version of the work. Birtwistle's willingness to excise a large section of the original score itself conflicts with the idea that every moment of the piece emerges as a necessary consequence of its immediate context. Yet it is that very loyalty to context that provides the sanction for the music's disregard of many of the libretto's textual repetitions. Perhaps the most startling feature of *Gawain*'s score in these regards is its utilisation of large-scale, *literal* musical repetition, notably at the Green Knight's second entrance in Act I, and also in transitional passages that span the acts ([18] and [73] in Act I and [135] in Act II). In the words of Rhian Samuel, these episodes 'seem to emanate more from the composer's fascination with the rehearsal of Time . . . than from the libretto'.[107] Yet eight years earlier Birtwistle had firmly rejected literal repetition, claiming that, 'I would never copy something out again from another page'.[108] These curious aspects of *Gawain* – prioritising evolving continuity at one moment and block repetition at the next, with little consistency displayed towards the libretto – point to a damaging rift of compositional intention.

In a review of the 1994 revival, Andrew Clements expressed some regret at the disappearance of *Gawain*'s boldest formal experiment: 'the new masque . . . totally lacks the numinous weight of the original, the feeling of a ritual during which the narrative flow of the action is put into abeyance. As a result, the opera loses some of its mystery and weakens its ability to transcend mere story telling.'[109] Clements suggests here that the earlier version of the masque did not content itself with the *depiction* of a ritual, but actually in a significant sense *became* one.[110] He thus raises the possibility that what is widely identified as a 'ritualistic' quality in Birtwistle's music is not simply a matter of mimicking the formal patterns of ritualistic behaviour – its 'routinized, habitual, obsessive . . . qualities'[111] – but involves the assumption of a genuinely ritualistic function. Whether this is possible is open to debate. T. S. Eliot believed that drama 'can never coincide with ritual, for in the theatre we are spectators, not participants'.[112] This point is elaborated in a careful comparison by A. E. Green:

> Both drama and ritual deal with social relationships, and both do so in the most direct way possible, through the enactment of those relationships by living people . . . [But] the means they have in common are applied to divergent ends . . . While theatre confines itself to saying things about social relationships, ritual also does things with them; and what it does is to reinforce or change them.[113]

This suggests that, while drama merely *affects*, ritual contrastingly *effects*. Drama may involve or move, and its impact may even prompt one into action, but that action is not effected in the drama itself. To engage in ritualistic observance, on the other hand, is to act out social relationships directly.

In fact, I will presently suggest a level at which attending a theatrical (or musical) performance *does* take on a ritualistic status. The real difficulty with the idea that Birtwistle's 'ritualistic' pieces constitute actual rituals, is the fact that their ritualistic properties have more in common with the unfamiliar rituals of alien or ancient cultures than with those prominent in modern Western society. Like Antonin Artaud, whose work in the theatre during the 1930s was increasingly dominated by stereotypically 'ritualistic' paraphernalia – 'masks, "puppets many metres high", incantation, and rhythmic movements'[114] – Birtwistle's concept of ritual is essentially an exotic one. When Birtwistle talks about ritual, he emphasises its 'mystery' – as in his description of the ritualistic aspect of *Secret Theatre* as, 'like looking at something that is carefully constructed . . . but you don't quite know what the rules are'.[115] But to those who participate in them, rituals are generally familiar rather than strange. In modern Western society one might think of the wedding ceremony, for instance, or the communal Sunday lunch: there is little mystery about either of these. The mysterious 'ritualisms' of Birtwistle's works are therefore better thought of as 'portraits of rituals', as Paul Griffiths has put it. Their 'ceremonial element' and 'ritual formality of action and content'[116] are viewed from the outside, rather than understood from within; it is represented, rather than actual.

Griffiths argues that the same is also true of Stravinsky, and thus aligns Birtwistle with the strong seam of exotic primitivism that threads its way through musical modernism, from *Le sacre du printemps* to Boulez's *Rituel*, via Messiaen. The appeal to 'primitive ritual' has served a useful purpose for modernist composers, for the imagined combination of systematic order and brutal or violent acts in such rituals can be used as a sort of primordial legitimation for music that possesses the same qualities. The modernist agenda thereby comes to appear both suprahistorical and supracultural. Theodor Adorno, in his *Philosophy of Modern Music*, famously disputed the existence of any such legitimation, and, in typically colourful terms, painted Stravinsky's turn to primitivism as a retreat from the realities of the present: 'hypostatized bourgeois culture drives man to seek refuge in the phantasm of nature, which in the final analysis reveals itself as the herald of absolute suppression. The aesthetic nerves tremble with the desire to regress to the Stone Age.'[117] Adorno missed what is perhaps the more obvious objection to the 'arcane ritualisms' of modern-ist composers, though; namely, their tendency to perpetuate a colonial view of non-Western cultures as animalistic, dehumanised and inhabiting a realm that stands opposed to the 'real'. The modernist appropriation of ritual is potentially highly culturally offensive.[118]

Often, the description 'ritualistic' is applied indiscriminately to Birtwistle's music when another would do just as well. As I have suggested, there are good reasons to avoid it – as Michael Nyman does in his delicate description of *Punch and Judy*, not in terms of ritual, but as 'a game, with clearly defined rules and set progressions'[119]. This is not to dispute the existence of a more genuinely 'ceremonial' quality in some of Birtwistle's music. But this quality arises from a real affinity with modern, familiar rituals, not from the imitation of some stereotyped exotic practice. I expand upon this in the next chapter.

The one work by Birtwistle actually to mention ritual in the title – *Ritual Fragment* – is something of an exception to all that has just been said. Here, as in Boulez's *Rituel*, the title refers to the work's memorial function: Birtwistle's piece was written following the death of Michael Vyner, artistic director of the London Sinfonietta. Rather than evoking some mysterious exotic practice, the 'ritual' of the title indicates the proximity of the piece to a real ritual in our society, the memorial service; and performances of it by the Sinfonietta movingly take on this function. The piece reminds us, too, how genuine ritual is not typically strange or mysterious but on the contrary appears 'natural', a commonly understood part of social existence.

The essence of ritualised activities is not their foreignness, but the way in which they are distinguished and privileged relative to other activities in society. As Catherine Bell puts it, 'ritualization is a matter of various culturally specific strategies for setting some activities off from others, for creating and privileging a qualitative distinction between the "sacred" and the "profane", and for ascribing such distinctions to realities thought to transcend the powers of human actors.'[120] It follows from this that the ritual aspect of musical performance lies not so much in the content or formal organisation of a particular work, as in the activity of attending the performance taken as a whole. In this, the audience very much takes the role of participants. To perceive a concert as ritual 'we need to begin by examining it, not just as organized sound, but also as an event taking place within our society, at a particular time and in a particular place, involving a particular group of people'.[121] Attendance at a concert or opera performance fulfils all of Bell's stipulates, and while its privileged status as a form of activity is widely recognised its rituality is not typically dwelt upon *per se*. There is an element of invisibility about ritual activity that allows it most effectively to function as 'a celebration . . . of the shared mythology and values of a certain group'.[122]

When Birtwistle's music is described as ritualistic, it is more often because of the kindredness of its procedures and tone to a popular idea of exotic or ancient ritual. But Birtwistle has also sometimes involved himself with the more literal ritual of the concert. The most obvious example of this involvement is the event entitled 'Spring Song' that he and the Pierrot Players mounted in 1970 at London's Queen Elizabeth Hall. In this concert, Birtwistle's own works were interspersed between music by David Bedford, Julie Kendrick, Lord Berners and Satie. The aim, as stated in the programme, was

> to conceive a concert as an overall structure which can be palpably experienced by the audience. To this end, Birtwistle has specified that the programme proceed until the end without the punctuation of applause, and that its formal bilateral design, arranged symmetrically around the interval, be underlined through lighting and spatial organisation. Rather than merely separating the halves of a programme, the interval becomes part of the total musical experience.[123]

The event thus strove to acknowledge aspects of the 'ritual' of the classical concert – emphasising its standard duration by treating it as a single span, and structuring the musical content around one of its defining features, the interval. This represented a move away from the assumption that the classical concert format constitutes a 'neutral' space for the presentation of music. 'Spring Song' had no direct successor, but a similar impulse may be detected elsewhere in Birtwistle's output. His fondness for fanfares, for instance, reflects an interest in one of the more familiar ways in which the ritual of a musical or theatrical performance is sometimes initiated. Fanfares appear explicitly in *Monody for Corpus Christi* (the second movement) and *Three Movements with Fanfares*, but more pertinent here are those he has written specifically to open a concert, which include one for the new opera house at Glyndebourne, and one written for a concert celebrating a Shakespeare anniversary. The latter, *Fanfare for Will*, is a hugely energetic, even flamboyant, work of just over two minutes, with a prominent first trumpet part – presumably a reflection of the fact that it was written shortly after the 'trumpet concerto', *Endless Parade*. It makes a perfect opener for a concert.

Birtwistle's interest in the ritual of the concert is also evident in the movement and spatial deployment of instrumentalists involved in many of his later works. Such techniques mimic the role-play of ceremony and ritual; but they are also 'ritualistic' in a stronger sense, in articulating, and thus drawing attention to, the performing space – something quite unusual in classical instrumental music. Along similar lines, the stylised nature of the story-telling in the earlier stage works serves to articulate conventions central to the ritual of *theatrical* performance. Stephen Pruslin's description of *Punch and Judy* as 'a stylized and ritualistic drama'[124] is best taken as referring, not to some mysterious or arcane primitivism, but to the way in which the piece points up the artificiality of 'realistic' theatre. As Michael Nyman points out, this is in contrast to

> most new serious operas which present B-feature plots and attempt psychological and physical naturalism in a losing battle with an artificial convention. *Punch and Judy* originates from the premiss that, to beat opera at its own game, a more or less total artificiality must be achieved . . . Away with cardboard humans, on with live puppets.[125]

In *The Second Mrs Kong*, written some thirty years after *Punch and Judy*, puppets are replaced by an articulated model from a film set and a seventeenth-century painting. But the focus upon the contrived artificiality of theatre is the same. Russell Hoban's libretto, which draws many of its details from the same author's short novel *The Medusa Frequency*, tells of the impossible love of King Kong and Vermeer's 'Girl with the Pearl Earring' (known in the opera simply as Pearl): Kong journeys from the underworld in order to find Pearl, but reality intervenes (in the form of a mirror) and prevents the fulfilment of their yearning. Hoban's libretto is peopled not by 'real' persons but by imaginary ones – dramatic characters, painted images, mythical figures. Thus a central feature of the ritual of theatrical performance, the audience's temporary belief in *illusory representations*, is itself drawn into the premise of the story. In contrast to *Punch*, there is now also a detectable element of self-parody. Two of Kong's companions in the 'World of the Shadows', Orpheus and Eurydice, inevitably appear referential to Birtwistle's own works. So do other aspects of the scenario: for instance, its casting of several singers in different but related roles in the second act (this device appears in one form or another in all the earlier stage works); and the appearance of such familiar themes as riddles, journeying and death. While Hoban's text contains neither the intricate modular structure of the librettos to *Punch* and *Orpheus* nor the network of textual repetitions found in *Yan Tan Tethera* and *Gawain*, it does include a number of repetitive set pieces that humorously parody the cyclical elements so prominent in these earlier works.

It would be incorrect, though, to view *The Second Mrs Kong* as simply another exploration of well-mined dramatic topics and treatments. For one thing the dramatis personae, though no more than figments and thus unlikely possessors of well-rounded psychologies, are in fact treated as 'genuine individuals . . . Even the characters that bear mythic names have a genuine personality.'[126] This contrasts sharply with the more stylised 'types' that populate earlier stage works. *The Second Mrs Kong* is in essence a love-story, and Hoban invests his characters with the psychological refinements that this necessarily entails. Secondly, the cyclical elements that feature in the long opening scene in the 'World of the Shadows' (initially involving all 'the dead' except Kong, then only Vermeer and his models) do not seek to contain the drama, but rather are enactions within the story. The placing of one or more characters outside each repetitive scheme, commenting upon it, emphasises that each is a performance by the dead themselves, rather than some contrived feature of Hoban and Birtwistle's narration. It is as if the dead are all cast-offs from earlier Birtwistle operas, unable to organise their tedious posthumous existence except through cyclic repetition – as Anubis says, 'one at a time . . . the way we always do it'.[127] The effect of both of these devices – the realistic characterisation of imaginary figures, and the depiction of the dead acting out repetitive cycles – is to ironise the stylised aspects of the story-telling in Birtwistle's own stage works.

Birtwistle is a willing accomplice in this, even though it is he rather than Hoban who is the butt of the joke. No excessive musical formalisation impedes the breezy naturalism of Hoban's characterisation, while the text's ironic cyclic sequences are supported by lightly handled musical repetitions. The prevailing simplicity of Hoban's narrative, its bizarre subject-matter notwithstanding, appears better matched to the smooth continuities and ever-generating invention of Birtwistle's idiom than was Harsent's libretto for *Gawain*. The impression of a happy marriage of text and music would not be accurate, however. Birtwistle's setting is neglectful not of the larger formal shape of the libretto but of its local specifics. Throughout *The Second Mrs Kong*, the music flirts moodily with both drama and words – occasionally responsive and even pictorial (as in the fight that ends Act I), but more often haughtily indifferent. Watershed moments in the plot are often recognised by a dramatic crescendo or apprehensive pause, yet between these moments the music goes its separate way, repeatedly ignoring the slapstick paciness of the action on stage in favour of an intense, brooding lyricism. The conjunction can be strangely compelling – particularly as the opera's final scene, movingly confirming the impossibility of Kong and Pearl's love, suggests that it is not the *music* that has been negligent up to this point, but the fripperies of the *drama*. Greater discomfort is caused by Birtwistle's word setting. Madame Lena's approximately notated speech song in the second scene of Act II is a welcome contrast to vocal lines that are otherwise consistently awkward and angular, and which frequently neither clearly belong to the orchestral music nor bear any expressive relation to the text's light-hearted frivolities. Inaudibility of the text is not a problem unique to this opera, but Birtwistle's carelessness in this respect here extends to some of the libretto's pivotal moments, which are either mangled by contorted melody or despatched with unseemly haste.

In reviewing *The Second Mrs Kong*, Tom Sutcliffe wondered 'why [Birtwistle] should want to make operas at all, being clearly so uninterested in the human voice's natural characteristics'.[128] The answer here (and, to varying degrees, also in *The Mask of Orpheus*, *Yan Tan Tethera* and *Gawain*) must have less to do with the faithful musical realisation of a dramatic text and more to do with the specifically compositional opportunities that a theatrical collaboration provides. For Birtwistle a libretto presents not words but dramatic situations; and a libretto's cogency as a narrative, far from demanding a correspondingly coherent musical response, largely *relieves* music of precisely that responsibility. In essence, Birtwistle 'makes operas' because the librettist's dramatic text provides a suggestive excuse for musical invention, one to which due obeisance need be paid only intermittently. This arm's-length approach is reflected in Birtwistle's comment that the drama of *The Second Mrs Kong* 'sits' on the thick texture of the score.[129] Weightier moments in the drama may receive a little extra cushioning (to continue the metaphor), but otherwise inter-action between them is limited. Paradoxically, then, despite the uncompli-cated (and, in Birtwistle's stage works, unprecedented) linearity of both text *and* music, the story-telling of *The Second Mrs Kong* still eludes the principal conventions of realistic music theatre. The piece is as multiplici-tous and internally divergent as any of Birtwistle's earlier works. In this respect, the submerged orchestral pit of the opera house, which assumes a primarily *supportive* role on the part of the music, is potentially both mis-leading and damaging.

Just as earlier works' complexities remain identifiable in *The Second Mrs Kong*, so the latter work's linearities are far from entirely unprecedented. Single, linear narratives underpin all Birtwistle's stage works, however jar-ringly discontinuous and formalised their moment-to-moment progress. *Punch and Judy*'s story remains intact in Pruslin's libretto, tracing a neat dramatic curve that peaks in the nightmare following the third Melodrama. Similarly, despite its complexities *The Mask of Orpheus* follows a grand linear progression, 'from the birth of Orpheus and his mastering of speech, then song, to the silencing, by Apollo, of Orpheus's singing skull'.[130] *Bow Down*, too, organises its multi-levelled telling around a single, faithful enaction of the basic story. Narrative sequence is rarely completely submerged beneath ritualistic repetition.

Nor should the *departure* from narrative simplicity automatically be treated as a withdrawal from the engagement with reality – as if the manip-ulations and distortions to the story-telling serve a purely formalist purpose, comprising no more than an empty display of the narrator's vir-tuosity. After all, the rituals of a culture form the corner-stone of its real-ities. As Francis Bacon suggests in relation to painting, reality is sometimes best served by transcending a literal rendering:

> I believe that realism has to be invented. In one of his letters Van Gogh speaks of the need to make changes in reality, which become lies that are truer than the literal truth. This is the only possible way the painter can bring back the inten-sity of the reality which he is trying to capture. I believe that reality in art is something profoundly artificial and that it has to be recreated. Otherwise it will be just an illustration of something – which will be very second-hand.[131]

Accordingly, the consistent complication of representation in Birtwistle's theatres may have the effect not of a retreat from reality but of enforcing a renewed engagement with it.

2 Roles

At the beginning of his *Poetics* Aristotle lists 'music composed for the flute or lyre' as one of a number of 'forms of imitation or representation', alongside literary genres such as epic and tragic poetry, comedy and the dithyramb.[1] He thus reminds the modern reader that not all traditions and cultures have maintained the sort of clear-cut categorial distinction between music and the theatre that has become customary in more recent centuries. Birtwistle's interest in dismantling these categories is clearly demonstrated in some of the stage works discussed in the previous chapter, most notably *The Oresteia* and *Bow Down*. But then, for Birtwistle the distinction between music and theatre has perhaps never really existed. In contrast to other prominent figures of the post-war European avant-garde, he has never striven after an illusory musical purity – a music free of all reference to spheres of activity external to its own material. On the contrary, he has stated explicitly that, 'I regard instruments as actors and I'm intrigued by their role-playing.'[2]

While this stance may place Birtwistle somewhat apart from some of his contemporaries, it is entirely consistent with more long-established trends in Western music. The majority of allegedly 'purely musical' forms in the classical music tradition can be traced back to genres that involved some element of theatre – song, dance or the church ritual. And even as musical forms attained increasing autonomy from these earlier functions, their expressive import remained bound to codes of musical meaning developed primarily in song and opera. The routine equation of absolute music with speech-like utterance or affective state – often identified with that of 'the composer himself'[3] – is dependent upon precisely this liminal 'theatricality'.

Yet while eighteenth- and nineteenth-century music is frequently suggestive of individuals in a drama or in conversation, a literal instrumental embodiment of those individuals is rare. Identities tend to be encoded in thematic material rather than the qualities of a particular instrument, and that material may be shared between many instrumental parts. The classical concerto, for instance, often viewed as presenting a clear-cut conversation between soloist and orchestra, usually blurs these allegedly distinct roles: musical material is typically shared by both principal participants, and tonal harmony additionally dictates a constant, mutually supporting harmonic relationship, thereby preventing any real antagonism. In Birtwistle's music, on the other hand, the dramatic interaction of musical personae is more vividly and literally evoked by particular instruments or instrumentalists, and so reaches well beyond nineteenth-century narrative practice.

Birtwistle's exploration of musical roles ranges more widely still. For instance, the interaction of a *number* of soloists is as likely to be explored as the more typical classical arrangement of the single soloist pitted against a tutti. When, as has increasingly been the case more recently, Birtwistle's scoring does approximate to the standard concerto format, the putative soloist is frequently rendered ambiguous, rather than foregrounded as the principal musical protagonist. Sometimes, Birtwistle's music shuns a straightforward dramatic representation in order to conduct a more detached examination of the very business of enaction: instead of representing illusory characters, instruments are shown taking on a variety of functions. Alternatively, a play of individuation may be initiated, in which the grounds for identifying the primary musical agents are constantly shifted, necessitating a perpetual redrawing of musical roles.

Each of these approaches to the idea of musical roles is considered in this chapter. Most of Birtwistle's instrumental music is receptive to interpretation in one or other of these terms. The present discussion, rather than mounting an exhaustive survey, focuses on a representative selection of works. The intention is to give an indication of the wide scope that prevails more generally.

Dramatic protagonists

Refrains and Choruses (1) • *Tragœdia* (14) • *Meridian* (36) • *Five Distances for Five Instruments* (87)

That Birtwistle was interested to take the association of instruments with individuals in a drama beyond the vagaries of nineteenth-century practice was clearly announced in his first published work, *Refrains and Choruses*, for wind quintet. The horn – the only brass instrument of the group – is singled out for special treatment. It flirts occasionally with the larger collective effort, but for the majority of the first two-thirds of the piece it remains excluded from the fleeting alliances formed between the other four instruments. Michael Hall describes the piece as a 'conflict between capricious individuality and the solidarity of the group', and he discerns an unambiguous shape to the drama:

Gradually the horn's capriciousness becomes more and more assertive until . . . it becomes almost uncontrollably headstrong. The *peripeteia*, or turning point, comes when (at the climax of the piece) the other instruments acting as a united chorus virtually silence the horn. Roles have been exchanged. In that moment the chorus plays the assertive part. Thereafter the horn becomes absorbed into the chorus and the drama is over.[4]

In fact, Hall's description does not do justice to the work's last sixty bars, when the horn is indeed more reconciled with the ensemble but the drama is by no means 'over'. It is interesting that Birtwistle's own short programme note to *Refrains and Choruses* makes no reference to an overarching 'plot', but focuses instead entirely upon the piece's refrain structure (which Hall does not discuss).[5] Nevertheless, Hall accurately encapsulates the music's sharply defined presentation of exclusion and incorporation. As in many of Birtwistle's works, the theatre in *Refrains and Choruses* is motivated first and foremost by the physical and sonic characteristics of different instruments. The isolation of the horn reflects the fact that it is not a woodwind instrument; and this principle of singling out instruments on the basis of their individual peculiarities is continued in a number of later works, including *Tragœdia*, *Meridian* and *Five Distances*. Birtwistle's relationship to the clarinet represents a different manifestation of this sensitivity to the distinctive qualities of individual instruments. This was his own instrument; its prominence in Birtwistle's output reflects his close understanding of its idiosyncrasies and capabilities. Birtwistle's feeling that, 'like voices in an abstract play, the voices of the instruments are important',[6] aligns him with Stravinsky, of whom Adorno commented, 'the instruments . . . instead of playing a subservient role, now begin to speak for themselves . . . Their own characters declare their independence of the overall intention and are thereby made new and fresh . . . The voices of his instruments are like animals whose very existence seems to express their names.'[7]

In sharp contrast to Birtwistle's programme note for *Refrains and Choruses*, that for *Tragœdia* is explicit about the work's oppositional instrumentation: 'the instruments are divided into three groups: wind quintet, harp, and string quartet. The cello and horn, being the "odd men out" of their respective groups, act as individual opponents within the conflict, while the harp acts as linking continuo.'[8] As in the earlier work, the horn is singled out as a soloist, and so is the cello, for it is the only instrument in the string quartet not played under the chin. Birtwistle's note describes the way in which these various instrumental personae interact in each section of the work; the score confirms that winds and strings are frequently kept musically distinct, and that the horn and the cello have more prominent parts than the other instruments.

Fig. 2.1. *Tragœdia*: role-play in main formal sections

Prologue:	soloists plus harp
Parados:	instrumental choirs (horn works with harp)
Episodion – Strophe I:	horn plus harp alternating with horn versus strings (brief occasional comments from wind)
Episodion – Anapaest:	two soloists (sharing melodic line), with harp and claves
Episodion – Antistrophe:	cellos versus wind (with horn occasionally joining latter)
Stasimon:	prominent harp with flute and violin 1 melodies (unpitched attacks in soloists, pedal notes in other instruments)
Episodion – Strophe II:	succession of different ensembles, involving soloists and instrumental choirs
Episodion – Anapaest:	ditto
Episodion – Antistrophe II:	strings (claves, wind and harp join at end)
Exodus:	closely similar to Parados

In *Tragœdia*, however, these interactions are given added dramatic point by the work's explicit references to Greek tragedy. In addition to the title – the Greek word for tragedy – each section of the work is named after one of tragedy's main structural components, as described by Aristotle in his *Poetics*. This suggests a closer association with the practices of the spoken theatre than the instrumental interplay of itself necessarily implies. The individual sections of *Tragœdia* (detailed in Figure 2.1) broadly conform to the function that Aristotle expected of them in Greek tragedy:

> The separate sections into which the work is divided are as follows: prologue, episode, exode, and choral song, the last being subdivided into parode and stasimon . . .
> The prologue is the whole of that part of a tragedy that precedes the parode, or first entry of the Chorus. An episode is the whole of that part of a tragedy that comes between complete choral songs. The exode is the whole of that part of a tragedy which is not followed by a song of the Chorus. In the choral sections the parode is the whole of the first utterance of the Chorus, and a stasimon is a choral song without anapaests or trochees.[9]

As Figure 2.1 indicates, the contributions of soloists and ensembles reflect Aristotle's injunctions. The Prologue is essentially soloistic, preceding the first 'choral' entry (that is, the whole ensemble) in the Parados. Birtwistle limits himself to two Episodions and one separating Stasimon: in the former, he follows the practice of Greek tragedy by involving both soloists and chorus; the Stasimon, on the other hand, once again puts the instruments of the 'choirs' centre stage.

It might appear from this that *Tragœdia* could itself be understood as a sort of abstract Greek tragedy – a miniature tone poem, as it were, that, while refusing to specify individuals or situations, mimics the personae of tragedy and the sorts of interactions that take place between them. Birtwistle's note does not altogether dispel this impression:

> The work is intended to bridge the gap between "absolute music" and theatre music. It contains a specific drama, but this drama is purely musical . . . The work is concerned with the ritual and formal aspects of Greek tragedy rather than with the content of any specific play . . . [Its] instrumental organization . . . is simply a reflection on the level of instrumentation of the drama which is also expressed in the form of the work.[10]

There are good reasons, however, for stopping short of such an interpretation. For a start, Aristotle's structural formula for tragedy is itself notoriously deficient, to the extent that some critics have viewed the chapter in which it appears as being of spurious authenticity. Stephen Halliwell calls Aristotle's model 'a crude approximation to what we find in many of our texts', and suggests that Aristotle may merely have been offering plain definitions for dramatic and theatrical terms already in common use, rather than a detailed or scrupulous account.[11] Birtwistle additionally departs from Aristotle in a number of respects. For instance, the division of each Episodion into a Strophe and an Antistrophe owes more to Messiaen's *Chronochromie* (1960) than to the structure of classical tragedy, as defined by Aristotle or anyone else. In Greek tragedy, the strophe and antistrophe form the main components of *choral* verse, not the soloistic episodes into which Birtwistle introduces them. (An antistrophe has exactly the same form and metre as a strophe, and Greek choral lyrics typically comprise strophe-antistrophe pairs, rounded off by a concluding 'epode'.[12] Messiaen's work follows this structure closely.) The Anapaests that Birtwistle locates at the centre of his Episodions are an additional inauthentic embellishment. An anapaest is not a section of a play but a rhythmic metre (short-short-long). Its martial quality means that in tragedy it is more often found in the parados than in the episodes.[13]

Birtwistle's condensation of the central part of the theatrical form – reduced to just two episodes and one stasimon – is perhaps a more serious impediment to any musical embodiment of the dramatic interactions of tragedy. The appeal of symmetrical form seems to have swayed Birtwistle here. More than two episodes would have given greater opportunity for a sense of evolving plot, as in Greek tragedy, but it would simultaneously have reduced the impact of the piece's symmetrical design. As Birtwistle himself says, 'the essence of the work's structure is symmetry – more specifically, bilateral symmetry in which concentric layers are grouped outward from a static central pillar'.[14] An analogy can be made with the verse and refrain element of *Refrains and Choruses*: both pieces give an important place to a repetitive formal principle that prevents their progress from being fully explained in terms of the directed linearity of dramatic plot. Symmetry informs *Tragœdia*'s instrumentation too, for Birtwistle writes for *two* choruses rather than one, each placed either side of the harp. A double chorus of this sort was not wholly unknown in Greek tragedy: occasionally a representative subgroup might split from the main body to form 'a second, subsidiary Chorus'.[15] Birtwistle's choruses, however, frequently seem more opposed than agreed, despite their occasional joint efforts (as at the start of the Parados and the Exodus). Their attitude to the soloists is also sometimes antagonistic, as in the aggressive confrontation of cello and wind at the end of Episodion I. This is in sharp contrast to the Greek chorus's more conventional role as 'spectators of the action, humble in rank, taking a limited part in but rarely initiating action, sympathizing with one or other of the chief characters, and commenting on or interpreting the dramatic situation'.[16]

Indeed what fascinates about *Tragœdia* is precisely the resistance exerted by its constituent personae to the outlining of straightforward characterisations. The cello, for instance, is frequently called upon to bolster the string quartet, sharing its material and dynamic level. At such moments it seems inappropriate to treat the cellist as the principal actor that, elsewhere, it so clearly is. Nor can one readily generalise about the other allegiances formed by the work's various participants – be it of the soloists to each other, the soloists to the 'choruses' from which they are respectively drawn, the choruses to each other, or both soloists and choruses to the harp. The central Stasimon is an interesting case-study in this respect. While the soloists are here confined to pianissimo, unpitched attacks (the cello plucking on the wrong side of the bridge; the horn player striking claves), making them wholly subordinate to the wide-ranging melodies spun by flute and first violin, they nevertheless participate in the role-play, striking up unexpected rhythmic relationships with members of the 'opposite' choir. Any interpretation seeking to establish a close connection between *Tragœdia*'s solo instruments and the main characters of Greek theatre would have to reckon with moments such as these. The Stasimon additionally brings the harp to the fore, with a part far more elaborate than the reiterated pedal notes of previous movements. The harp's prominence here 'marks the centre of instrumental and of formal symmetry',[17] and thus acts as a signal, as it were, of the degree to which the structural principles of Greek tragedy have been left behind in the pursuit of quite different formal imperatives.

Dispensing with the idea that *Tragœdia* presents a literal musical embodiment of the structure of tragedy makes it easier to see how the practices of ancient Greek theatre are suggestive of other interpretations of the piece. For instance, the unequal status of cello and horn (the cello doubles as chorus member, whereas the horn does not) is not unfaithful to the Greek practice of differentiating between the main actors in tragedy. In the ancient Greek theatre, a scale of relative importance separated the first actor (called the protagonist) from the second and third (respectively the deuteragonist and tritagonist): the protagonist received the most important parts and the tritagonist took on the least.[18] This reflects the development of tragedy from monodrama, an earlier form that combined a single actor representing many roles with a chorus. The introduction of a second and third (and, rarely, a fourth) actor was a gradual process, and the protagonist retained his special status. It also remained common, even in later tragedy, for several roles to be assigned to single actors.[19] This means that the modern assumption of a direct, one-to-one mapping between dramatic participant and role is neither authentic to ancient Greek practice nor necessarily the most fruitful way to interpret Birtwistle's 'dramatic' instrumental music. Birtwistle's interest in the assumption of many roles by a single participant is apparent in his own *Monodrama*, where a soprano, described as 'Protagonist' in Stephen Pruslin's libretto, also takes two other roles; similar multiple representations may well be at work in Birtwistle's instrumental works. It is certainly difficult to identify in *Tragœdia* the sort of unambiguous singular personalities that, for instance, Elliott Carter bestows upon the four players in his String Quartet No. 2. Each of the instruments in Carter's work 'is given a particular expressive character and its own repertory of speeds and intervals',[20] allowing the composer to liken each to 'a character in an opera'.[21] In Birtwistle's music this identity between instrument (or instrumentalist) and dramatic character is rarely as securely maintained.

Tragœdia's explicit referencing of a particular theatrical genre sets it apart from later works, even if its connection with Greek tragedy, like *Punch and Judy*'s, is less comprehensive or respectful than is sometimes claimed. Nevertheless, the piece has a direct successor. *Meridian*, written six years later, might be considered a 'sequel' in the filmic sense; for, as Birtwistle explains, it retains the main soloists of the earlier work: 'When I wrote *Meridian*, I took those three instruments – harp, horn and cello – out of the *Tragœdia* context and put them in the new context: the context is different, you see, but the role of the instrument is the same.'[22] There is even a cinematic 'flashback': just less than halfway into *Meridian* ([35]) Birtwistle borrows the whole of the anapaest from the earlier work's Episodion I, altering only the pitches of the percussive attacks garlanding the cello and horn's sustained melody.

This quotation, together with a number of formal repetitions linking the beginning and end of *Meridian*,[23] makes it tempting to seek further parallels to *Tragœdia*'s loosely Aristotelian form. That none is readily identifiable is largely due to the very different 'context' to which Birtwistle refers. *Tragœdia*'s soloists are joined in *Meridian* by a mezzo-soprano soloist, who sings verses from Thomas Wyatt and Christopher Logue, and a highly idiosyncratic ensemble, comprising three oboes, three clarinets, two harps and piano, two percussionists and six sopranos. Each of the four verses of Logue's 'The Image of Love' is separated by instrumental interludes, and the whole is preceded by the Wyatt texts set for solo and choral voices. The roles of the horn and cello are dramatically affected by this new context. In contrast to the neat alternation of 'soloist' and 'chorus' in *Tragœdia*, in *Meridian* one or both of the soloists are present practically throughout (only the first verse of the Logue poem sees them both silent, possibly as a means of focusing some initial attention upon the text). *Meridian*'s wind- and percussion-based ensemble also prevents the soloists from receding into choral anonymity, in the way that the cello, at least, sometimes does in *Tragœdia*. Their presence as soloists is as a result largely unrelieved. The vague precedence of the horn over the cello noted in *Tragœdia* is also greatly heightened in the later work. The horn appears alone on a number of occasions while the cellist has a comparable solo only once, directly after the *Tragœdia* quote (and possibly prompted by the strongly assertive treatment of the cello at the same place in that piece).

So, far from re-creating their old roles, as Birtwistle contends, these instrumental soloists function quite differently in *Meridian*. They are, above all, less ambiguous as characters. By failing ever really to shed their soloistic status, the cello and horn retain a measure of integrity as dramatic personae that is withheld from the same instruments in *Tragœdia*. This impression is strengthened by the presence of the singer, with whom the solo instruments frequently interact as an equal. In Western classical music a solo singer is typically treated as representative of him or herself as an individual, contributing to the music not just as a functional, sounding component but as an individuated, autonomous person. An instrumentalist, on the other hand, more readily yields his or her real individuality – becoming transparent, as it were, in the cause of a collective musical effort. Yet, in their close association and interaction with the singer, *Meridian*'s horn and cello also assume something of her resilient individuality. Indeed, the poetic texts, about love and song, have encouraged commentators to go further and attribute specific characteristics to the instrumental soloists, such as that they represent lovers,[24] or even, specifically, Orpheus and Euridice.[25]

The interpretation of *Meridian*'s solo instruments as lovers may also have been influenced by a piece that Birtwistle wrote shortly afterwards, in which there is yet another prominent horn part. *The Fields of Sorrow*, for chorus and instrumental ensemble, sets a text that, while not explicitly about lovers, could certainly be construed as such ('They wander in deep woods . . .'). The chorus is supported by undemonstrative woodwind and pianos; and the horn is paired off with a closely shadowing vibraphone, in what has been described as 'an image of the lovers locked in perpetual embrace'.[26] Programmatic explanations of the important horn part in the slightly later *Epilogue*, on the other hand, are harder to come by. It may be that the horn's prominence in all these pieces, *Meridian* included, reflects simply the continuing attraction for Birtwistle of its sound, rather than any particular narrative intention. It would be entirely consistent with Birtwistle's attentiveness to the particular sonic qualities of different instruments were sonority sometimes to override considerations of plot or character elaboration as primary compositional premise.

Much later, with the composition of *Five Distances for Five Instruments*, it again became clear to the composer that 'the horn's function could be special'. Indeed the composer specifically states that, 'It was the identification of each instrument's characteristics that was my first concern when I began to write.'[27] This is reflected in the work's title, whose reference to 'five instruments' rather than a wind quintet indicates that the instruments' coherence as an ensemble is not guaranteed. The instrumentalists are instructed to sit 'as far apart as is practically possible', and the work proceeds in large part as a series of double duets which are either rhythmically determined, in the case of instruments sitting adjacently, or rhythmically freer, in the case of instruments sitting opposite each other. The horn, sitting in the middle of the ensemble, is excluded from this duetting for much of the piece. The parallel with Birtwistle's earlier wind quintet, *Refrains and Choruses*, where the horn was similarly excluded, is unavoidable.

Interestingly, though, where the earlier piece has been interpreted in terms of a headstrong individual endangering a wider harmoniousness, in *Five Distances* the other wind seem unaffected by the horn's exclusion. In fact, the horn appears to be struggling for recognition. It is almost as if, in the absence of the sort of grounding relationship that each of the other instruments has with its duetting partners, the horn does not amount to a character at all. Read along these lines, the piece appears to be aligning itself with the philosophical idea, hugely influential both in relation to the operation of language and also (more pertinently) the very nature of human subjectivity, that identity lies in relationships and the play of difference, rather than any immanent properties.[28] As the horn finally manoeuvres itself into a rather grudging duet with the bassoon (and the other instruments are obliged to form a trio), it is almost as if we are being instructed in a new form of post-structuralist role-play.

This may be an unwitting aspect of the piece. Birtwistle's point of departure for the piece was 'the identification of each instrument's characteristics', presumably determined 'immanently' rather than 'relationally'. But in his recent music it is common for Birtwistle to depart from such initial schemes in the process of composition. As he says with reference to *Five Distances*: 'In the course of composition, intuition comes into play; contexts are arrived at which are illogical. Well designed systems are often broken.'[29] There is all the more reason, then, when striving for a plausible interpretation of a piece, to distinguish carefully between Birtwistle's stated initial compositional strategies and stimuli, and what emerges as the final product.

Ceremonial actors

Verses for Ensembles (25) • *For O, For O, the Hobby-Horse is Forgot* (49) • *Ritual Fragment* (80)

In *Five Distances*, being able to *see* the instrumentalists helps in the realisation of the role-play. The various affiliations forged between the instruments are not readily heard, and the gestures and eye contact made necessary by the piece's complex system of cues form an integral part of the drama. The work's very title indicates the centrality of stage placement to its machinations. Not that a visual aspect is by any means new to Birtwistle's instrumental music. Many of his pieces specify a stage layout, either in order to articulate symmetries in the instrumentation or to highlight instrumental roles.

Some take an extra step in requiring musicians to move during performance. This latter idea first appeared in Birtwistle's music in *Verses for Ensembles*, and it is likely that he viewed it as a natural extension of *Tragœdia*'s attempt 'to bridge the gap between "absolute music" and theatre music'. Indeed, the structure of *Verses for Ensembles* can be loosely mapped onto that of *Tragœdia*,[30] although the score itself provides no evidence of the influence of a specific dramatic form. It is the symmetrical instrumentation and stage layout of the earlier piece that is more clearly capitalised upon. Five wind players, five brass instruments and three percussionists are positioned on a four-level stage, and movements around the stage are carefully indicated in the score. The wind move between two

facing rows of seats perpendicular to the edge of the stage; the percussionists move back and forth between two rows of instruments facing the audience; and the brass sit in between wind and percussion, also facing the
audience. Additionally, four solo desks are positioned at front and rear
corners, which can be occupied by wind, horn or trumpets.

As well as developing ideas incipient in *Tragœdia*, Birtwistle may have
been influenced in *Verses for Ensembles* by 'theatrical' devices in the works
of European avant-garde composers. Berio's *Circles*, dating from 1960,
carries the multiple meanings of its title to the activity of the musicians on
the stage, which includes

> setting the percussionists into frantic gyrations around their instruments . . .
> requiring the singer to move in a half circle from her initial position in front of
> the instrumentalists until she is absorbed into the ensemble, and in the last few
> bars asking the second percussionist to trace circles in the air with a clap-
> cymbal.[31]

This stage movement is not simply surface gesture: it visually articulates
the musical relationships between the participants. As the vocalist moves
nearer the instrumental ensemble, her part 'is drawn more and more into
the musical ambits of the instruments'.[32] A starker take on a similar idea is
found in Boulez's *Domaines*, which was premiered in 1968, shortly before
Birtwistle started work on *Verses for Ensembles*. In Boulez's piece, six
instrumental groups are arranged in a circle and a solo clarinettist is positioned in the middle: 'The clarinet soloist chooses the order in which he
will play six passages of "original" material, and he plays each in the
"domain" of one of the instrumental groups. The instrumental group
whose domain the soloist is occupying then plays its own commentary on
his "original".'[33]

The principle of visually reinforcing musical processes and structures
by relocating performers during the piece inevitably brings music closer to
the spoken theatre, where it is conventional for the main participants to
move freely round the stage. It also enhances the music's 'theatricality' in
two more specific senses. Firstly, it foregrounds the instrumentalists as
individuals. The staticity of most performances of classical music contributes to the sense that the individuality of each instrumentalist is temporarily suspended (or becomes transparent) for the sake of the collective
musical effort. Allowing instrumentalists to move reincorporates their
integrity and autonomy as individuals as part of the performance. With
attention focused on the instrumentalists as cogent individuals, there is
reduced room for ambiguity (of the sort found in *Tragœdia*, for instance)
as to whether the dramatic agents portrayed in the music are or are not
coterminous with the performing musicians.

Secondly, the incorporation of movement in musical performance establishes connections with traditions of performance that make no clear distinction between music and formalised movement. In the Western world, certain sorts of religious ceremony provide the clearest examples of performances in which it is difficult to detach the musical material from its spatial presentation. Introits are sung as the choir files into its stalls; responsorial chant articulates the different spatial locations of celebrant and congregation (and thus, indirectly, their different ceremonial roles); and antiphonal polyphony draws attention to the sheer size of the space generally reserved for religious ceremony. If only by association, there is something unambiguously ceremonial about *Verses for Ensembles*. As Michael Hall has noted, the layout devised by Birtwistle actually bears some resemblance to a church, with its choir stalls and lecterns.[34] Birtwistle has described the work as 'a territorial piece',[35] wherein particular music is 'allotted to a space':[36] the idea is 'that *that* music happens here, in *this place*, and it doesn't happen in another place'.[37] Place and musical material are profoundly interdependent.

Birtwistle has also suggested that this aspect of *Verses for Ensembles* has an analogy in *Punch and Judy*, where, for instance, 'the murders all happen in one place; Choregos only sings in one place and so on'.[38] This comparison is not completely accurate. To understand why, it is necessary to examine more closely the effect on Birtwistle's instrumental theatre of the identification of certain music with a certain place. As noted at the start of this chapter, convention has it that musical characterisation resides principally in musical material, rather than particular instruments. This means that the instrumentalists in *Verses for Ensembles*, rather than performing certain *actions* as they take up the music allotted to a particular space, are more accurately thought of as assuming different *roles*. They possess no role independently of the particular position that they occupy on the stage. Even the distinct sonic qualities of their instruments cannot be relied upon to provide an element of consistent characterisation throughout the piece. The wind players do not bring their instruments with them as they move to new positions, but take up different ones; the percussionists likewise change instruments whenever they move. It is as if the different, spatially separated musics are costumes or masks that the instrumentalist 'actor' dons in the course of the performance. In *Punch and Judy*, on the other hand, the characters' dramatic roles are obviously established prior to the various spatially specific activities that they engage in. Each character's personality transcends the individual actions he or she may be required to undertake in different parts of the stage.

If *Tragœdia* presents a 'musical drama', as Birtwistle describes it, *Verses for Ensembles* more analytically portrays the very business of *enactment*. It represents not just roles, but the *assumption* of roles. This only reinforces the work's ceremonial qualities, of course. Where realist drama does its best to disguise the distinctness of the role from the individual performing it, in ceremony that distinctness – the fact that many other people have performed the role before, and many others will do so in the future – is positively celebrated.

A later work more explicitly invokes the idea of ceremony: *For O, For O, the Hobby-Horse is Forgot* is subtitled 'a ceremony for six percussionists'. The journeys undertaken between stands in *Verses for Ensembles* are here distilled into the more confined movement of each performer between a wide range of percussion instruments; but even without the ambitious relocation of the earlier piece, there remains a sense in which the music is identified as much with a space (namely, the location of a particular instrument) as with a particular performer. In addition, a larger use of space remains in play, for the six percussionists are positioned symmetrically, a layout frequently exploited in antiphonal exchanges.

This is just the undertow to a far more manifest level of ceremonial activity, however. Four of the six percussionists, each with identical instruments, form a Chorus; the remaining two are called King and Queen and have a different selection of instruments. The interaction of all six takes place not just in terms of sounding material but also through a complex system of arm positions and movements. Frequently one arm will be involved in striking an instrument while the other will assume one of eight 'stick-positions' indicated at the front of the score. The King and Queen guide the activity of the Chorus with a combination of sounding and gestural (which is to say, non-sounding) cues, determining the onset and close of sections, tempos, dynamics and the particular combination of chorus members involved. Their parts are sometimes precisely determined, at other times left to the choice of the two performers, meaning that the piece as a whole swings between a hierarchical situation where the Chorus members must basically hang on the whim of the King and Queen, and a more equal arrangement where there is a sense of all participating in some mutual endeavour.

Despite the lack of movement around the stage, the formalised gesturing of all six percussionists has something of the same individuating effect, simply by virtue of drawing attention to the individual bodies causing the musical sounds. The title of the work, which is borrowed from Shakespeare's *Hamlet*, suggests a more specific basis for interpreting the work's role-play. 'For O, for O, the hobbyhorse is forgot' are the last words spoken by Hamlet before the dumb show in Act III, Scene ii; the dumb show itself includes prominent roles for a King and a Queen. Birtwistle makes clear that the piece 'was written after working on *Hamlet* and with the dumb show in mind, but only in mind, for this piece does not intend to characterise or to play out the psychological drama':[39] it would be wrong, therefore, to attempt to correlate the specifics of Shakespeare's dumb show with Birtwistle's piece. But, at the same time, Shakespeare's 'play within a play' – his *representation of* an enaction – forms a neat parallel to Birtwistle's own exploration, in this and other works, of the assumption of roles. The specific idea of the dumb show also points up some of the distinctive characteristics of *For O, For O*'s role-play. The scoring, for a start, inevitably affects the projection of roles: musical tradition still dictates a strong association between pitch configurations and dramatic-expressive states, rhythm and sonority conventionally being of secondary importance. The percussion instruments do indeed seem 'dumb' or 'mute' compared to the soloists of *Tragœdia* and *Verses for Ensembles*. The work's fascinating interplay of sounding rhythm and physical gesture, the latter involving not just the symbolic stick positions but also non-sounding striking motions, also positions it closer to mime or dance than the spoken theatre. It cannot be coincidental that *For O, For O* was written at roughly the same time as *Pulse Field*, which Birtwistle wrote for the Ballet Rambert in collaboration with the choreographer Jaap Flier. The percussionists' movements are not placed at the service of sound or directed towards the articulation of types of musical material, but participate on equal terms. Indeed, substantial passages of the work involve just movement; others involve movements that are fully integrated into a rhythmic structure that is only partly sounded. As Hans Keller noted in a short review of the piece, it is sometimes as if Birtwistle 'hears' the physical gesture.[40] The work's close sees the systematic replacement of sound by movement as the Chorus's quaver beats are gradually replaced by silent strokes. This ceremony ends as pure dance.

The previous chapter argued that Birtwistle's music was on the whole better understood as portraying rituals and ceremonies than literally comprising them. That is certainly true of *For O, For O, the Hobby-Horse is Forgot*, the formalised movements of the percussionists enhancing the sense that the audience has chanced upon a mysterious, barely understood ritual observance. *Ritual Fragment*, on the other hand, carries a more literal ceremonial function as a memorial piece to the London Sinfonietta's artistic director Michael Vyner. It continues the idea of a 'territorial' music, where certain music is located in a certain place. The work's fourteen instruments are arranged in a semicircle around a central solo position: one by one, the instruments move forward as soloist, and then return to the semicircle. Each soloist is modestly 'characterised' by a brief motive which typically announces their arrival at the solo position and also appears sporadically when they are not in the limelight. Yet the melody spun out by successive soloists is conceived by the composer as at least partly autonomous of specific instruments: as Birtwistle says in his Performance Notes, it is 'a solo part, played by ten of the players in succession', and it contrasts markedly with the accompaniment, which is largely made up of loosely co-ordinated ostinato figures. (Michael Hall has revealed that the solo part seems to have been written first, before any of the accompaniment.[41])

Ritual Fragment thus picks up on an idea underlying the earlier *Secret Theatre* yet less systematically exploited there, namely that melody occupies a particular location on the stage. While the instruments in *Ritual Fragment* do possess individual characteristics, their differences are moderated and partly suppressed when they step forward to take the solo part. The effectiveness of the work as a collective tribute by the musicians of the Sinfonietta is not simply a matter of the opportunity it gives for a succession of soloistic turns; rather it is encoded into the very substance of the instrumental parts, which allow both for a distinctive individuality and its partial suspension in ceremonial remembrance.

Negotiated identities

Monodrama (20) • *Four Interludes for a Tragedy* (24) • *Signals* (33) • *Chanson de Geste* (46) • *Secret Theatre* (65)

The idea that Birtwistle's instrumental music involves ambiguities of instrumental role has already been touched upon in this chapter. In *Tragœdia* it was noted that a solo instrument's function may not be wholly fixed, making a direct analogy with the main actors of Greek tragedy difficult. Other works, discussed in the previous section, abandon more fully the dramatic imperative of consistent role-play in order to emphasise instead the contrived nature of enaction.

Sometimes this sort of play with instrumental identity appears to result more from the compromises and modifications that arise, unforeseen, in the process of composition, than any deliberate intention on the part of the composer. That a confusion of role-playing conventions *is* a creative and compositional concern for Birtwistle, however, was made clear in Chapter 1. The stage works use a number of strategies to this end. In *The Mask of Orpheus* the tripartite projection of the main characters immediately confuses the realist presumption of a one-to-one mapping of actor to dramatic role. It is difficult to treat the three manifestations as representative of a single person. But nor are they readily understood as representing three distinct characters: their close interaction when they appear together suggests that there remains a residual singularity of identity, however prismatic its representation. A good example of this is the very beginning of the second scene of Act II (the '1st Cry of Memory'), where Euridice Singer and Euridice Puppet share a single languorous line, and later hocket intimately (Example 2.1). Similar ambiguities of role are caused by the second act's recasting of singers in different parts, in a way that makes no attempt to hide itself, and indeed carries a degree of dramatic import. Both situations – more than one voice per role, and more than one role per voice – are also found in a number of the other stage works.

This sort of representational device is not uncommon in modern theatre, where it may be used to express allegorical or other forms of hidden meaning. The ancient Greek theatre provides a further precedent; for there, as we have seen, several roles were regularly assigned to single actors. A different but equally subtle theatrical situation may be found in kabuki, the popular Japanese theatrical form renowned for its elaborate costumes. In kabuki, stage assistants frequently appear on stage during the performance. They are costumed and carefully choreographed into the performance, yet form no part of the narrated drama. Birtwistle's negotiations with instrumental roles may have been influenced by all of these theatrical parallels. Yet there is a sense also in which he is merely magnifying an aspect of all Western instrumental music. Some recent musicology has argued that we make sense of music precisely by conceiving of it in terms of dramatic action, and that this conception involves not a single ascription of roles (or 'agency') but many, shifting and often mutually contradictory, ones:

> A listener follows the music by drawing on the skills that allow understanding of commonplace human actions in everyday life . . . [However, this understanding is characterised by] a pervasive indeterminacy in the identification of musical agents . . . As the listener discerns actions and explains them by psychological states, various discriminations of agents will seem appropriate, but never a determinacy that rules out other interpretations . . . A single listener's experience will include a play of various schemes of individuation, none of them felt as obligatory.[42]

Orchestral music can be used as an example. At times it is appropriate to treat individual instruments (most probably in the wind or brass) as the principal 'actors' of the drama: the human actions and states that their music embodies appear to be those of an individual instrumentalist. At other times, however, it seems more appropriate 'to think of the whole

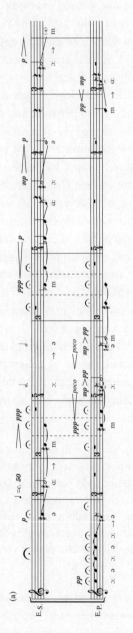
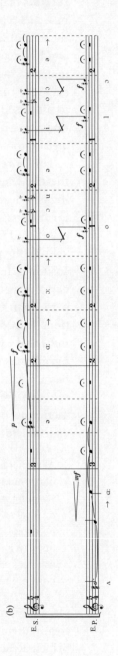

Ex. 2.1. *The Mask of Orpheus*: (a) Euridice Singer and Euridice Puppet at start of Act II, Scene ii; (b) Euridice Singer and Euridice Puppet in Act II, Scene ii, [56]

texture of a piece as the action of a single agent'.[43] The location of a sense of individualistic agency shifts uncertainly from single instrument or section to the collective effort of the orchestra as a whole. Something of this quality has already been identified in *Tragœdia*. There we are sometimes encouraged to hear the instrumental 'soloists' as distinct individuals, usually because their music has a conflictual or confrontational relationship to its surroundings. In cases where the horn and cello merge or meld into their surroundings, on the other hand, it is just as plausible to redraw one's 'scheme of individuation' as to insist that these instruments retain their soloistic status. As part of their respective 'choruses' the horn and cello are just that, chorus members – not principal actors attempting to team up with their choral subordinates. Music's predominant aurality appears to be one of the factors that allows such a redrawing of roles without the grating artificiality that it would bring in the spoken theatre.

Indeterminacy of agency is more determinedly explored in other pieces. In 1967 Birtwistle collaborated for a second time with Stephen Pruslin, the librettist of *Punch and Judy*. The work that resulted, *Monodrama*, takes as its model 'the earliest form of Greek tragedy in which one actor assumes numerous dramatic functions'.[44] In *Monodrama* a soprano soloist doubles in the roles of Protagonist, Prophetess and Herald. She is joined by a second figure, Choregos, who is represented by a male voice delivered through a loudspeaker. At one level, as in *Punch and Judy*, Choregos simply performs the function that the chorus would take in the Greek monodrama. But he is more intimately related to the Protagonist than this might imply. Stephen Pruslin describes the Choregos as the female Protagonist's 'alter ego . . . They are the inseparable poles of any dualism: male-female, reason-intuition, objective-subjective, external-internal.'[45] So the soprano is at once multifaceted *and* partial, carrying many roles yet complete only in combination with the other participant in the drama.

Birtwistle was unhappy with the work and withdrew it. The ambiguities of identity with which it was concerned are still perceptible, however, in the *Four Interludes for a Tragedy* for basset clarinet and tape, which are derived from the solo instrumental 'Interstices' in *Monodrama*. In these short pieces, it is the relationship between live and recorded music that is of interest. At one level, the tape part may be seen as a necessary substitute for the withdrawn context of the larger work: in the words of Michael Hall, it 'creates the illusion of a chorus always mysteriously there in the background'.[46] The ascription of two distinct roles is certainly encouraged by the contrasting qualities of the two parts: the tape's simple, resonant sounds, gradually rising and then falling in each Interlude, cast the impulsive angularity of the clarinet into high relief. (Birtwistle has explained that different compositional processes were used in the construction of each part: 'what's on the tape is structured according to a random process; the clarinet plays something which is the opposite to random'.[47]) Whether the two actually comprise wholly distinct roles is another matter. The disembodied sound of the tape seems more akin to an 'environment' in which the clarinet is suspended, than a second dramatic persona. Indeed, its vaguely nightmarish quality (consistent with the quotation from Djuna Barnes that prefaces the score: 'With shocked protruding eyeballs, for which the tragic mouth seemed to pour forth tears'[48]) suggests that it represents a diffusion of the clarinet's own identity. The clarinettist's expressionistic utterances reflect its confusion about the extent of its own subjectivity in what it perceives about it.

Two later pieces, both subsequently withdrawn by the composer, take rather different slants on the potential for role-play afforded by the format of solo instrument and tape. Each involves a considerable element of choice on the part of the live performer. *Signals* again pits clarinet against tape sounds, the clarinet this time 'choosing from five possible sets of responses' in answer to signals from the tape.[49] Each set of responses, or 'Strain', also leaves much open to performer decision. Indeed, taken together they present a veritable panoply of variables to be decided upon by the performer: in Strain 1 the positioning of repeats; in Strain 2 degrees of ritardando and accelerando; in Strain 3 variants of a melody; and in Strains 4 and 5 routes through complex matrices of material.[50] Compared to *Four Interludes*, then, the clarinettist here is very much portrayed as an autonomous and unambiguous musical agent, deciding and acting in just the way that Aristotle required of the dramatic character: 'Character is that which reveals personal choice, the kinds of thing a man chooses or rejects when that is not obvious.'[51] Birtwistle clearly felt unhappy with the work and it was never published; nevertheless, three years later it found a direct successor in *Chanson de Geste*, whose title (literally, 'Song of Deeds') makes manifest the element of autonomous agency implicit in *Signals*. The deeds in question are choices that the amplified solo instrumentalist (originally a double-bassist, but later left unspecified) must make, 'according to certain prescribed rules',[52] about the material to be played. Michael Nyman's description elaborates:

> The tape, or pre-recorded continuo, as the composer has termed it, contains two basically contrasting elements – a continuous feature and an intermittent, more percussive one. The performed part also has two elements, and these correspond to those of the tape: the CANTUS, a continuous unbroken melodic line: and a series of six PUNCTI, interjectory complexes from which the performers derive part of the material they play.[53]

The six 'Puncti' are, in fact, borrowed almost verbatim from the fifth Strain in *Signals*. Where in the earlier piece each variable-route matrix followed on almost immediately from the previous one, separated only by brief sustained pitches, in *Chanson de Geste* they are inserted as intermittent features against the sustained cantus. Their location is only approximately indicated on the playing score: there is therefore a less determined relationship between the deeds of the instrumentalist and the sounds of the tape than was the case in *Signals*.

For anyone familiar with *Secret Theatre*, the resonances that Michael Nyman's description of *Chanson de Geste* finds in the later work, notwithstanding the decade that separates the two pieces, are striking. *Secret Theatre*'s principal conceit – the combination of two different kinds of music, one predominantly linear (the cantus), the other predominantly 'vertical' or rhythmic (the continuum) – is in many ways foreshadowed by *Chanson de Geste. Secret Theatre*, in fact, is readily seen as something of a summative statement, written as it was for the composer's fiftieth birthday concert, and incorporating many earlier ideas about instrumental role-play, as well as forging associations with earlier pieces written for the London Sinfonietta (principally *Carmen Arcadiae Mechanicae Perpetuum* and *Silbury Air*). The terms cantus and continuum themselves have histories in Birtwistle's music, even before *Chanson de Geste*: research undertaken by David Beard has revealed that Birtwistle's unpublished third opus, *Three Sonatas for Nine Instruments*, was originally entitled 'Sonata cantus choralis';[54] and as early as 1969 Michael Nyman was reporting Birtwistle's interest in 'a new kind of continuo (perhaps "continuum" would be a better word) which would act as a permanent backing to a projected large-scale orchestral work'.[55] *Secret Theatre* fails only to take up the strong element of aleatoricism that characterises *Signals* and *Chanson de Geste* – and which may have been the reason for their withdrawal by the composer. Bestowing such a degree of choice upon a performer is perhaps the most powerful way of asserting his or her identity as a musical agent; after all, individual performer and musical material thereby become entwined to an unusual degree. But it simultaneously limits the possibility of engineering more subtle and ambiguous identities. Such subtlety and ambiguity are to the fore in *Secret Theatre*.

This is clear from the way in which Birtwistle treats his two types of music. As in earlier works, stage separation is used to articulate musical difference: the cantus is placed to one side of the bulk of the ensemble (the continuum). Instruments are drawn from the continuum to play in the cantus, suggesting (as in *Verses for Ensembles* and *Ritual Fragment*) that there is a distinction to be drawn between individual instrumentalists and the musical role that they perform. Yet in contrast to those earlier pieces, the movements between stage areas follow no methodical pattern but are governed by arcane rules devised by the composer – the very 'secret theatre' to which the title refers.[56] Nor do all of the instruments participate in the cantus. Some remain seated in the continuum for the entire piece, though occasionally they show clear affinities to the cantus's musical material. The impression that the instruments are not simply acting out a predetermined ceremonial routine is furthered by the inclusion in the score of part of Robert Graves's poem *Secret Theatre*.[57] According to Birtwistle, the poem was discovered after the piece had been fully conceived (originally the work was to be entitled 'Mystery Play'[58]); but he acknowledges that if you read the poem you also learn something about the music.[59] The music should not be assumed to correspond in its detail to the progress of the poem, then. Nevertheless, Graves's fantastic vision of a dreamed theatre – 'an unforeseen and fiery entertainment' as Graves puts it, spontaneous and thus utterly *unceremonial* – may suggest some possible interpretations for its role-play.

At the most basic level, Graves's reference to a flute ('a flute signals, / Far off') appears to be reflected in the prominent role taken by the flute at the outset of the work. It is the first instrument to play in the cantus, and also the first to return to the continuum; after about four and a half minutes a series of three-note flute 'refrains' ([12]), played initially from the continuum and then from the cantus, serves to round off one of the work's larger paragraphs.[60] A more ambitious interpretation has been tentatively proposed by Jonathan Cross, which connects continuum and cantus with, respectively, the 'humming audience' and 'stage' of Graves's poem.[61] *Secret Theatre*'s role-play is accordingly conceived in terms of the relationship of dramatic actors with their audience. The poem talks of 'mounting the stage as though at random', and this is certainly an apt description of the unpredictable succession of instrumentalists that take up the cantus positions. Cross additionally likens the melodic continuity of the cantus to the continuity of dramatic narrative.[62] However, viewing the instruments of the cantus as analogous to actors on a stage is not wholly consistent with one of the cantus's principal musical features, namely its almost exclusive adherence to different types of unison. As Birtwistle makes clear in notes written prior to the composition of the piece,[63] unison implies not the multiplicity of roles normally found on the theatre stage but a singularity of voice: 'The CANTUS . . . will consist of several instruments speaking as a single voice (choral unison) . . . Individual single voices (single instruments) could play in the CONTINUUM.'[64] To judge from Birtwistle's comments, multiple individuation of the sort found on stage during a theatrical performance would appear to be characteristic of the *continuum*; the unified nature of the cantus, meanwhile, is in certain respects more analogous to the anonymous collectivity of the attentive audience. In the event, the 'individual single voices' in the continuum are largely absorbed into composite ostinato figures involving several instruments: the analogy of audience and stage is unsustainable either way.

This sort of interpretative difficulty is entirely characteristic of *Secret Theatre*. While it would surely be perverse to understand the piece *without* reference to some realm of human action and interaction, that sense of tangible agency is touched by enthralling and perplexing ambiguities. Birtwistle's reference to 'a single voice', for instance, might suggest an interpretation that treats the cantus as a single protagonist acting against a collective or depersonalised backdrop. The cantus's predominantly melodic character strengthens this reading. As Andrew Clements comments, *Secret Theatre* is 'in a very obvious sense . . . a vast exploitation of the time-honoured principle of melody and accompaniment',[65] and this principle is conventionally connotative of the individual (melody) acting in an environment (accompaniment).[66] Birtwistle's use of the word 'cantus' suggests, specifically, an analogy with *song*,[67] and the consistently high register of the cantus allows an even closer comparison with the restricted vocal range of a single individual (specifically a woman, or a child) where a wider registral compass would permit a comparison with no single human voice type. The cantus thus signifies the human body, and perhaps also *words*, where the 'continuum' has no similarly human resonance. Yet Birtwistle is also adamant in his pre-compositional notes that the cantus is *not* to be perceived as primary in this way. The continuum may attempt to wrest the musical foreground from the cantus, and accordingly Birtwistle talks of not one but 'two beings in the same labyrinth'. The fact that cantus and continuum frequently appear to be in a state of perpetual collision, mutually indifferent, rather than engaged in a shared dramatic endeavour, seems to support this conceptualisation. It is not until about five minutes into the piece, with the antiphonal exchanges that immediately precede the flute's three-note motives, that we find the first real sign of mutual recognition (4 bars before [11]). This makes it difficult to map cantus and continuum onto either the model of single protagonist plus chorus (where the one is typically highly attentive to the concerns of the other), *or* the model of single protagonist plus environment (where again there is the presupposition of a closer relationship between them).

The singularity of the cantus is itself not to be taken for granted. Birtwistle at once subsumes a number of instruments into a single musical identity *and*, by moving each instrumentalist visibly and often singly, emphasises the constitution of that identity by a number of performers. In the score Birtwistle lists his instruments as 'Dramatis Personae', further emphasising the element of inviolability at the level of individual instrumentalist, regardless of their deployment in ways that would seem to relieve them of their individual identities. The fact that, with the exception of the two violins, every instrument of the fourteen-piece ensemble is different, means that their individual 'voices' are particularly well projected.

It is not totally impossible to reconcile this focus on the character of individual instruments with the work's apparently conflicting larger principle, which identifies musical roles not with instruments but with particular locations on the stage. As in the more overtly ceremonial pieces, each instrument is conceived not so much as a character but as an *actor*, who assumes different roles according to the stage location he or she inhabits. In contrast to *Verses for Ensembles* and *For O, For O*, however, the actors in *Secret Theatre* are treated not as neutral figures, but as individuals with personalities *in addition to* the roles they assume. The piece combines both a representation of enaction – the assumption of roles by instrumentalists – *and* a representation of the characters of the participants in that enaction. Tendencies amongst the individual instruments to transgress their allotted roles, as if their real personalities sometimes assert themselves over those they are acting out, are suggested by the liaisons that periodically occur between cantus and continuum. For instance, about seven and a half minutes into the work, the bassoon, still sitting in the continuum ensemble, emerges as the music's principal melodic agent, leading the rather awe-struck cantus instruments ([23] – see Example 2.2). The bassoon here gives every indication of wanting to have the role that has been denied to it – and in the process the 'actor' lets slip his or her true character. The bassoon's act of defiance sparks off a period of intense negotiation between cantus and various instruments in the continuum: first the strings ([26]) and then the vibraphone ([33]) revolt against the segregation of roles imposed upon them. *Secret Theatre* is as much about the fissures in the represented enaction – the failure to achieve a watertight allocation of roles between the two ensembles – as about the roles themselves.

Secret Theatre, then, suggests a variety of 'schemes of individuation'. In this, if Fred Maus is to be believed, it merely plays upon a property found in a great deal of music; but, unlike other music, *Secret Theatre* brings the various schemes' competing claims to the fore to such an extent that their mutual inconsistencies cannot be overlooked – as we might routinely do in the Beethoven quartet that Fred Maus analyses. *Secret Theatre* doesn't just

Ex. 2.2. *Secret Theatre*: bassoon leading cantus instruments, [23]

involve these inconsistencies – it is arguably 'about' them. This is perhaps where we find the real connection with Graves's poem. The central, first-person protagonists in the poem play no single role in the 'fiery entertainment' but instead are constantly redrawn: firstly comprising part of the audience ('in the seventh row of the stalls'), then stage-hands ('we mount the stage as though at random, / Boldly ring down the curtain'), then performers ('then dance out our love'). In Birtwistle's piece, as in Graves's poem, roles and functions are melded and interchanged seamlessly, adhering to the malleable logic of dreams, rather than the rational allocations of the woken mind.

Soloists

Melencolia I (48) • *Endless Parade* (71) • *Antiphonies for Piano and Orchestra* (86) • *The Cry of Anubis* (93) • *Panic* (95)

Secret Theatre appeared to confirm an overriding interest, evident in many earlier scores, in the negotiations of a *number* of instrumental roles. Since then, however, Birtwistle has increasingly focused on a more traditional means of presenting musical protagonists: the concerto. Birtwistle has never used the term 'concerto' in a title, but informally he has often described works that combine an instrumental soloist with a large ensemble in this way. Recent years have seen important pieces for trumpet, piano, tuba and saxophone soloists.

These pieces typically capitalise upon the unconditional focus on a single soloist to make particularly explicit connections with individual personae. At the same time, though, they take steps to prevent that figure holding sway over all around it – as tended to happen in the nineteenth-century concerto. Such a rigid allocation of roles would be an anathema to Birtwistle. This pattern is already established in Birtwistle's first work to juxtapose a single instrumental soloist and ensemble, *Melencolia I*. Here, the soloist (a clarinet) is clearly articulated both by its differentiated musical material and by the distinctiveness of its sound against the harp and double string orchestra that form its accompaniment. And the impression that it is representative of a single, lone individual is bolstered by the engraving by Albrecht Dürer from which Birtwistle took his title for the piece. Dürer's *Melencolia I* depicts a winged woman, seated amidst numerous arcane symbols of learning and science, and forlornly leaning her head on her left hand. Birtwistle came across the engraving in Günter Grass's part-autobiographical novel *From the Diary of a Snail*,[68] where it serves as an analogue for Grass's own meditations on melancholy. The clarinet, then, can be seen as a generalised melancholic individual, the musical evocation of whom draws upon aspects of Dürer's image, of Grass's self-reflections and of Birtwistle's own personality. The danger of an unrelieved foregrounding of the clarinet, however, is guarded against by the extreme reticence of its musical materials. Both the clarinet and the strings play music that is, by and large, exceedingly slow and undemonstrative. In the music's determined avoidance of the concise phrasing and regular accentual or intonational qualities characteristic of speech-like melody, the soloist is deprived of one of its principal means of stamping an all-encompassing mark on the proceedings. Similarly, the strings' rather faceless progress for the majority of the piece, which would seem to indicate a relegated role – providing, perhaps, 'the "environment" through which the clarinet travels'[69] – is disturbed towards the piece's close. In one of the work's most striking gestures, the individual string instruments suddenly break free of the anonymous confines of dense tutti textures in a shudder of fragmentary, un-coordinated solo phrases. This gesture of individuation suggests the lurking presence amongst the strings of a stronger element of agency than had hitherto been recognised – as if the work's 'environment' had all along been hiding a multitude of individuals. The harp, meanwhile, whilst by no means as continuously present as the clarinet, has musical material of sufficient individuality to encourage the attribution of a further, distinct role. Its alternating allegiances with clarinet and strings suggests that it is a Choregos-like figure, a master-manipulator – guiding, nudging and cajoling the other instruments, and bringing the whole proceedings to a halt with an abrupt last word.

It was eleven years before Birtwistle wrote another piece for soloist and tutti. *Endless Parade* in certain respects presents a closely analogous instrumental situation to *Melencolia I*: a solo trumpet is starkly offset by accompanying string orchestra, and is additionally shadowed, prodded and pushed by a vibraphone. Birtwistle himself underlined the similarities with the earlier work in a programme note to *Endless Parade*, in which he comments that, 'as in the earlier piece, the solo and tutti . . . do not operate in dialogue as in a traditional concerto; instead they use simultaneous independent material, with a shared compositional object'.[70] Birtwistle's note likens the vibraphone's role to that of the harp in *Melencolia I*. In fact, *Endless Parade*'s vibraphone appears rather less assertive, largely preferring to gloss trumpet and string figures; in the few places where it strikes out independently, it possesses little of the harp's penetrating presence. The vibraphone can, in any case, hardly be expected to keep the trumpet's brash persona in check, for, simply in terms of volume, the trumpet dominates all around it. This fact, together with the trumpet's almost continuous presence throughout the piece, suggests that *Endless Parade*'s soloist represents the observer of a winding parade that Birtwistle mentions in his programme note – an image he offers as an explanatory 'metaphor' for the piece:

> I became interested in the number of ways you could observe [the parade]: as a bystander, watching each float pass by, each strikingly individual yet part of a whole; or you could wander through side alleys, hearing the parade a street away, glimpsing it at a corner, meeting head on what a moment before you saw from behind.[71]

Several recurrent motives in the trumpet strengthen its identity as an autonomous individual – imprinting its own personality, as it were, on its narration.[72] The strings do their best to prevent this single perspective becoming overwhelming: their music is generally more volatile than was the case in *Melencolia I*, and occasionally a single string instrument strikes out alone (as at [33]), as if in a defiant attempt to escape being reduced to a figment of the soloist's world-view. Despite the trumpet's extroversion, however, it too ultimately falls short of the expatiatory confidence characteristic of the nineteenth-century soloist. Moments of sustained melody are few and far between: instead the trumpet's material is consistently fragmentary and halting. Although the trumpet is cast in the role of narrator, its part seems openly to acknowledge the difficulty it has in achieving a speech-like cogency. Its contributions are expressive of frustration at its lack of articulacy, rather than of any more confident command of the larger proceedings.

Beyond this, the vaguely uncomfortable quality of the piece may be put down to a more straightforward technical matter which Birtwistle himself acknowledges in his programme note: namely, the piece's 'limited sound palette'.[73] The combination of trumpet and strings makes difficult any negotiation of relative prominence, and the strenuous efforts of the strings to compete on equal terms can be wearing on the ear. The work has a monochrome quality. Birtwistle was undoubtedly constrained in this respect by the terms of Paul Sacher's commission: the work was written expressly for trumpeter Håkan Hardenberger and the strings of Sacher's Collegium Musicum in Zurich. At the time, this seemed an unlikely combination of instruments for Birtwistle. The prioritisation of a single instrumental sound has particular consequences for some of Birtwistle's compositional preoccupations. There is a risk, for instance, that such relative instrumental inflexibility will hamper the repetition schemes and antiphonal exchanges that in other contexts vivify his musical forms, and which are frequently dependent on stark instrumental contrasts. Similarly, the sinewy heterophony that clothes Birtwistle's melodic writing may be threatened if one line asserts overriding priority. These potential conflicts are present not just in the concerto works but also in the vocal music, where the unrelieved foregrounding of a singing voice may result in a similar textural rigidity.

Antiphonies for Piano and Orchestra brings these issues into particular focus. The title announces a concern with the very formal device that undue emphasis on a single instrument might endanger; the whole question of melody, meanwhile, is problematised by the solo instrument's relative inadequacy in this regard. In the event, the drama of the piece is motivated more by the second of these issues than the first. Contrary to the expectations raised by the title, the piece takes a rather informal approach to structure, intermingling short-winded antiphonal exchanges with rather hectic through-composed passages. What at first appears one of the work's weaknesses – the more or less constant presence of the piano, unrelenting for listener as well as pianist – actually indicates the piece's principal concern: the plight of sustained melody. The limitations of the piano (which is sometimes tellingly reinforced by tuned percussion and harps, creating a sort of 'composite instrument'[74]) are enlarged to become characteristic of the piece as a whole. Attempts by the orchestra to establish a sustained cantus line are quickly thwarted: either instantly curtailed, as at the very start of the work (bb. 24–5), or 'choked' by fluctuating dynamics (for instance b. 190 ff., about ten and a half minutes in). Even the most extended cantus line, which occurs dramatically towards the end of the piece (b. 651), and seems to require the orchestra to summon up all its resources, rapidly fades. In this way, the orchestra dramatises the piano's failure to achieve a sustained melody – precisely the feature which conventionally serves to imprint an expressive agenda upon a musical situation. The hopelessness of this situation is mitigated only at the work's close, where solo orchestral instruments strike up with more decorative melodic writing. If one were to locate an unproblematic presentation of instrumental personae in this piece, it would be here, rather than in the 'soloist's' part.

Slow Frieze, a later work for piano and ensemble (written for Joanna MacGregor, who premiered *Antiphonies*), takes the pressure out of this situation by treating the piano essentially as part of the ensemble, a far more reticent contributor to the overall proceedings. Other recent pieces to prioritise an instrumental soloist are less ambiguous about the personification intended therein. The titles of both *The Cry of Anubis* and *Panic* encourage a connection to be drawn between the mythical characters to which they allude and the pieces' soloists (respectively, tuba and alto saxophone). In the case of the former, the said character is drawn straight from Birtwistle's opera *The Second Mrs Kong*. In the opera, Anubis is the gravel-voiced boatman who ferries souls to the underworld – a figure rather outside the main action, who perhaps attracted Birtwistle's attention, but allowed no further elaboration within the confines of Hoban's libretto. There is in fact no explicit musical connection between the two works, and the tuba part in the orchestral work gives reason to suggest that Birtwistle's Anubis is rather different from Hoban's: the slightly petulant, schoolmasterly character of the opera is here transformed into a more muted, melancholy figure. As Jonathan Cross has noted, the relation of tuba and orchestra is relatively intimate and integrated, in contrast to the 'simultaneous independent material' found in the earlier concerti.[75] The tuba, while characterising the work's sound world up to a point, is more readily absorbed into the orchestral sound than *Antiphonies'* soloist ever could be. This allows musical textures to be flexibly negotiated, rather than being determined in advance. As a result, the work resembles an orchestral tone poem as much as a concerto. The situation may be compared to that in Richard Strauss's *Don Quixote*. There, the prominent solo cello part is not wholly commensurate with the mishap-prone knight. Rather, the cello shares its representation with other instruments in the orchestra, right from the very first soloistic presentation of Quixote's themes, which is shared between cello and clarinet. Similarly, in *The Cry of Anubis*, the tuba is best taken as a spokesperson for the wider orchestral portrayal, rather than a soloist on whom falls the burden of a sustained expressive discourse.

Birtwistle prefaced the score of his next substantial work, *Panic*, with three half-remembered lines from a poem by Elizabeth Barrett Browning:[76]

> O what is he doing the great god Pan
> Down by the reeds by the river.
> Spreading ruin and scattering ban . . .[77]

Here there appears little doubt about the soloist's identification with the work's protagonist, for the saxophone's raucous progress frequently swamps the intricate musical invention in the accompanying wind band – thus very literally 'spreading ruin and scattering ban'. (It is difficult, too, to detach the solo part from the specific saxophonist (John Harle) for whom it was written. More than any other of Birtwistle's concertos, this work is a showcase for a particular performing individual.[78]) Birtwistle calls the piece a 'dithyramb', which in classical Greece was 'a choric hymn, with mime, describing the adventures of Dionysus'.[79] Later the term came to be used more loosely for any wild song or chant. *Panic* is not Birtwistle's first dithyramb: one had earlier appeared in *Punch and Judy*, in the sinisterly celebratory build-up to Punch's first murder of Choregos. Its raucous combination of high winds, bawling toy trumpet and percussion, the latter two following their own tempos, directly foreshadows *Panic*. In fact, Pan is in many respects a direct successor to Punch: an individual whose ego is rampantly out of control, his behaviour displaying the polymorphous perversity of the small child rather than the more finely tuned characteristics of a matured adult.

Even here, though, where the instrumentalist seems so unambiguously representative of the protagonist alluded to in the work's title, there is an intriguing and, this time, disturbing ambiguity. For *Panic* can be understood to refer not just to Pan but to a particular myth about Pan. The irrepressible prominence of the saxophone brings an unavoidable emphasis upon the *pipes* that Pan is typically portrayed as playing (as in Browning's poem, which is actually called 'A Musical Instrument'). The myth relating the origin of those pipes is one that, for contemporary readers, has a highly sinister undertow. It is related at the end of Book I of Ovid's *Metamorphoses*:

> Then the god said, 'In the cool Arcadian mountains, there was among the Nonacrian Hamadryads one very famous Naiad; the nymphs called her Syrinx. She had escaped pursuing Satyrs more than once as well as all the gods the shady forest and the fertile country holds. She worshipped the Ortygian

goddess with her devotion and with her virginity too . . . On the way back from the Lycaean hill, she was seen by Pan, his head decked out with sharp pine, and he spoke to her words like this . . .'; he had still to speak the words, and tell how the nymph had spurned his prayers and fled through trackless places till she came to the peaceful stream of sandy Ladon; and how there she begged her liquid sisters, when their waters had stopped her flight, to transform her, and, when Pan thought Syrinx was pressed against him, instead of the nymph's body he was holding marsh canes; and how, as he sighed, the winds he had stirred in the reeds made a low sound, like a complaint; and how the god, taken by this new art and by the sweetness of the sound, had said, 'This conversation with you will remain with me', and so, for unequal reeds fixed together by a joint of wax, he had preserved the name of the girl.[80]

The fable thus tells of the origin of the Greek name 'syrinx' for what we now call Pan-pipes. But it is also a tale of attempted rape; of Syrinx being forced to surrender her life in order to escape the lusting Pan. The screaming and wailing of the saxophone in Birtwistle's *Panic* take on quite a different connotation in this light. If *Panic* is about Pan – and there seems to be little disagreement about this amongst either commentators or composer – then it is necessarily also about Syrinx, whose voice is heard whenever Pan picks up his pipes. Indeed, her protesting 'complaint' is unrelentingly kept to the forefront of the texture for the entire work. The saxophone is thereby neither clearly representative of Pan *or* Syrinx, but symbolises instead some horrible combination of the two – pursuer and victim, lusting abandon and sheer terror, rolled into a single, garish utterance.

As we have seen, one of Birtwistle's principal strategies for undermining the dominance of his soloists is to deny them the conventional vehicle for asserting an expressive agenda: namely, speech-like melody. In *Panic*, on the other hand, for all the complexities affecting the saxophone's identity, little attempt is made to challenge its authority over the proceedings. Even so, it is not so much speech that is connoted by its material, as screaming and shouting. Basic vocalisation (be it that of Pan or Syrinx, or a combination) replaces syntax and symbol; in a sense the protagonists' voices are *returned to music* – quite literally in Syrinx's case. Birtwistle's wildly gestural and literally incoherent material determinedly resists the various conventions that would have us read the saxophone's role-projection in terms of expressive speech. Whatever the work's other shortcomings – and its indirect portrayal of violent masculinity is, at the very least, problematic – it remains in intriguing ways consistent with the more subtle negotiations of roles found in many of Birtwistle's earlier works.

3 Texts

Birtwistle's fondness for opera has typically been understood as a manifestation of his more general interest in theatre. The operas are less often considered in terms of the interaction established between words and music, or the qualities of the singing voice. Yet non-operatic vocal works have a prominent place in Birtwistle's output, comprising about a third of the published œuvre. Words and the singing human are, for Birtwistle, no mere pendant to a musico-dramatic situation but, by any standards, comprise major compositional concerns in their own right.

Several of Birtwistle's vocal works have a predictably 'dramatic' quality, and the opening section of this chapter looks at some of the ways in which Birtwistle achieves a *narrational* tone in these pieces. A smaller number of works dabble more determinedly with avant-garde text-setting techniques; separate sections of this chapter assess Birtwistle's use of textual fragmentation and his explorations into the *sound* of texts. Particular attention is given in these discussions to the ways in which strategies that at first appear intent on disrupting comprehensibility can also give rise to new meanings.

Despite Birtwistle's occasional use of such techniques, he has not undertaken the sort of systematic exploration of the significatory possibilities of text-setting found in the works of some of his contemporaries. Indeed, by comparison with the vocal music of composers such as Berio or Babbitt, Birtwistle's approach seems strikingly conventional. It may be this that has led to many of Birtwistle's vocal works being neglected and overlooked by both performers and commentators: the majority of the non-operatic vocal music, from the early 1960s to the present day, remains little known. Distinctive tensions and paradoxes nevertheless lie behind the surface conventionality of Birtwistle's text setting – particularly that of his more recent songs. The final section of this chapter attempts to unpick some of these under-recognised characteristics.

Narration

Narration: A Description of the Passing of a Year (8) • *Nenia: the Death of Orpheus* (34) • *La Plage: Eight Arias of Remembrance* (44) • *Carmen Paschale* (13) • *On the Sheer Threshold of the Night* (57)

Opera presents one possible model for texted music: a text may be brought together with music as a means of heightening its narrative component. It is little surprise, given Birtwistle's interest in operatic story-telling, that a number of his other vocal works should place some form of narration centre stage. This is of course not an unfamiliar role for song, which has long been used as a vehicle for narrative text. In part, song becomes narration simply according to what sort of text is set: some tell stories, others do not. But the narrational profile of a song is also affected by the way in which the text is set to music. Although it has been persuasively argued that music invariably has a 'disintegrative effect' on words – the latter suffering, according to Lawrence Kramer, an inevitable 'topological distortion of utterance under the rhythmic and harmonic stress of music: a pulling, stretching, and twisting'[1] – such disintegration nevertheless occurs in widely varying degrees. Many writers on texted music have sought to recognise this by making a distinction between lyric and dramatic settings.[2] The former aims primarily at a musical reflection of a text's mood or wider meaning, in which case a degree of verbal intelligibility may be surrendered. The latter, on the other hand, brings music together with words in order to heighten the telling of the text. In this sort of setting it is more important that the words can be heard; the effectiveness of the song depends upon a listener being able to appreciate how the music is emboldening what is being told in the words. This sort of distinction is not just applicable to the classical repertoire. Richard Middleton has developed a tripartite taxonomy of different word-music relationships in popular song. Two of his three categories are 'affect' and 'story'. According to David Brackett, the first treats 'words as expression', which means that the singing voice 'tends towards "song"'; the second treats 'words as narrative', in which, accordingly, the singing voice 'tends towards speech'.[3]

The speech-like quality of dramatic song can be manifested in a number of ways, and Birtwistle's narrational pieces intermittently entertain these conventions. Syllabicism – the use of one note to one syllable – is central. In fact, for at least one of Birtwistle's contemporaries, Luciano Berio, syllabic song is connotative of speech to the extent that it is barely music at all, disregarding as it does the complex acoustic content of individual syllables.[4] Birtwistle's stance is less extreme. His early work for a cappella chorus, *Narration: A Description of the Passing of a Year*, which sets passages from the fourteenth-century romance *Sir Gawain and the Green Knight*, is predominantly syllabic, each syllable additionally frequently separated from its neighbours by short rests. This prevailing syllabicism is relieved only occasionally, enlivened by moments of rather predictable word-painting (for the words 'sing' and 'fly', for instance). Such madrigalisms are, of course, consistent with the 'narrational' cast of the setting as a whole; and both the madrigalian flavour and the narrational clarity of the piece are furthered by the predominantly homophonic treatment of the eight-part chorus. The work is, however, a madrigal in slow motion. The attention paid to individual syllables results in a protractedness that, for all the care taken in other respects, endangers the coherence and intelligibility of the text. Not for the only time in Birtwistle's vocal music, a respectful-ness towards one aspect of the text (in this case, its syllabic structure) is undermined by an extreme neglect of spoken rhythms.

A later vocal work that is also overtly a 'narration' involves speech more directly. In *Nenia: the Death of Orpheus*, a soprano – accompanied by cro-tales, piano and three bass clarinets – assumes three roles: Orpheus and Euridice, who both sing; and the Narrator, whose part is mostly spoken. *Nenia* thus establishes an unambiguous connection between speech and narration. The piece proceeds largely on the back of the Narrator's story, with the two singing protagonists providing sporadic lyrical interjections in the form of each other's name. In spite of this apparent pre-eminence, however, the spoken part finds itself engaged in a complex negotiation with the *musical* context in which it is situated. It is, for instance, strictly rhythmically notated. This imparts a sense of metrical confinement, dis-torting the spoken syllables. Furthermore, as the piece proceeds sung pitches become increasingly frequent. These sung notes sometimes occur in the middle of words, so endangering the cogency of the Narrator's text. Finally, some of the more violent episodes in the story are related so rapidly that they dissolve into garbled noise. In these various ways, the Narrator's speech is contaminated with music. Only the single, most basic quality of speech remains adhered to for the work's entirety – its syllabi-cism. The narration remains syllabic even when Orpheus briefly takes up the story in the middle of the piece. His deliberate, marcato line suggests a tentative foray into a newly learnt mode of expression.

Syllabicism is not the only way in which Birtwistle may allude to narra-tion in his vocal music. A respect for the sequential form of a text also nat-urally helps to preserve its narrational profile. While poetic texts typically remain intact in nineteenth-century song, twentieth-century composers have sometimes dismantled them, as if in recognition of the change they will in any case necessarily undergo in being combined with music. Birtwistle has not been immune from this tendency in modern text-setting: some examples will be discussed later in this chapter. By and large, though, his settings of pre-existent texts refrain from such fragmentation and rearrangement. This would be less remarkable were it not for the stark contrast it presents with prominent aspects of his instrumental forms, with their re-arrivals and reprises. In fact there is something of a mismatch in this respect between the operas, whose librettos are suffused with textual repetitions and temporal disjunctions, and the non-operatic vocal works, which typically take a strictly unidirectional route through the chosen text. Sometimes, Birtwistle's slavish adherence to the original textual form appears rigid and arbitrary, when other musical decisions seem so intent upon undermining the semantic component of a text.

La Plage: Eight Arias of Remembrance situates itself fascinatingly in this regard. Like *Nenia*, this work was written for Jane Manning and the ensemble Matrix, with its distinctive line-up of three clarinets, piano and percussion (in this work, marimba). It is based on a tiny short story by Alain Robbe-Grillet, which tells of three children walking along a beach.[5] The story's appeal for Birtwistle must have resided partly in its combination of a thread of linearity (the traversing of the beach) with more isolated and repetitive events – birds taking off and landing, and the ringing of a distant bell. In essence it is a story about nothing happening, a static narration. But, rather than set the whole story, Birtwistle retains only the isolated statements of the children, which comment on the bell. These are sung by the soprano on a single pitch and without notated rhythm, each statement closing a short instrumental 'aria'. In choosing *selectively* from a pre-existent text, *La Plage* is unusual in Birtwistle's vocal works. The sequential order of the children's comments is retained, however, raising the possibility that the intervening instrumental music is somehow a substitute for Robbe-Grillet's omitted narrative. That programmatic intentions were not wholly absent from Birtwistle's mind is clear from the piano part, which in the first and seventh arias portrays (with a sombre minor ninth) the bell that the children are discussing. Whether one is able to go further, and identify the gliding of the sea birds in the music of arias 1, 3 and 8 (perhaps in the three clarinets) is less clear.[6] The fact that we may feel encouraged to do so is perhaps what is relevant. At the same time the fragmentary use of the original text, and the breaks between arias, make *La Plage*'s narrative continuity ambiguous. The instrumental music is consistently very soft and slow, and its reticence means that a narrative connection between the children's isolated statements is never forced. It is, to a large degree, left open to the listener whether to build a narrative from the sung comments or not.

The veiled quality of the narration in *La Plage* is also partly due (at least for non-francophone listeners) to Birtwistle's use of the original French rather than a translation. Elsewhere – notably in the Celan settings of recent years – Birtwistle has preferred to use English translations of foreign texts. On the occasions when he retains an unfamiliar language, especially if it is an ancient one, the narrational qualities of his settings are dramatically challenged. The motet *Carmen Paschale*, for four-part chorus and organ, is a good example. It sets a little-known ninth-century Latin Easter hymn, which Birtwistle found in Helen Waddell's collection of *Mediaeval Latin Lyrics.*[7] The work contains some of Birtwistle's most intelligible choral word-setting: briskly syllabic and largely homophonic textures convey the text effectively. In addition, the music is sometimes frankly illustrative, with celebratory 'alleluias' and 'aves', and birdsong in the organ to accompany the sustained, repeated setting of 'philomela melos' ('song of the nightingale'). Yet the marrying of such attentiveness with a Latin text that few are likely to understand complicates the work's narrational profile. The work contains features apparently designed to optimise spontaneous comprehension, yet the use of Latin withdraws the linguistic familiarity on which such comprehension would depend.

A much later choral work, *On the Sheer Threshold of the Night*, which Birtwistle subtitles 'madrigal for 4 solo voices and twelve part chorus', and which also takes its text from Waddell's volume, compensates more actively for the unfamiliarity of the Latin in its attempt to communicate the poetic narrative. The poem, written by Boethius in the sixth century, relates part of the Orpheus legend. Birtwistle correspondingly designates four soloists with the roles of Orpheus (a male alto and a tenor in rhythmic unison), Eurydice (a soprano) and Hades (a bass). These solo roles are placed symmetrically on the stage, Orpheus in the centre of the chorus, Eurydice and Hades at either end. As in *Nenia*, Orpheus and Eurydice intone each other's names throughout the piece; Hades, on the other hand, takes the words ascribed to him in the poem. This illustrative role-play makes up for the opaqueness of the Latin narrative, the bulk of which is carried by the chorus; indeed Birtwistle appears to take the Latin text as licence for all manner of text-setting strategies, many of which impede rather than assist the intelligibility of individual words. Passages of single-pitch recitation, albeit of a rather halting sort, intermingle with more sustained, melismatic passages that stretch individual words out of all recognition, and with contrapuntal textures that completely obscure the text. As a result, Birtwistle's diligent procession through the entire poem becomes a purely conceptual matter. That Birtwistle does not mean the words to be understood is confirmed by his inclusion of Waddell's English translation alongside the Latin at the very end of the work, providing a sudden emergence into verbal comprehensibility.

Even the violence committed by Birtwistle's setting upon the Latin text, however, may work to assist the narration. Near the end of the piece the text is fractured into isolated syllables. These are enunciated homophonically by the entire chorus, but they form little more than shards of barely reconstructable syntax. The text is thus rendered totally incomprehensible; at the same time, though, Birtwistle's setting imbues the music with an appalled, literally speechless quality quite in keeping with the terrible events related by Boethius' narrative.

Fragment

Entr'actes and Sappho Fragments (11) • *Four Songs of Autumn* (74) • *...agm...* (54) • *Words Overheard* (68)

The end of *On the Sheer Threshold of the Night* suggests just one way in which the disruption of a text's meaning through its fragmentation may nevertheless convey a sense consistent with the text. It was noted earlier that Birtwistle's generally respectful treatment of the form of his texts seems at odds with the complex and disrupted progress that characterises some of his instrumental works. Of course, a total congruence of musical and poetic form is only one solution amongst many when planning their interrelation: fruitful tensions may arise from formal discrepancies between text and music. But the tendency of continuous texts to guarantee an element of reassuring linearity can seem incongruous in Birtwistle. In *Meridian*, the singer's literal renderings of Logue and Wyatt, with verses intact and well separated, appear absurdly innocent of their bizarre musical surroundings.

In a number of Birtwistle's vocal works, however, the disruption of narrative continuity extends to the texts themselves. In the works of other composers, such textual fragmentation serves a variety of ends. It can hold a purely formal appeal, textual materials being submitted to the same sorts of systematic organisation as the musical materials (as in some of Milton Babbitt's vocal music, for instance[8]). Or it can be deployed as an act of textual analysis, seeking out and highlighting hidden levels of connection and meaning in the original text (Berio's *Circles* is a good example of this sort of strategy[9]). Lawrence Kramer sees such devices as reflecting many avant-garde composers' 'attempt to get beyond the expressive tradition that begins with the text-centred styles of the Renaissance and their imperative "to express and paint in tones the outer world of nature and the inner reality of man"'.[10] In all instances, the general effect of textual fragmentation is to allow greater flexibility in the sorts of interaction that may be established between language and music. Disrupting syntactic or semantic continuity in a text undermines the concreteness of verbal imagery, and this in turn enables a more effective pull and tug between musical and verbal meaning. Ordinarily our cultural logocentricity inclines us to attribute to the text the governing role in song – particularly classical song, where the poem typically predates its musical setting. The music may be considerably more sophisticated than the poetry, yet its nature is largely determined by it. Only when denied a self-contained or self-explanatory verbal text does it become possible to countenance a more even-handed relationship (or, indeed, one in which roles are reversed). In such a situation, the way in which the words are deployed in their musical context becomes crucial to determining their sense.

Three works from different periods in Birtwistle's compositional career attest particularly strongly to a concern for the fragmentary text; two of these even allude to the idea of fragment in their titles. *Entr'actes and Sappho Fragments* (1964), *Cantata* (1969) and *...agm...* (1979) each set poetry by the sixth-century BC Greek poet Sappho, whose extant work survives only in fragmentary condition. Taken together, these three works trace an evolving journey in Birtwistle's treatment of Sappho's poetry. The earliest, *Entr'actes and Sappho Fragments*, uses English translations from the early years of the twentieth century.[11] These translations tend to smooth over the gaps in the original sources, filling out the extant fragments into relatively substantial three- or four-line verses. The translated verses are presented largely intact in Birtwistle's piece. *Cantata*, in contrast, uses shorter segments of translated text. This is presumably partly in order to balance them with the single-line tombstone inscriptions that Birtwistle sets alongside the Sappho.[12] *...agm...*, for sixteen voices and large ensemble, continues the paring-down process, Birtwistle now seeking to symbolise at a number of levels the fragmented originals. In *...agm...*, three or four words are occasionally recognisably strung together, but on the whole single words, or parts of words, are treated separately. Birtwistle was assisted in this approach by new translations by Tony Harrison, which more faithfully reflected the state of the sources. Much of *...agm...*, however, preserves the original Greek.

The translations of Sappho used in *Entr'actes and Sappho Fragments* may misrepresent the surviving sources, but the work effectively symbolises the latter's piecemeal state in other ways. The piece began life as *Entr'actes*, a cycle of five movements with coda for harp, viola and flute. This cycle was later incorporated as the first part of the expanded work; the Sappho settings, which are scored for soprano, flute, oboe, violin, viola, harp and percussion, then follow, alternating with reworkings of the original 'Entr'actes'. Birtwistle has likened the resulting structure to that of Boulez's *Le marteau sans maître*, with its interleaved cycles of vocal and instrumental movements.[13] The alternation of song and instrumental music in itself hints at the text's partialness: it is as if the Sappho fragments are insufficient to stand by themselves, instead requiring 'completion' by

Ex. 3.1. *Entr'actes and Sappho Fragments*: voice at start of Cantus V

instrumental music. Birtwistle's vocal style, by turns faltering and volatile, contributes further to the fragmentary impression. The first, fourth and fifth of the settings wrench asunder the words of the translated poem, separating them with rests and treating them to contrasting dynamics or articulations: great pressure is placed on the semantic cogency of the text as a result (Example 3.1). The second and third are marginally more cohesive, but the extreme melodic contortions of the vocal line suggest that this cohesion is achieved only forcibly – as if the singer has to do everything in her vocal power to weld words that are more inclined mutually to repel than to attract (Example 3.2). An expressionist anxiety looms large in these settings.

Textual fragmentation does not always serve such expressionist purposes in Birtwistle's music, however, as is indicated if *Entr'actes and Sappho Fragments* is compared to a much later work. The *Four Songs of Autumn*, for soprano and string quartet,[14] set English translations of four Japanese haiku – texts comparable in their brevity to the Sappho translations in *Entr'actes and Sappho Fragments*. There are also strong parallels between the imagery of the verses used in the two pieces, with their shared focus on nature and the seasons. Yet the *Four Songs* display little of the emotional fraughtness of the Sappho settings. Wide intervals and angular lines are largely absent in the vocal part, and the string quartet remains subdued throughout. Instead, more modest musical intervention acts against the coherence of the poetic text. In the first song, for instance, the soprano line is loosely repetitive, comprising a cycle of pitches that occurs four and a half times in slightly permutated form.[15] The repetitive pitch structure interacts arbitrarily with the words, segmenting the text in unpredictable fashion. The third song partitions the text even more obviously. A repeated vocal rhythm (an accented demisemiquaver preceding a

Ex. 3.2. *Entr'actes and Sappho Fragments*: voice at start of Cantus II

quieter, more sustained note value) splits the poem into groups of two syllables – quite regardless of either its meaning or its inherent rhythmic properties. This modest fragmentation helps dissipate the semantic grip that the words might otherwise exert over the music: the repeated rhythm is strongly suggestive of 'music' encroaching on the space previously inhabited by verbal meaning. The song reminds us that a genuine meeting and mediation of music and words, while potentially symbolically expressive of the sort of mental disarray evoked in *Entr'actes and Sappho Fragments*, need not have such connotations.

The idea of the fragment is present at another level in *Entr'actes and Sappho Fragments*, one that makes a virtue of the work's complex compositional history. At three places in the second, newer half of the work, Birtwistle introduces isolated bars from the original *Entr'actes*.[16] These are verbatim repeats – despite the fact that they appear in different instruments – and Birtwistle highlights them in the score by placing them in bold inverted commas. Birtwistle, here, has sought to create something of a musical analogue to Sappho's own fragments. Both the quotation marks and the exactness of the repetitions (the latter contrary to Birtwistle's normal practice of *varied* repetition) emphasise the origin of these brief passages in *other* music – fragments of something else, rather than an organic part of the ongoing musical discourse. Just as Sappho's fragments have been found on the shreds of papyrus used to wrap mummies, so we chance across shreds of an old, discarded piece (*Entr'actes*) in unwrapping the later *Entr'actes and Sappho Fragments*.

Entr'actes and Sappho Fragments thus alludes to the fragmentariness of Sappho's poetry at a number of different levels. The translated verses themselves, however, remain resolutely intact. The same is true in *Cantata*, Birtwistle's second setting of Sappho.[17] *...agm...*, in contrast, extends the musical commentary on Sappho's texts to the very manner in which the texts themselves are deployed – the work's title itself indicating this emboldened focus upon fr[agm]entation.[18] Instead of preserving the sources and their new, more faithful translations, Birtwistle's setting *continues* the process of disintegration. Sappho's poetry is shattered into its constituent components, words and syllables floating independently, and frequently randomly. At the very start of the piece, for instance, four singers from the sixteen-voice chorus are instructed to intone a small number of Greek syllables, repetitively but 'at random'; this forms a murmuring accompaniment to the isolated words and parts of words from Harrison's English translations in the other voices. The principle of unpredictable succession and recurrence also informs the setting at the large scale, with both English and Greek textual elements occasionally reappearing. Notable amongst these is the word 'flashback', which appears at the very start of the piece and then, rather self-referentially, at a number of later stages. Clearly, there is a strong parallel between such textual treatment and the formal and motivic recurrences that characterise Birtwistle's instrumental music. The piecemeal condition of the Sappho fragments that Birtwistle uses in *...agm...* limits their semantic functioning; and Birtwistle's extensive use of the ancient Greek, incomprehensible to most listeners, emphasises the sense in which the texts comprise not language in any ordinary sense but raw vocal material that may be submitted to an abstract, formal structuring.

This is not to deny the text all semantic function. On a couple of occasions Harrison's translations of Sappho's words appear to comment ironically on the text-setting itself – as when a long section of sustained textures is peremptorily halted by the first tenor's rather impatient '. . . 'and so on' (just before [11]); or when the unison statement of 'all together' is spoilt by some laggardly tenors (four bars before [24]). Elsewhere, Birtwistle's juxtaposition of isolated words highlights their widely varying semantic potency. 'Alone', for instance (third bar of [7]), has a resonance quite lacking from the mundane 'did', 'then' or 'from' that occur a few pages earlier. About halfway through the piece, Birtwistle's setting seizes celebratorily on 'be my light' ([26]), much as such a resonant phrase must have been seized upon when archaeologists searched though the shredded papyrus for the first time. However, even the *translated* words are sometimes unintelligible in Birtwistle's setting, drawn out to the point that they dissolve into sound, or fragmented so that they become indistinguishable from the Greek. The impossibility of reconstituting meaning is forever present in the piece – making Birtwistle's musical setting in some respects more faithful to the Sappho fragments than any literary edition, where the neat, self-contained appearance of the verse can give a misleading impression of cogency and authenticity.

The random succession of words found in parts of *...agm...* has its closest counterpart not in a work that uses someone else's words but in one that uses the composer's own. In *Words Overheard*, an eight minute work for soprano and chamber orchestra, Birtwistle sets his own text, which is written in a 'stream-of-consciousness' style, mostly out of short snatches of between one and four words. Vague narrative traces present at the outset of the work ('she would smile . . . and on that day . . . when we had met . . . she was so . . . well . . . I . . . did not wait . . .') eventually dissolve into dissociation and obsessive repetition. The impression is of a once-coherent text that has been dismantled and almost randomly reassembled – a procedure conspicuously absent from Birtwistle's settings of other poets, apart from ...*agm*... . The text of *Words Overheard* has been published separately;[19] but this misses the point of the piece. If Birtwistle did pen a self-contained poetic text, it was left behind at some earlier stage in the work's conception. In fact *Words Overheard*, which is subtitled 'a composed fragment', gives every impression of words and music having been generated side by side, neither one preceding the other. The words make little impression by themselves, with the exception of the little flourish of alliteration and assonance at the beginning. Their clipped and resolutely syllabic musical setting suggests instead that they are fragments of a longer, unheard spoken narrative. Even in this piece, then, where the disruption of textual coherence is so unusually evident, there is a sense of being referred back to some underlying, unheard textual continuity.

Phōnē

Ring a Dumb Carillon (12) • *Deowa* (62) • *The Fields of Sorrow* (39) • *Cantata* (28)

Words Overheard shares with ...*agm*... an uncharacteristically fragmented text, but it is less inclined than the earlier work to dwell on the sounds of words or syllables. Its brisk syllabicism gives little opportunity for the ear to interrogate the *sound*, as opposed to the sense, of the words. This is peculiar, for Birtwistle's text is full of exploitable phonetic content. The opening phrase is a good example, the music giving no special prominence to the assonance and alliteration so laboriously evident in the text (Example 3.3). The treatment of diphthongs during Birtwistle's long vowels is also left totally unspecified, and the double consonant 'ts' (ending 'nights') is illogically assigned to a pitch, where in speech it would be unvoiced. The slightly later *Songs by Myself* for soprano and seven instruments, which (as the title suggests) are also written to texts by the composer, contain the same strange disjunction. Birtwistle's words are

Ex. 3.3. *Words Overheard*: voice, opening phrase

rich with vivid and colourful phonetic content, but his musical settings blithely ignore the fact.

This is not a phenomenon unique to the later songs. *Ring a Dumb Carillon*, for soprano, clarinet and percussion, sets 'A Matter of Prophecy', a poem by Christopher Logue. The opening of the work seems to revolve around the common vowel sound of the poem's first two words: 'He sleeps'. The soprano's long note values highlight the vowel, and a soft clarinet note appears to sustain it immediately afterwards. Later occurrences of the same vowel sound in the first verse of Logue's poem go unnoticed, however; and this establishes the pattern for the rest of the work, which consistently refuses to capitalise upon Logue's copious assonances and alliterations, and concentrates instead on the volatile rhythmic relationships between the three participants. Indeed, for all that convention would dictate the musical primacy of the voice in a texted work, in this piece it is the *clarinet* that 'carries the monody'[20] and from which the other parts are proliferated. Birtwistle says that he was attracted by some of the imagery of Logue's poem, but that the work is essentially a dramatic piece and that the poem, conversely, 'isn't particularly dramatic'.[21] This suggests that the poem exists at one remove from the musical drama, and Birtwistle's negligence of Logue's words bears this out. The extremely deliberate pace of most of the setting shifts attention to the words' vowels merely by default. Throughout, the intelligibility of the text is thoroughly obscured.

There are more obviously intended explorations of word sound in Birtwistle's output, however. *The Mask of Orpheus*, pre-eminently, sees a literal and very deliberate exploration of the transitional spaces between sound and word: from the opening of the work, where Orpheus painstakingly finds his way from spoken sound to sung word; to the wrenching spoken utterances and shrieking vocalise of the Oracle later in Act I, to the artificial language of Apollo throughout the opera, forged from the component sounds of the words 'Orpheus' and 'Euridice'. The first and second of these examples amply demonstrate that non-verbal vocal utterance need not necessarily signal (as it partly did in ...*agm*...) a retreat from expressivity in favour of a purely formalist approach to vocal sound. Orpheus' and the Oracle's vocalisations are powerfully expressive, by association with the many everyday ways in which a feeling or a state of mind is

Ex. 3.4. *Deowa*: motives with syllables

vocally expressed without recourse to words. Similar examples of non-verbal vocalise are found in the other operas, especially in the parts of Morgan in *Gawain*, and the 'wild and wordless' Kong in *The Second Mrs Kong*.

It is, however, the third device in *Orpheus* – Apollo's language – that was most clearly taken up in the work written immediately after the opera's completion in 1983. *Deowa* is a short piece for soprano and clarinet, each of whose parts comprises an angular melody, proceeding in sustained counterpoint against the other. The singer's text consists entirely of syllable sounds extracted from the title and variously reassembled – a clear parallel to the way in which Apollo's language was constructed in the opera. The melodic invention is given added coherence in each part by the recurrence of tiny motives, which are absorbed into the melodic lines. In the case of the voice, these motives are often attached to particular syllables (see Example 3.4). In contradistinction to Apollo's language, there appears to be no attempt in *Deowa* to build a vocabulary from the repertoire of syllables, and this lack of syntactic distraction encourages a more complete focus on the *sound* of the text. Yet in spite of this freedom from the demands of language, Birtwistle stubbornly retains the *syllable*, rather than its constituent phonemes, as the basic unit for his setting. 'A' as in 'acorn', for instance, is a diphthong, but no account is taken of this in Birtwistle's setting. A revealing comparison may be made with Berio's *O King* for mezzo soprano and five instrumentalists, a work written some fifteen years before *Deowa*. In Berio's work the sung text is similarly made up of constituent parts of the phrase abbreviated in the work's title: 'O Martin Luther King'. However, Berio, rather than resting content with the syllables provided by the phrase, begins merely with its six vowels, altering the one diphthong amongst them to the pure vowel sound [o]. Only after laying bare this lowest phonetic level does Berio admit the consonants that complete the syllables of the four-word phrase. In this way, Berio conducts a much more thorough analysis of his text's phonetic content.

Deowa is in some ways closer in spirit to English vocal polyphony of the late fifteenth and early sixteenth century than to the experiments of other twentieth-century composers. In the music of the Eton Choirbook, which dates from the late fifteenth century,[22] liturgical texts are given extremely protracted, melismatic settings, so that for much of the time one hears merely a counterpoint of vowel sounds. It has been suggested that this text-setting style is connected to the richness of spoken vowel sounds at the time, in comparison to modern day 'received pronunciation'. As John Potter comments,

> For specifically musical reasons a great deal is lost [in modern performances of sixteenth-century music] by ignoring the plurality of accent and the rich variety of tone colour that this implies . . . The colour and shape of the language become the main determinants of vocal colour, rather than the notions of 'beautiful' tone quality which are at the heart of modern 'classical' singing . . . Diphthongs, so rich in earlier varieties of English, mean that the text is always in motion at the level of the syllable.[23]

In *Deowa*, then, Birtwistle similarly presents the singer with the opportunity to invest the text with 'motion' by means of her treatment of the diphthongs. The idea of vowel sounds being altered according to accent or dialect also finds some reflection in Birtwistle's piece, for the component syllables of the title are interpreted in different ways: thus the 'a' is both 'a' as in acorn and 'a' as in apple; the 'o' is both 'oo' as in 'hoop' and 'o' as in 'orange'.

Deowa explores in a particularly intense way the sounds of a word, while leaving room as well for the play of a particular voice. The transmutation of word into voice is more explicit still in *The Fields of Sorrow*, for chorus, winds, vibraphone and two pianos. The chorus relates Ausonius' melancholy evocation of a gloomy, wooded scene,[24] in a manner that exemplifies Birtwistle's narrational idiom – syllabic, homophonic and with an almost complete lack of melodic inflection. But two soprano soloists latch on to and echo isolated vowels and syllables from the main text in such a way as to blur the distinction between textual enunciation and untexted vocalise. Towards the end, roles are reversed: the two soloists deliver the closing line of the poem in a hauntingly protracted manner, following which the chorus gently hums the piece to its close. By this stage it is clear enough that the function of the words is as much to 'randomly' generate vowel sounds as it is to convey a poetic narrative.

For a piece whose title gives such prominence to the activity of singing, *Cantata* has been little discussed from this point of view. Commentators have focused instead upon the formal novelty of the work, namely a 'Refrain' that appears five times and allows for a variety of realisations. But, as the title implies, *Cantata*, which is scored for soprano and small ensemble, is really a piece about singing. The vocal line comprises a judicious blend of types of song. Sustained single notes, set to individual syllables of text, seem less intended to emphasise patterns of vowels than to provide plenty of room for the particular vocal quality of a singer to 'tell'. The leisurely flow of words is also frequently interrupted by vocalise. Perhaps most strikingly, the vocal line is saturated with portamenti, which help to smooth some of the sharper angles in Birtwistle's melismatic writing, and, in their more protracted form, appear to represent a deliberate statement of resistance against the scalic increments that ordinarily confine the singing voice in notated music. Given that the piece was written for the Pierrot Players it is natural to assume that Schoenberg's *Sprechstimme* was an influence here.

These glissandi also permeate the string writing in the accompanying ensemble – one of the ways in which the ensemble may be seen as emboldening the specifically *vocal* quality of the music. Another is the music's prevailingly high tessitura: only rarely does the piano venture into its deepest register, and overall the piece is dominated by the sounds of glockenspiel, celesta, and high winds and strings. As a result, Birtwistle's characteristically ambitious soprano writing appears less of a textural afterthought, and sounds less awkward, than is sometimes the case in other pieces. The treble-dominated sound of the piece effectively mitigates the uneasy or distressing associations that atonal writing for the high soprano voice can evoke. (This aspect of Birtwistle's vocal writing is discussed further at the end of this chapter.) Thus, the closing text of the piece, sung against the final statement of the Refrain – 'No longer will my mouth utter sounds / nor the clapping of hands follow' – is not simply a rather droll reference to concert convention. For it is precisely the 'uttering of sounds' with which *Cantata* appears concerned, to an uncommon degree.

Expression

Prologue (37) • *Epilogue* (42) • *Pulse Shadows* (Nine Settings of Celan) (99) • *Songs by Myself* (66) • *An die Musik* (75) • *Four Poems by Jaan Kaplinski* (82)

The first section of this chapter pointed to the concern of some of Birtwistle's vocal works with narration, a concern shared with the operas. This may manifest itself simply in terms of a respect for the sequential form of the text, and a tendency to syllabicism. Or it may involve a more explicitly dramatic conception, as in *On the Sheer Threshold of the Night*, with its designated solo roles. This more dramatic relation to the text is also apparent in *Prologue* and *Epilogue*, two short works for male voice and small ensemble. Their texts are drawn from the spoken theatre: *Prologue*

Ex. 3.5. *Epilogue*: 'ding-dong bell'

sets the opening of the Watchman's speech from Aeschylus' *Agamemnon*; *Epilogue* takes Ariel's song 'Full fathom five' from Act I of Shakespeare's *The Tempest*. Each work forms a miniature dramatic scena, in which the singer represents the character whose text is sung, and the instrumental music is representative of both the character's physical surroundings and his own psychological state. The settings are in certain respects responsive to the semantic content of the text, dwelling on words of importance and emboldening the vocal part with appropriately timed gestures and changes of texture in the instrumental music. So, in *Prologue* Aeschylus' Watchman gives particular emphasis to 'weary', 'night' and 'watch', the last being further emphasised by a distinctive, fanfare-like flurry in the two trumpets. Dramatic realism is even more evident in *Epilogue*, with its whispered 'Hark! now I hear them' and frankly illustrative 'ding-dong bell' (see Example 3.5). Such literalism has not always been a feature of Birtwistle's vocal 'dramas'. In *Ring a Dumb Carillon,* for instance, which Universal Edition's catalogue describes as 'a dramatic scena', the drama arises principally from the abstract rhythmic interaction of voice, clarinet and percussion. Christopher Logue's vivid poem provides an added ingredient to the melee of stimuli, but its grip on the vocal part is moderated by what might be understood as 'purely musical' concerns.

To hold back from the sort of explicit, dramatically responsive relationship of music to text found in *Prologue* and *Epilogue*, however, does not necessarily imply the abandonment of all connection with a text's semantic content. As mentioned earlier in this chapter, there exists a second, distinct category of text-setting, one that is more 'lyrical' than 'dramatic'. Lyric song is aimed less at tracing the course of events related by a text (as both *Prologue* and *Epilogue* do) than at a musical reflection of a text's mood or wider meaning. Lyric poetry in any case often contains no 'story' that could be outlined in a musical setting: instead, it may involve a more static succession of images or ideas. Music's function in relation to such a text is not so much the heightening or dramatisation of its content, as the providing of an interpretation – the making specific of a meaning that remains fluid or ambiguous in the text itself. The difference between dramatic and lyric song is thus one of degree rather than kind. Writers such as Lawrence Kramer have argued persuasively that *all* text-setting forms an act of interpretation, a selective reading: 'A song . . . does not *use* a reading; it *is* a reading, in the critical as well as the performative sense of the term: an activity of interpretation that works through a text without being bound by authorial intentions.'[25] No text-setting can pretend to be wholly authentic to the poem. Nevertheless, where that interpretative presence may sometimes remain tacit and unannounced, in lyric song it comes to the fore. Composers in this tradition are driven less by the belief that their music delivers a wholly faithful rendering of a poem than by the sense that, in the words of Kramer, 'song brings poetry to life not by resembling it, but precisely by being different'.[26]

The abandonment of a close adherence to a poem's narrative unfolding means that, in lyric song, the intelligibility of the text is less of a priority. The voice moves away from the emulation of speech, and becomes instead primarily a vehicle for melody – for it is melody that has traditionally been the locus of the composer's expressive interpretation of the poem. As Hegel put it, '*Lyric music* . . . expresses individual moods of the soul melodically.'[27] A statement by Arnold Schoenberg typifies the perspective of the lyric song-writer:

> Even Schubert does not set off words singly in any marked fashion according to the weight of their meaning. Rather, by means of a comprehensive melody, he may pass over a salient textual feature, even when it is most important in regard to poetic content and poetic substance. It should not be surprising, then, that a genuine melody will arise relatively seldom from a procedure which strongly emphasizes the text.[28]

Birtwistle's more recent songs are notable for their unapologetically melodic cast. They have steered clear of both the simpler delivery found in *Narration* and *La Plage*, and the fragmented or phonetics-oriented settings of *...agm...* and parts of *On the Sheer Threshold of the Night*, in favour of a sustained cantabile that is strongly suggestive of an expressive relation to their texts.

This is not the only way in which these songs declare their adherence to a lyric tradition. A shift in Birtwistle's attitude to text-setting is indicated by his choice of poetry in recent years. One might contrast his earlier interest in Sappho's verse – verse that has been described as possessing a 'cool neutrality' ideally suited to filling out a specifically musical design[29] – with the more recent turn to modern European poets such as Rilke and Celan, whose striking and disturbing imagery raises the expectation of a fully expressive engagement. Indeed, both of these writers form part of a tradition of German poetry, running from Hölderlin to Trakl, that has been the life-blood of the so-called 'art song' since the early nineteenth century.[30]

Ex. 3.6. Nine Settings of Celan, 'Night': voice, bb. 39–43

Taken together, these features of Birtwistle's recent songs have encouraged critics to discern in them an 'expressive lyricism' that positions them in a tradition of serious song extending back through the second Viennese school to the early nineteenth-century lied.

As the above quote from Schoenberg indicates, earlier composers have been aware of the conflict that tends to arise in lyric song, between melodic expression and respect for the text. In his cycle of songs *Das Buch der hängenden Gärten*, for instance, Schoenberg's expressive interpretation of texts by Stefan George demanded a vocal style that risked warping them out of all recognition; in the words of Lawrence Kramer, 'the musical gestures of the voice are almost too fluid, too autonomous, to be reconciled with utterance'.[31] Birtwistle's recent songs persistently deal with this same tension, fighting shy of the extreme 'antitextuality'[32] of avant-garde techniques but nevertheless resisting on several fronts any close resemblance to speech. The Nine Settings of Celan, whose composition spans a period of nearly a decade, may be treated as representative. In the completed cycle, parlando syllabic settings ('Psalm', 'Tenebrae' and 'Night') feature prominently alongside more angular, melismatic ones ('Thread Suns' and 'White and Light', for instance) – reminding us that Birtwistle, like Webern before him, does not see syllabicism as an irreconcilable obstacle to properly lyrical expression. (In fact Webern's text-setting, for all its apparently abstract relation to the text, is consistently syllabic – far more so than Birtwistle's.[33]) Similarly, the Celan settings often display a perceptible attentiveness to spoken rhythms and accents – as at the end of 'Night' (shown in Example 3.6), where the syllables 'stone', 'made', 'o-[ther]' and 'tar-[get]' are given appropriate emphasis by being placed on the strong metric beat. At the same time, though, these concessions to verbal intelligibility are compromised by other aspects of the settings. The consistently protracted way in which Birtwistle proceeds through his texts, for instance, means that individual syllables risk losing their identifiability – at least for anyone who does not have the poems in front of them as they listen. 'An Eye Open' provides a particularly extreme example, each syllable prolonged to an extent that seems deliberately intended to *prevent* comprehension of the poem. And a sensitivity to prosody can be neutralised by melodic contours that contradict the intonational emphases characteristic of speech. In Example 3.6, for instance, the metric emphasis visible on the page is projected only weakly by the melodic line – particularly at the second syllable of 'other', which receives melodic emphasis over the first. In general in the recent songs, Birtwistle's melodic contours are resolutely unspeech-like, for all that their rhythmic qualities may be determined in response to the text. Wide melodic intervals frequently serve to obscure textual cogency, as they did earlier in *Entr'actes and Sappho Fragments* (see Example 3.2). Even when Birtwistle adopts a more recitational, single-note style, he consistently forces his soprano line into its upper register, far removed from the pitch level of ordinary speech. The first half of 'Night', for instance, is delivered on a single high G and its immediately adjacent notes. (This reflects words of the poem – 'shard note, thin' – while paradoxically obscuring their enunciation.) On a number of occasions this prevailing high tessitura appears to be dictated by the functioning of the E at the top of the treble stave as a sort of pedal note or focal pitch: this note opens four of the nine songs, and only plays anything less than an important role in the first and last songs of the cycle. In a number of ways, then, textual enunciation and musical invention exist in audible conflict in these songs.

As I have suggested, such is the condition of lyric song. However, it would be wrong to view this as the exception rather than the rule in Birtwistle's vocal writing, affecting only the recent 'lyric' settings: in fact, the contrary seems to be the case. An uncertainty about the relative status of words and music affects Birtwistle's more overtly 'dramatic' works as well. In *Prologue* and *Epilogue*, for instance, moments of obvious dramatic responsiveness to the text are combined with a turgidity in the setting that makes comprehension extremely difficult. On the one hand, the illustrativeness of the music suggests that we are expected to understand what the singer is saying; on the other, that speech appears to be relegated by other musical concerns. The question of textual audibility has been a more publicly contentious issue in relation to Birtwistle's operas. Following the first performances of *Gawain*, a letter was printed in *Opera* magazine objecting to Birtwistle's neglect of 'rule number one of operatic composition – to set the text so that the words can be heard by the audience'.[34] As the letter made clear, Andrew Clements's preview of the work had anticipated and defended this aspect of Birtwistle's writing, claiming that some of his vocal lines 'were never designed for audibility'.[35] But it is not easy to sustain

Clements's argument precisely because Birtwistle appears ambivalent on the matter. This was demonstrated more recently by the Sphinx in *The Second Mrs Kong*: her easily heard quips form a brief oasis of immediate verbal communicativeness in an otherwise highly logophobic musical environment. Throughout both *Gawain* and *The Second Mrs Kong* the music flirts moodily with both libretto and drama, at times haughtily indifferent, elsewhere responsive and even pictorial. In *Gawain* critical moments in the libretto can be exceedingly casually responded to, as at Morgan's culminating revelation of the identity of the Green Knight and subsequent explanation of the purpose of Gawain's ordeal. Morgan's highly-strung neurosis is surely not sufficient excuse for the garbled word-setting at this point.

Of course, the inaudibility of a text in vocal music is not intrinsically a failing. There are instances where composers have deliberately set aside audibility as an issue. Louis Andriessen, for example, sets texts by Plato and Augustine in his works *De Staat* and *De Tijd*, but by retaining the ancient languages of the originals he ensures that most modern listeners will never be put in the position of straining to reassemble them while they listen. Other strategies in these works strongly reinforce this deliberate inaudibility: in *De Staat*, the treatment of the singers as just another part of an instrumental ensemble of great stridency and volume; in *De Tijd*, the setting of each and every syllable of text to a prolonged semibreve, by analogy with the cantus-firmus technique of medieval polyphony. The text's function in the music is limited to the bestowing of a certain associative weight, a seriousness of purpose, and a specificity of message that the instruments could not achieve by themselves. Birtwistle follows a similar path, to good effect, in *...agm...* and parts of *On the Sheer Threshold of the Night*.

Something of the ambivalence found in the recent operas comes through in Birtwistle's recent songs. Here, as I have suggested, Birtwistle is working in a tradition where there is less expectation of continual audibility, and by and large Birtwistle's settings skim over individual words in pursuit of a more generalised correlation to an underlying meaning or tone. (The fact that Birtwistle is happy to have the Celan settings performed in English *or* German – the published score prints Celan's original poems beneath the translations of Michael Hamburger – is indicative of this approach.) However, at the same time some of the recent songs adopt a recurrent cliché of Birtwistle's earlier text-setting practice, namely the spoken close. Spoken last lines are found in *Ring a Dumb Carillon*, *Punch and Judy*, *Cantata*, *Epilogue* and *Nenia*, and they are also strongly implied by the simple, even-rhythmed syllabicism found in *Meridian* and *On the*

Sheer Threshold of the Night. Songs by Myself takes up the latter device; and the gesture is hugely magnified in *Pulse Shadows*, in that the whole of the last song, 'Give the Word', is delivered in a perky speech-song, 'quasi parlando'. Presumably intended to impart an elegant conclusiveness to the works in which it appears, this device can function less beneficially. The sudden clarity of the spoken voice carries the implication that the listener is assumed to have been attending to and comprehending the text all along, an assumption that other aspects of Birtwistle's text-setting in these works seem to have abandoned. It would be easier to accept unintelligibility as an integral part of a text-setting style were the ready intelligibility of speech not so tantalisingly part of the equation. The rather naïve word-painting that features throughout the Celan cycle (see, for instance, the florid melismas accompanying the words 'flower' and 'heaven-ravaged' in 'Psalm' or, still more predictably, 'sung' in 'Thread Suns') has a similar effect – suggesting that the setting is, after all, serving a literal, narrational function, rather than the more distanced interpretation that legitimates the neglect of the text's specificities in other places.

The reversion to speech, or the sudden snatch of word-painting, appear as intrusions into a vocal style that is otherwise largely innocent of the specific significance of the particular words it is carrying. The five *Songs by Myself*, for soprano and seven instruments, exemplify this style. Birtwistle says that the texts he sets in these songs were 'dredged from the silt of my subconscious during spates of holiday melancholy'.[36] They are dense with vivid imagery and consonantal play, as at the start of the third song: 'Cold statements thaw time's stillness, / but once the daydream's midnight / belled slow refrain ends'. Birtwistle's vocal line, however, makes little attempt to distinguish between words, and passes over their phonetic content without comment. Words are strung along a melodic line like beads on a string: the relationship is convenient but far from necessary, and the beads could readily be substituted by others (see Example 3.7). It could be argued that the vocal line's unrelieved, gluey monotony is appropriate to the obsessive, melancholy staticity of Birtwistle's texts. Still, an instructive comparison can be made with the much earlier *Monody for Corpus Christi* (discussed more fully in Chapter 6). Here, the text-setting is similarly distanced from the specificities of the words, but the teeming invention of the instrumental ensemble distracts attention from it, asserting itself as the musical foreground. In *Songs by Myself*, on the other hand, the voice and its words largely remain the focus of attention. Instrumental textures are mostly constructed from circular ostinati or other 'accompanimental' figuration, and thus appear to take a supporting role. As a result, the various levels at which the instrumental music might be seen to convey

Ex. 3.7. *Songs by Myself*, No. 3: voice, bb. 6–17

textual meanings (some of which have been elegantly elaborated by Arnold Whittall and Michael Hall[37]) are frequently obscured by the meanderings of the voice.

By comparison with *Songs by Myself*, the sporadic word-painting of the more recent Celan settings seems unexpectedly illustrative. These settings are, in fact, characterised overall by a greater commitment to their texts, a commitment that also manifests itself in the more varied text-setting styles already mentioned, and in a more assertive role on the part of the instrumental ensemble (which comprises two clarinets, viola, cello and double-bass). So, the general connection that can be made between the slow, twining melancholy of Birtwistle's music (here the willingness of the clarinets to contribute to the music's melodic component alongside the voice is important) and 'the anguish, the darkness, the shadow of death' that is a feature of all Celan's poetry[38] is emboldened in some of the settings by a more perceptible attentiveness to the specific content of individual poems. In 'Psalm', for instance, the 'negative theology'[39] of Celan's text ('No one moulds us again out of earth and clay, / no one conjures our dust. / No one.') is well caught in a setting that drifts between defiant flurries on the clarinets and the sullen bleakness of low double-bass and harmonics on the viola and cello. In another of the syllabic settings, 'Tenebrae', the clarinets again angrily convey the desperation of Celan's imagery, and the viola's 'pesante' double-stopping ensures that the 'clawed and clawing' of the poem's fourth line pervades the whole song. Celan's 'Psalm' and 'Tenebrae' are relatively accessible texts: a little background knowledge of Celan's first-hand experience (as a Rumanian Jew in Nazi Germany) of persecution and genocide is sufficient to fill out their meanings. 'Todtnauberg' is another poem with identifiable autobiographical connections, for it relates to Celan's 'intense intellectual relationship'[40] with

Heidegger, and Celan's hope that Heidegger would one day retract the public support he had offered Hitler's regime. As Michael Hall has noted, the sense of a dialogue is conveyed in Birtwistle's setting by having the soprano both sing and speak the text in rapid alternation, one version in the original German, the other in Hamburger's translation. Birtwistle's 'Performance Notes' for the song ask that the spoken text should be 'delivered as if reading from a text which is barely visible, resulting in an added feeling of hesitancy'; for Hall this hesitancy suggests 'that reconciliation had only been broached and there was still an element of doubt in Celan's mind'.[41] The sustained clarinet lines and anxious staccato figures on the strings which underpin the voice's schizophrenic exchanges give the song considerable tension.

Admittedly, it is difficult to tell to what extent these are genuine examples of interpretative sensitivity to Celan's text, as opposed simply to chance coincidences: it will always be possible to identify some element of a text that can act as a rationale for some element of the music to which it is set. There is certainly enough else in Birtwistle's musical settings that recourse to the poem cannot so easily explain. Some of Celan's other poems are more inscrutable, however; as Hamburger has written, Celan found realism and reportage too simplistic, and 'wanted poetry to be open to the unexpected, the unpredictable, the unpredeterminable'.[42] In Birtwistle's settings of these less accessible poems, what is more apparent than any congruency of specific content is their musical emphasis of the texts' surreal strangeness. This is the case in 'With Letter and Clock', for instance, where dully throbbing clarinet semiquavers create a disturbing, hallucinatory impression – one that responds to the surface imagery of 'swimming light' and 'strange, painful rings', rather than seeks out deeper, hidden meanings. The shadowy harmonics and *sul ponticelli* of the equally elusive 'Night' have a similar effect, the setting seeming to share in a listener's likely bewilderment at Celan's text.

The course of action taken by Birtwistle in 'With Letter and Clock' and 'Night' – preferring to emphasise the poetry's strangeness rather than attempt a more overtly interpretative teasing out of meaning – is perhaps the more responsible one. For all that certain correlations can be drawn between music and text in some of these songs, there is a strong sense in which Celan's poems remain untouched by them. It remains questionable, for a start, to what extent Celan's poetry has any meaning *at all*, independently of the specific semantic force of each individual word: a song technique that proposes largely to dispense with the specificities of the individual word (its rhythmic and intonational qualities, its phonetic content, its semantic import) in pursuit of some more general musical expression may consequently have little to build upon. Michael Hamburger writes that 'the difficulty and the paradox [of Celan's poetry] demands a special attention to every word in his texts',[43] and he notes how Celan's focus on the individual word led him 'to coin new words . . . and to divide other words into their component syllables'. In the later poetry, the process of condensation means that 'verse lines and whole poems tend to be shorter and shorter'.[44] Meaning resides as much, possibly more, at the level of the individual word, as at the level of the verse or the poem. Birtwistle's settings, with their tendencies for textural homogeneity and disregard for clear enunciation, repeatedly blur and dilute the vividness of Celan's word play. This problem is anticipated in an earlier song, *An die Musik*, for soprano and ten instruments. Here Birtwistle sets a poem by another 'difficult' modern German poet, Rainer Maria Rilke, which proceeds in terms of distinct and frequently disjunct images, rendered in a variety of syntactically adventurous forms. The poem finds no musical correlate to its own meticulous precision of imagery. Birtwistle's setting divests the words of their particular intensity, stringing them unconcernedly onto a rhapsodic melodic line whose aims and effect seem wholly divorced from the original text. That this is less disabling here than is sometimes the case in Birtwistle's vocal writing can in part be put down to the careful musical integration of vocal line and instrumental ensemble. The sense, difficult to avoid in *Songs by Myself*, for instance, that the singer is some kind of rambling, hallucinatory interloper upon the proceedings is correspondingly diminished.

Both Rilke and Celan make considerable use of punctuation and line division to heighten the projection of their verbal imagery. In the poetry of both, single words frequently stand alone; and, as Michael Hamburger has demonstrated, hyphens and enjambment are crucial to the 'polysemy' of Celan's poetry. Such devices are highly suggestive as to musical treatment, in terms of both timing and relative emphasis,[45] but Birtwistle's response is inconsistent, reflecting the text's written structure at one moment but passing over it at the next. In the Celan settings, breaks between verses are generally marked by short instrumental passages; the refrains contained in two of the poems ('With Letter and Clock' and 'Tenebrae') are also predictably reflected in the music. The internal structures of verses are not so clearly projected, Birtwistle's vocal melody frequently serving to smooth over the craggy progressions and sharp edges of Celan's verse. Again, an earlier work, the *Four Poems by Jaan Kaplinski* for soprano and thirteen instruments, forms a direct precedent to this aspect of the Celan cycle. Kaplinski's poems, which focus upon images from the natural world, are written in short lines of one or two words, encouraging the reader to

Ex. 3.8. *Four Poems by Jaan Kaplinski*, 'Ant Trail': voice, verses 4 and 5; and format
of original text

what pulls
you upward
is it
your weight

what pulls
you down
is it
your wings

savour even the simplest words. Birtwistle's setting, on the other hand,
seems perversely intent on homogenising Kaplinski's pithy imagery – as
can be seen in the vocal line reproduced in Example 3.8.

According to Michael Hall, the entire vocal line to the Kaplinski songs,
like the melodic parts to several other works of the period, was written
first, wholly independently of the instrumental accompaniment, and
'without hesitation'.[46] This can be heard in the final product, in which the
soprano's expressive melody is starkly offset against the sustained pedals
and more subterranean cantus lines of the instruments. The ensemble is
more assertive in the brief interludes that separate the four songs; but in
fact the work overall has a strongly 'instrumental' cast. As Example 3.8
suggests, the serpentine vocal part has a stronger connection to the similarly foregrounded instrumental melody of a piece like *Ritual Fragment*
than it does to the sound or the sense of Kaplinski's words. And Birtwistle's
large ensemble, which includes a piano and a harp, is virtuosically
exploited to evoke a wealth of finely honed, atmospheric textures, some of
which are strongly reminiscent of *Gawain* (which Birtwistle had completed shortly before). Indeed, it is notable that most of Birtwistle's songs,
like Stravinsky's, eschew the traditional piano accompaniment in favour of
an instrumental ensemble. This in itself seems to imply a dilution of the
exclusive attention normally accorded the singer and his or her words.

There seems ample evidence in all this to support Andrew Clements's
claim that 'seeking words to fulfil a musical function he had already
defined precisely in advance' was a regular practice of Birtwistle's.[47] And
yet Birtwistle has returned repeatedly and regularly to song writing. This
suggests that poetry is more important to him than the scenario painted
by Clements would suggest. How is one to reconcile this with the appar-

ent shortcomings of Birtwistle's text-setting – the fact that its *neglect* of the qualities of a text is as (if not more) apparent as its sensitivity to them? One possibility is to reconceive the connection between poetry and music in these works. Instead of seeing the music as directly expressive of the poetry, it might be viewed as an *after-effect*. In other words, the poem is thought of primarily as a stimulant to the creative act, and not in any strong sense an important presence in the final product. Having written music *in response to* the poem, Birtwistle then 'drapes' the text across the completed composition as a sort of label or tag. (The gluey melisma that is so characteristic of Birtwistle's word-setting seems consistent with the imagery of 'draping'.) The words remain as a reminder of the song's initial stimulus, but they do not form its central facet. A loose parallel might be drawn with Webern's vocal works in which, according to Edward Levy, 'the text serves as an impetus for specifically musical impulses . . . [and therefore] the music proceeds according to its own determinants; the text may help set the length of the piece and its parts, but specific words may fall, by and large, fortuitously'.[48] Webern's own reflections on the process confirm this interpretation, emphasising as they do the degree to which his text-setting was the product of a propensity on the part of texts to spark the creative process, rather than of a desire to write vocal music per se:

> Please understand me correctly: I have *never* gone out looking (as it were) for a 'text', with the intention – indeed *I could never have such an intention* – of writing something vocal (a song, a choral piece, etc.). It was never thus; *the text was always provided first!* Given a text, then of course 'something vocal' should be the result.[49]

Of course, such a musical response to a text might seem not to require a voice at all. There are numerous examples of purely instrumental pieces being stimulated by, and taking their titles from, poetry – Debussy's *Prélude à l'après-midi d'un faune* and Schoenberg's *Verklärte Nacht* amongst them. But maybe a virtue can be made of Birtwistle's retention of the voice in these songs, superfluous though it can seem. The presence of the voice indicates, specifically, that a purely instrumental reaction is insufficient in the face of a poetic text. Rather, the after-effect of the poem takes the form of *an urge to sing*, to engage in vocal performance. It is this urge, this necessary reaction, of which many of Birtwistle's later songs are expressive, as much as the poems themselves. The singer has read the poem and is moved to sing as a consequence: the reciting of the poem's text as she sings occurs largely automatically, an involuntary by-product of the vocal response. The words are 'already processed', meaning having been drawn from them at an earlier stage, prior to the making of music.

In many respects this interpretation merely extends the sort of argument put forward by Pierre Boulez in the 1950s. Responding to the argument that unintelligibility in song signals a bad compositional technique, Boulez asserted with characteristic brusqueness:

> If you want to 'understand' the text, then read it, or get someone to speak it for you: there will be no better solution. The more subtle [musical] working that I am now suggesting implies a previous knowledge of the poem. I reject the idea of 'musical reading' or reading with music.[50]

Boulez thus argues that song should come to represent a later stage in one's acquaintance with a text, rather than the initial, naïve encounter that has traditionally been presumed in classical song. Boulez uses this argument principally as a defence against the accusation of inaudibility: his settings are still strongly and overtly responsive to individual images and structural features of the poetic text (as has been demonstrated by Célestin Deliège in a detailed analysis of *Improvisation sur Mallarmé I*[51]). Birtwistle's songs sometimes go further in distancing the sung texts from the possibility of immediate comprehension. The apparently mind-numbed, hallucinatory rendering that characterises the delivery of the text in a number of the recent songs – the third of the *Songs by Myself*; 'Heart of Rain' in *Four Poems by Jaan Kaplinski*; 'White and Light' from *Pulse Shadows* – reinforces the impression of a text memorised yet in other respects only vaguely remembered, colouring the entire musical proceedings, but hardly governing them.

I have suggested that these songs are expressive, not so much of the content of their poems, as of a more generalised need to sing, a need occasioned by poetry. There is one other level, though, at which these songs 'are expressive' – or to put it more simply, at which they signify. This concerns the treatment of the human voice. Song's capacity to convey a content simply on account of the way in which the voice is deployed rests on truisms about our relations to vocal sounds and behaviour in everyday life: for instance, that certain voice types carry strong associations with character types or social roles; that certain sorts of vocal sound (as classified by dynamics, register, timbre) are immediately connotative of emotional states; and that for every speaking person the pleasure or discomfort involved in making certain sorts of vocal sound are intuitively empathised with in the performances of others. The conventions of composed song frequently rest on such everyday associations and rarely override them.

Some of the relevant factors in play in Birtwistle's vocal music may then be listed. These include: an almost exclusive use (in the solo vocal works) of the soprano voice; the exploitation of a wide registral compass and a particular fondness for the upper part of the soprano register (rising as high as E and E flat above the soprano stave in *An die Musik* and the *Four Poems of Jaan Kaplinski*, and consistently perching at and around the top of the stave in the soprano songs as a whole); vocal lines of unusual angularity and 'awkwardness'; and the absence of any clear distinction between vocal and instrumental idioms and musical material. From this, it is difficult to avoid the same conclusion that Dai Griffiths reaches in relation to Webern's vocal writing, namely that,

> Webern was doing something *very nasty indeed* with and to the female voice ... The voice is becoming like a machine: constricted, precise, tuneless, losing her trace of personality and any mark of authenticity. And then there's the weight of resonance: why was Webern so taken with the soprano range? – was it to do, technically, as it were, with what it is for a vocal line to 'sit on' the rest of the sound? – was it some notion of female hysteria, or some personal obsession?[52]

For some, the proposal that Birtwistle's songs are expressive of the subjection of women – the songs' vocal writing symbolising, first and foremost, a woman in a highly distressed condition – will be hard to accept. This sort of vocal writing has become, to a degree, stock in trade for musical modernists, a fact that might be held to signal its absorption into a more semiotically neutral 'musical language'. It could be argued that the connotations of such extreme vocal behaviour in ordinary life, while possibly important to our understanding of nineteenth-century song or opera, are filtered out in the context of a modern musical idiom.[53] Wherever one stands in this argument, the vocally strained quality of many of Birtwistle's solo songs, and the uncomfortable difficulty and density (and consequent intonational uncertainty) of the choral music, are inescapable. At times these qualities overwhelm the subtler levels of meaning at play in Birtwistle's texted music, becoming an awkward obstacle to a listener's appreciation. No attempt to come to grips with these works can proceed without acknowledging the real difficulties that Birtwistle's treatment of the voice sometimes presents.

4 Times

Time

Précis (4) • *Chronometer* (41) • *The Triumph of Time* (43) • *The Mask of Orpheus* (60)

When, in the early 1970s, Birtwistle asserted that 'new concepts of time are my main compositional preoccupation',[1] it was a claim that had particular force. Preoccupied as he then was with the Orpheus myth, a myth in certain respects 'about' time and the impossibility of reversing it, time and the related themes of pulse and journeying inevitably emerged as prominent concerns in a number of works of the period. Recent years have seen other preoccupations move to the fore, but Birtwistle's interest in time has not disappeared. This is indicated by the subtitle of the recent orchestral work *Exody*, '23:59:59' – that is, the second before midnight. Time, and the temporal, are of prime importance to works throughout Birtwistle's compositional career.

Birtwistle is not alone in such an interest. Many twentieth-century composers – including Stravinsky, Messiaen, Carter and Stockhausen – have declared a fascination with the relationship between music and time.[2] This can be seen, in part, as a consequence of the abandonment of tonality. Tonal harmony ensured a type of musical organisation so closely congruent with prevailing models of time – which is to say, one that was continuous, connected, motional and unidirectional – that there was no reason to question the fit of one to the other. But in the absence of tonal syntax and tonal forms, and thus potentially also the qualities of musical organisation that they ensured, matters became more complicated. Harmonic idioms and musical structures arose that, through their staticity or disruptiveness, appeared to contradict time. This apparent paradox has frequently exercised the thoughts of modern composers.

Birtwistle's own commitment to formal procedures that sit uncomfortably with time is nicely demonstrated in the short piano piece *Précis*. Birtwistle's intention was to write a piece 'which turned back on itself yet has a sense of forward movement'.[3] This temporal paradox is manifested in a loosely palindromic structure. The work consists of five tiny sections: section 5 is essentially a retrograde of section 1, with octave displacements;

the brief flourish that separates sections 1 and 2 is softly repeated between sections 4 and 5; and sections 2 and 4, while less closely related, share a prominent use of paused sustained notes. Section 3 then forms the central panel of an arch-like form. Various aspects of this design signal Birtwistle's determination to manipulate or reconfigure time, rather than to submit to it. The retrograde relationship between the work's outer sections chafes with the received idea that temporal experience possesses a unidirectional flow, and may never be reversed. In the second and fourth sections, the striking contrast made by the paused notes against the busy figuration that surrounds them suggests not a reversing but a *freezing* of time – as if in anticipation of the moments of frozen action that will later occur throughout *Punch and Judy*. Birtwistle's meticulous tempo specifications, resonant as they are with the view of the Darmstadt composers that tempo should be treated as a separate musical parameter rather than remain subordinated to harmony or rhythm, also suggest a desire to control and manipulate time's flow.

These aspects of *Précis* are characteristic of countless avant-garde compositions of the fifties and sixties. They may now seem dated, representative of rather wishful thinking about the impact that clever formal devices might have upon the temporal experience of a listener. (How many people are likely to recognise the retrograde in the work's last section?) More interesting temporal conundrums arise in Birtwistle's piece, however. Stephen Pruslin has described *Précis* as 'a very personal response to the winds of change that blew from Darmstadt to Dartington in the late 'fifties',[4] and the influence of Webern's post-war followers makes itself felt in the form of a specifically temporal problem: namely, that it comprises a music so dense with information that it effectively defies its own time-span. A fleeting, once-only encounter with the piece will yield little. The work's content becomes clear only with repeated listening, or through analysis of the score, and both of these approaches involve the subversion of the music's own temporality – repeated listening involving the piece-meal assemblage of a memorised representation of the work, and analysis allowing the specific temporal presentation of sounds to be put to one side. Birtwistle's title – which implies that the piece takes the form of a temporal telescoping, a process of condensing or shrinkage – indicates an awareness of the way in which this music 'overrides' time.

Précis involves itself with matters temporal largely by virtue of formal properties and procedures that it shares with much other twentieth-century music. As already mentioned, Birtwistle's output includes many pieces that feature a more intensive engagement with time and the temporal. This sometimes takes the form of a *questioning* of conventional models of time – a direction already hinted at in *Précis*. Birtwistle's use of pulse, for instance, can work to undermine a listener's assumptions about the form of temporal experience, and does so in more psychologically pertinent ways than is the case in the early piano piece. Alternatively, Birtwistle capitalises upon a traditional view of temporal experience, by conceiving of his pieces as journeys. Both of these themes are considered in greater depth later in this chapter.

A smaller number of works refer explicitly to 'time' in their title; a closer examination of these forms a useful way of introducing Birtwistle's dealings with the topic. Nowhere is this reference to time more startlingly evident than in *Chronometer*, a substantial tape piece made in collaboration with Peter Zinovieff. According to Zinovieff, *Chronometer* 'is entirely made up from the sounds of clock mechanisms which have been computer-analyzed and regenerated onto 8 tracks'.[5] This computer-assisted transformation allows for timbral modification, speed changes and all manner of superimpositions of the ticks and chimes of some hundred diverse recordings. The transformations are insufficient, however, to make the sounds unrecognisable: the piece is at least as much 'about clocks' as it is about an abstract structure of pulses. The closing chimes from Wells Cathedral, with all their weighty cultural connotations, confirm the impression that this is Birtwistle's most unashamedly *representational* non-texted work.

The power of the piece cannot simply be ascribed to its illustrative qualities, however. Michael Hall has noted how the mechanism of Big Ben, present for most of the work as a sort of grounding ostinato, is sonically modified to resemble the limping thud of the human pulse.[6] The transformation, though, is not complete: the clock sound remains identifiable. In emphasising the proximity of clock and heartbeat, *Chronometer* identifies the most pervasive and persuasive way in which society projects measurable clock time as 'natural' – namely, by reference to pulse. The ticking pulse of clockwork is sufficiently close to the pulse of the human body that a seamless connection may readily be forged between biological mechanism and existing social rationalisations of change. It is a measure of the success of this move that we find it difficult to dispute the actuality of 'clock time', and that we have grown to believe that discrepancies between individual experience and the time of the clock must be explained as errors on the part of the individual, and not the 'time' that we compare it with.

Some thinkers, however, have asserted that to understand subjective existence in terms of the linear, measurable time of the clock is seriously to constrain it. The nineteenth-century philosopher Hegel, for instance, believed that science was at a loss to deal with the unrest of existence, and was therefore forced to use 'a paralysed form, viz. as the *numerical unit* . . . which . . . reduces what is self-moving to mere material, so as to possess in it an indifferent, external, lifeless content'.[7] For Hegel, existence was made 'lifeless' in this quantitative rendering. In Marx's writings, to bind individuals to quantitative or 'commodified' time was to deny them an important element of personal freedom. Under this view, 'time' itself becomes symbolic of the constraint of the individual by social forces.[8] This is the perspective that underpins Theodor Adorno's critique of Stravinsky's music. For Adorno, any concept of time that treated it as an object, at once a universal constraint upon existence *and* an unchanging thing with certain unquestionable properties, was a sinister ideological construct. The effect of such a concept was to contain and control the free consciousness of individuals.[9] In principle, music had the potential to alert people to the constraints of received concepts of time; but it decisively forfeited any such potential if it incorporated those concepts into its own material. For Adorno, Stravinsky's music, with its regimented pulsing and obsessive measuring and counting, succumbs to this fate. It takes chronometric time as its subject, yet tries to disguise it as neutral musical material.[10]

Adorno's notorious antipathy towards Stravinsky meant that it was left to others to seek out those aspects of Stravinsky's music that are susceptible to more positive temporal interpretations.[11] For all Adorno's unashamed partisanship, though, his approach to musical temporality, and the scepticism that underlies it about the very existence of 'a time', remain powerful as interpretative tools – tools that can fruitfully be applied to Birtwistle's own negotiations with time and change. From an Adornian perspective, *Chronometer* hovers dangerously on the precipice of total submission to the rationalised time of industrial society. Complete submission is prevented perhaps only because the sounds remain aurally identifiable as the product of actual machines, and are never totally elevated to the status of abstract musical material. The added presence of chimes, periodically punctuating the motoric ostinati of the clockwork, additionally suggests a glimmer of hope in what is in other respects an unremittingly pessimistic piece. The chimes of a clock, though obviously implicated in clock time (for they quantify its perpetual passage), also invoke *memory*, in a way that insistent local metrication does not. An hourly or quarterly chime implicitly refers back to a previous, remembered one. In Adorno's eyes, it is memory that holds the key to a transcending of clock time, for memory offers the opportunity of a 'gathering up' of experience, one that transcends the linear sprawl of existence connoted by the clock.

Pulse, far from being unique to this clock-dominated work, is central to much of Birtwistle's music. For Michael Nyman, writing in 1971, it was a defining characteristic of Birtwistle's style – one of the crucial respects (together with ostinato and 'a cadential language') in which Birtwistle's music retrieved 'elements forgotten by atonality and post-Webern serialism'.[12] In *Chronometer*, pulse is used to connote clock time. Elsewhere (as I will detail later in this chapter) it is as often deployed to suggest the *shortcomings* of conventional concepts of time as to confirm their reality. At the time of *Chronometer*'s composition, however, Birtwistle was also at work on a second time-related piece, one in which pulse is for the most part barely perceptible. In his large orchestral piece *The Triumph of Time*, Birtwistle takes a very different approach to time. Where *Chronometer* deals primarily with what might be called the 'quantitative' aspects of time, *The Triumph of Time* concerns itself with the 'qualitative'. The orchestral piece involves itself not so much with time's extent and length as with the form of its *motion*.

Ever since Newton's assertion that time, 'from its own nature, flows equably without relation to anything external',[13] it has been a commonplace that time 'moves'. Not all have agreed, however, with Newton's belief that time's movement necessarily takes a rectilinear form: in so far as time is something manifested in and measured by planetary movements it would appear, rather, to be strongly cyclical. Different social groups and cultures have tended to come down on one side or the other: rural, agrarian cultures, for instance, appear to emphasise the cyclical over the linear; urban, industrialised cultures vice versa. *The Triumph of Time* engages with both. The linear and the cyclical are held in mutual suspension. This is musically manifested in the subjection of different, recurring 'musical objects' to a continuum of degrees of change, 'so that, for instance, where A is an element that is circumscribed and never changes, one descends through a sequence of potentially unlimited degrees of change to the musical object which is a permanent state of change'.[14] In the course of listening to the piece, one becomes aware of elements that recur practically identically – for example, a three-note motive for amplified soprano saxophone which appears seven times throughout the piece; and a longer cor anglais melody that appears at the beginning, middle and end, on each occasion with slight modifications. But additionally there are recurring elements that have undergone greater degrees of transformation, so that their 'return' takes the form of a more subtle allusion. Examples include the percussion textures at [35], which are similar to those found two bars before [8]; the alternating ensembles at [22], which appear to be a grossly inflated version of the innocuous antiphonies at [3]; and the toccata-like burst of trumpets and percussion at [31], which resembles those found much earlier, shortly before [15] and after [18]. Indeed, it would appear that the chorale-like melody screamed out by the high winds right at the end of the piece is a further transformation of this last 'musical object', rather than (as Michael Hall has suggested[15]) the apotheosis of the less mutable soprano saxophone motive. (The abrasive trumpet and percussion music prior to [38] forms the transitional link between toccata and chorale.) Finally, the piece contains elements so radically altered that they appear completely unpresaged.

While Birtwistle was writing the piece, he found an analogy to his form in an etching by Brueghel, and eventually decided to use the title of the etching for his own work. Brueghel's *Triumph of Time* depicts, 'in the foreground, the overall image of the procession', a freeze-frame of an ever-changing succession of which neither the beginning nor the end is visible; and 'in the background, recurrent procedures that are continuously there if only seasonally – the maypole, a weather-vane, the tides'.[16] In one sense, time is 'triumphant' in Brueghel's etching precisely in being shown to be resistant to coherent representation. There is no 'correct' answer: the paradox is a product of the chafing of our useful but ultimately inadequate representations of time. This conjunction of linear and cyclical images of time finds a parallel in Birtwistle's music, in a way that was deemed novel in his output at the time. For while repetitive and cyclical schemes had been prominent in many of his earlier works, the sense, given by the steady flow of unrecognisably altered musical elements, of an underpinning linearity was less familiar. In 1975 Meirion Bowen wrote that, 'for the first occasion in Birtwistle's music, we are made dramatically aware of the temporal factor. In this, his first major goal-directed work, we are ever conscious that Time is passing, bringing Death.'[17] Since then, it is precisely the combination of the cyclical and the linear that has come to seem characteristic of Birtwistle's forms. Michael Hall, writing in 1984, designated the combination of 'perpetual recurrence' with 'a process which is circumscribed and unique' as the 'central organizing principle' that underlies all Birtwistle's music.[18]

Bowen's description of *The Triumph of Time* does not simply refer to linearity or process, however; rather, he identifies specifically the purposeful, goal-oriented tread of Time and Death. This is to make too close an analogy between Brueghel's linear procession and the musical form. Birtwistle's stated intention in writing the piece was to construct 'a piece of music as the sum of musical objects, unrelated to each other, apart from one's decision to juxtapose them in space and time'.[19] At one level, such a succession of disparate musical objects does indeed present a loose parallel to the diverse participants in Brueghel's parade. But it is the very heterogeneity of the musical succession that makes difficult the imparting of a sense of goal-directedness or common purpose. In music, an impression of singular goal-directedness is traditionally attained through the creation of tensions by the sum of musical materials, which receive full resolution only at the end of a piece. Every element of a piece contributes to this end. Such unity of purpose, let alone any moment of all-encompassing resolution or arrival, is difficult to discern in Birtwistle's grim juxtapositions. How, then, can we tell that Birtwistle's musical objects all share the same 'goal' – that they are all marching in the same direction, as Bowen's description suggests? If it is simply by virtue of their successive presentation in time, then there would no longer be any grounds to mark out *The Triumph of Time* as more 'goal-directed' than any other music, for in these terms *all* music may be understood to 'pass' a listener, unidirectionally. Without some governing syntactical system that regulates relative tension, music struggles to form any stronger resemblance to the purposefulness of a procession.

The impression that *The Triumph of Time* is goal-directed – a grave processional – is arguably due instead to surface features that are *connotative* of more genuinely organic music. The soft murmurings of the opening and the gradual gathering of activity and expansion of forces during the first third of the piece bespeak a coherent, collective effort; later (about twenty minutes in), ardent tutti passages effortlessly signify impending climax in the manner of many nineteenth-century musical forms. In so far as these features give the work a conventional shape, however, it is one discerned retrospectively, rather than perceived in the course of listening. It is difficult to feel the work's critical moments as 'led towards' or inevitable: on the contrary they tend to happen out of the blue, without warning. Birtwistle's quotation of his own *Chorale from a Toy Shop*, massively amplified for winds and brass, is a case in point: its introduction towards the end of the work's first half, intruding noisily into the proceedings, sounds as if it occurred to the composer on the spur of the moment, rather than formed part of some grand master plan.[20] Time triumphs in this piece, then, in a further sense: not because it guarantees any deterministic channelling of the course of events, but on the contrary because of its alarming tendency to deliver the unpredictable. Time leaves us reeling in its aftermath, as it were, struggling to make sense of what has happened as best we can.

Taken together, *Chronometer* and *The Triumph of Time* present a template for Birtwistle's subsequent engagement with time-related compositional concerns. Despite being written concurrently their approaches form a striking contrast. *Chronometer* is built on pulse. *The Triumph of Time*, by comparison, makes use of pulse only residually – indeed, at times

Birtwistle's orchestration appears to go out of its way to blur the pulsed ostinati that, characteristically, form the basis of his invention. Instead the orchestral piece negotiates with the form that time might take, and the paradoxes and problems that attend the representation of such form in music. Each of these contrasting approaches to time may be traced through later works, as I detail in later sections in this chapter. Pulse became a particularly overt concern in the later 1970s, partly as a result of its usefulness in Birtwistle's work at the National Theatre. And, while the metaphor of the procession is of only limited use in the case of *The Triumph of Time*, the possibility of representing different sorts of journeying, sometimes specifically treated as metaphors for different ideas about time, emerged as a crucial theme in several pieces during the eighties and nineties.

These later pieces do not always acknowledge their involvement with time quite as explicitly as *Chronometer* and *The Triumph of Time*. In the operas, though, time continues to feature as a prominent and central theme. Narrators have always been able to 'manipulate time' in their representations of events, and Birtwistle's librettists have consistently focused upon this narrational prerogative, presumably with the composer's encouragement. Some of the devices found in the operas are relatively standard. The many brief moments of frozen action in *Punch and Judy* – suggesting time 'stopped' – merely allude to the dramatic stasis of the operatic aria. Similar moments are found in *Gawain*, where Morgan's comments frequently freeze the action, thereby emphasising her role as manipulator of events. The bizarre combination of historical characters in *The Second Mrs Kong*, made possible through the supratemporality of the underworld, similarly has a venerable pedigree in narrative of all sorts. *Yan Tan Tethera* and *Gawain* both attempt manipulations of time of a more novel kind. Birtwistle says of *Yan Tan Tethera*, 'the whole thing is like a big clock mechanism, like one of those intricate clocks you get in Bavaria'.[21] On several occasions, a character's counting serves to accelerate time. Alan's and Caleb's competitive counting of their flocks prompts the passing of a year in little more than a minute; later, Hannah's lamenting counting-song sees the narrative through a whole seven years. What is distinctive about this idea is that the drama is not suspended while it happens: rather, dramatic action and narrated time are separated, which has the effect of highlighting the idiosyncrasies of the latter. An analogous situation is found in the masque at the end of Act I of *Gawain*, where Gawain's preparations for his journey are accompanied by the passing of a whole year. This device had a particularly heightened impact in the original, longer version of the masque.

There can be little doubt, though, that the most sophisticated operatic treatment of time in Birtwistle's œuvre is found in *The Mask of Orpheus*. As Michael Hall has observed, this is appropriate, for 'time is one of the essential ingredients of the Orpheus legend. All versions include the desire to reverse time, to return to a time when Euridice was still alive.'[22] In the introduction to his libretto, Peter Zinovieff expands upon the way this aspect of the myth informed his conception:

> In *The Mask of Orpheus* time is expressed, through memory, as echoes and distortions. The music, words and actions repeat previous sections and anticipate future ones. Echoes and pre-echoes persist throughout. The first words are almost the same as the last. This system allows the same event to be presented from different aspects at different times or even simultaneously.[23]

Zinovieff here amply enumerates the ways in which the work's complex narration works to focus attention on time itself. Additional, time-focused elements of the libretto include the explicitly named 'Time Shifts', and the identification of various phases of the rising and falling tides that govern the structure of Act III with past, present and future. Birtwistle's musical response to such features of the libretto varies. For instance, the Time Shifts, wherein Euridice's death is re-portrayed three times in mime, do not themselves receive a musical setting: the music at these moments (the beginning of Act I, Scene iii; and the beginnings of both Acts II and III) accompanies the second layer of dramatic action, which is different on each occasion. However, the *end* of each Time Shift is announced, purely musically, by a recurring 'Whisper of Change'. It is less easy to identify a musical correlate to the various temporal phases of the rising and falling tides in Act III. Music's limits with regard to the signification of past or future – which is to say its lack of tense[24] – perhaps inevitably confine aspects of Zinovieff's conception to the libretto alone.

On the other hand, the *music* sometimes suggests time-related images and ideas about which the libretto says nothing. It is difficult to hear some of the opera's electronic 'Passing Clouds' and 'Allegorical Flowers' without being reminded of *Chronometer*, and it is difficult not to presume that the earlier work was something of a model. *Chronometer* stood then, as now, as Birtwistle's only other electronic music, moreover produced in collaboration with Zinovieff himself. Not all the interludes foreground pulse to the same extent as *Chronometer*, but pulse *is* central to the Third Cloud and Third Flower, both of which involve the precise subdivision of stretches of time into different numbers of percussive attacks. The superimposed textures of *Chronometer* are lost in these interludes, as is the explicit reference to timepieces, but the ominousness of such insistent metrication is only emphasised by the inhuman precision with which the different rates of pulse are executed. The *distance* of precise temporal quantification from ordinary human existence is thereby emphasised, a move in keeping with the strikingly malleable treatment of time in the opera's story-telling as a whole.

The one place where the opera does adhere to a largely linear form of story-telling is in the second act. As mentioned in Chapter 1, Orpheus' methodical description of the seventeen arches spanning the valley to the world of the dead provides the opportunity for a cumulative and largely uninterrupted musical structure – further focused by the steady shift in emphasis, in each successive arch, from dream to nightmare. It appears doom-laden and predetermined from the start, and in this respect it forms the sharpest possible contrast with *The Triumph of Time*'s blindly unfolding 'linearities'. That such a relentless musical structure should dominate the act that portrays Orpheus' attempt, and ultimate failure, to surmount the flow of time, is entirely appropriate. The music indicates the impossibility of Orpheus' endeavour well before he himself admits it, giving the act as a whole its moving undertow of tragic inevitability.

Pulse

Pulse Field (51) • *Silbury Air* (50) • *Pulse Sampler* (59) • *Harrison's Clocks* (104)

It was noted earlier that pulse is a prominent feature of much of Birtwistle's music, and that it came especially to the fore in a number of works written in the mid- to late seventies. And it was suggested that, in contrast to *Chronometer*, these works appear intent on *avoiding* the connotation of clock time in their use of pulse. Only once has the avoidance of clock time explicitly been part of Birtwistle's compositional agenda, however. This was in relation to *Pulse Field (Frames, Pulses and Interruptions)*, the collaborative dance piece that he devised with the choreographer Jaap Flier and the dancers and musicians of the Ballet Rambert. *Pulse Field*, like *Bow Down* and *The Oresteia*, was an attempt to achieve a genuine integration of different forms of dramatic presentation. The work is written for nine instrumentalists and six dancers; the instrumentalists are symmetrically positioned around the edge of the stage, and both music and dance are partly determined by cues from the other. As the 'Composer's Note' in the score explains,

> *Pulse Field* . . . is essentially an attempt to reformulate and thereby to expand
> the relationships between music and the dance . . . Maybe, as essentially corpo-
> real music, it can help both dance and music to regain that parity and auton-
> omy which all too often is lost through the subjugation of one by the other.[25]

As in *Bow Down* and *The Oresteia*, it is pulse that forms the common
ground to the work's two constituent elements. The music is built around a
continuous structure of pulses, played by four percussionists, upon which
is sporadically superimposed non-pulsing material for three trombones
and two amplified double-basses. The pulses are usually played by only
one percussionist at a time, and are organised in terms of short periods,
within which the pulse remains constant. Between periods the pulse typically passes to another percussionist, and the speed of the pulse may
change to another of three broadly defined 'pulse tempos'. Some periods
contain no pulses and are simply marked by a single down-beat – this is the
case at the opening of the work, for instance. Additionally, the durations of
periods may change, so that the changes between instruments and speeds
do not occur at predictable intervals.

This suggests a forbiddingly complex structure, but in fact at every level
Birtwistle has striven to avoid quantitative prescriptiveness, in order to
achieve what the Composer's Note refers to as 'a non-mechanistic
approach to tempo'. At the larger level, no numerical tempo indications are
given for the length of periods. Changes in period length are indicated by
simple 'longer than before' and 'shorter than before' markings. At the
smaller level, numbers of pulses per period are not prescribed, a new
period simply being initiated by a strong cue on the part of one of the percussionists. The three different pulse tempos may each inhabit a range of
speeds, as indicated in the Performance Notes. And the same Notes state
that, 'Each pulse must be played in a "non-metronomic" manner.' As the
Composer's Note suggests, these strategies are intended to ensure what
might be thought of as a 'corporealising' of pulse:

> The ritual movement of Western classical dance has always been subservient
> to chronometric time, even in the apparently extreme irregularity of the
> Sacrificial Dance at the end of Stravinsky's 'Rite'. *Pulse Field*, operating with
> relative rather than absolute concepts of tempo and duration, seeks to replace
> the rhythm of the clock with something approaching that of the body.

In fact this is the strongest sense in which the influence of dance may be felt
in the piece (for the musical elements actually determined by the dancers
during performance are limited to fairly insignificant and short-lived contributions from the double-basses and individual percussionists). By
eschewing precisely calculated mathematical relationships attention is cast

instead onto the intuitive treatment of pulse changes by the *bodies* of the instrumentalists, with all their variability and 'imperfections'. The music comes to be less about chronometric structure, more a musical symbolisation of the biological pulses that govern human life. The pessimism of *Chronometer*, with its seductive identification of the ticking clock with the heart-beat, correspondingly has its counterpole in *Pulse Field*.

The idea that pulse is not intrinsically 'mechanical' or 'metronomic' is central to Birtwistle's music. Birtwistle states his case in no uncertain terms: 'pulse is something we associate with primitive music and popular music. It's something which is regular, it's something you get off on and you forget about. I tend to never let the listener get off on it. It's always reassessing itself.'[26] Birtwistle states his objection to regular pulse in terms of its lack of structural interest. This is a predictable position for a modernist composer to take. But perhaps more significant is the connection that concerned the composer in *Pulse Field*, between regular pulse and time. Regular pulse all too readily functions as an assurance of the containing actuality of chronometric time. Quite apart from its resemblance to the tick of the clock, pulse appears to possess qualities that are also customarily assumed of time – namely, motion and measurability. The unquestionable perceptibility of pulse's measured motion is then used as a substitute for the thing we seem unable directly to perceive: time itself. Pulse becomes an indicator of time's flowing and quantifiable reality.

In *Pulse Field*, Birtwistle was concerned to challenge 'the rhythm of the clock'. This same challenge is present in his use of 'reassessing' pulse in other pieces, even if it is less explicitly part of the composer's conception. *Silbury Air*, for instance, which was written for the London Sinfonietta and completed shortly before work started in earnest on *Pulse Field* and *Bow Down*, is highly dependent on pulse. But at the same time it complicates the connection between pulse and both motion and measurement. In so doing, it undermines the intimate association we are wont to forge between pulse and time.

The piece falls broadly into two halves: the first is dominated by pulsing, percussive mechanisms; the second cedes a greater part of the foreground to melody, but is still underpinned by obsessive ostinati. Its title refers to Silbury Hill, a man-made mound situated near Avebury in Wiltshire, which Birtwistle describes as an 'artificial but organic intruder of the landscape'.[27] The music is not intended as an illustrative evocation of the hill and its surroundings, but it is nevertheless clear that the 'organic artificiality' of the hill has its parallels in the music, not least in its rhythmic structure. This is governed by a four-part 'pulse labyrinth',[28] a complex network of interrelated tempos that governs the music's numerous changes of metre and speed. On the face of it nothing could be further removed from the total absence of precise tempo instructions in *Pulse Field*. Indeed in some ways these two closely contemporaneous pieces form a counterpart to the similarly divergent treatments of time found in *Chronometer* and *The Triumph of Time*. But there remains an underlying similarity between the two pieces. Birtwistle uses his pulse labyrinths in such a way that every new tempo is strongly related to the old one. Groupings or subdivisions of pulses may change, but some level of pulse remains constant at each moment of interruption. This pragmatic step – which makes the music easier to play, if harder to conduct – gives the tempo changes an 'organic' aspect, a decidedly corporeal quality, in spite of their surface 'artificiality'. There is no striving for the impossible metrication of the computerised interludes from *The Mask of Orpheus* here. The rather mechanistic quality of much of *Silbury Air* does indeed contrast markedly with *Pulse Field*, but these are blatantly man-made mechanisms, rudimentary and pleasingly explicable.

Silbury Air also shares *Pulse Field*'s problematisation of the connection between pulse and chronometric time, though it sets about it in different ways. Firstly, it refuses to allow pulse to settle into a measuring role, counting out the piece's progress in terms of durational spans. It has been argued that, in tonal music, metric pulse serves precisely this function, allowing 'precise judgements concerning duration and evaluations of proportions'.[29] Viewed as such, regular metre instantly consigns musical experience to the realm of clock time, denying it the possibility of standing over and against that realm. Birtwistle's rapid and abrupt tempo shifting, on the other hand, prevents pulse from assuming this measuring role, for the constant change of pulse throughout the first half of the piece denies any consistent unit upon which an adequate intuitive assessment of temporal span might be built. Secondly, Birtwistle's deployment of pulse undermines the motional qualities that in other contexts seem one of its most apparent properties. One of the arguments against the *absence* of pulse in so much twentieth-century classical music is precisely that it denies music its primary cause of motion, and thereby appears to contravene a property of time itself.[30] But if one is inclined to view such an objectified concept of time – the idea that time is a 'thing' with identifiable properties – as a social construct rather than some God-given existential constraint, this 'motionless' quality of modern music becomes rather less of a problem. Indeed, under these circumstances the *abandonment* of pulse may come to seem positively desirable. Alternatively, pulse may be retained, but treated in such a way that its connection to motion is thoroughly problematised. This is what Birtwistle does in *Silbury Air*. At the many moments of tempo

Ex. 4.1. *Silbury Air*: rhythmic structure, 14 before [9]

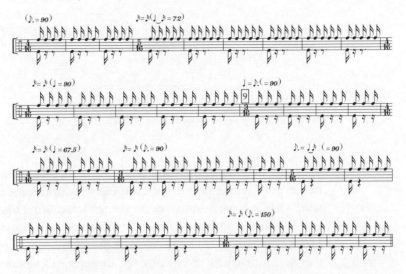

change in the first half of the piece, it might be tempting to refer to a change of 'pace'. But does the 5/16 four bars into Example 4.1 bring an unambiguously *slower* pace relative to the foregoing 4/16? The attacks marking the bar lines occur less frequently but the semiquavers remain constant, contradicting any impression of reduced speed. At [9] the situation is slightly different: here the semiquaver speed slows but the prevailing larger pulse in harp and upper strings continues unchanged. The complication to our motion-related intuitions remains the same. Of course, at moments such as these, it would be possible to refer to *two* ongoing speeds, one of which changes while the other continues unaltered. But that would also be to deny the existence of *any* strong connection between the music's pulsing and the flow of clock time – unless it were to be proposed that time's movement, too, could take two different speeds simultaneously.

The attempt to separate pulse from the linear time with which it is usually associated is felt more generally in the work's polarisation of pulse and melody. *Silbury Air* is determined to keep pulse untainted by the spectre of linearity. For the first half of the piece melodic lines are consistently kept subservient to the play of pulse dictated by the pulse labyrinth; it takes a unison wind melody of extreme urgency (Example 4.2), even-rhythmed but driving against the bar lines which govern the more percussive, accompanimental material, to precipitate the crisis that brings about the 'air' dominating the work's second half. This initially appears in the flute, over a reprise of the work's gently pulsing opening (at [29]), and then

Ex. 4.2. *Silbury Air*: wind melody, 22 before [28]

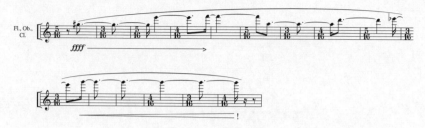

opens out into the other high winds in the music that follows. The opposition to pulse is maintained, however. The wind proceed at an independent tempo to the quaver ostinati in the strings, which form a gentle backdrop; and the air's progress is repeatedly interrupted by bursts of aggressive material that derive from the rhythmic brass fanfare that appeared twice in the work's first half. Eventually the flowering of woodwind melody is calmed, reduced once again to an even rhythm in a pale reflection of the passionate statement that initiated it (Example 4.3; compare with the start of Example 4.2).

The sheer quantity and prominence of pulse in *Silbury Air* sets it somewhat apart from even the most pulse-oriented of later works. For instance, *Pulse Sampler*, for oboe and claves, serves as a reminder that it is a *suspicion* of regular pulse that is most characteristic of Birtwistle – a dread of becoming predictable or hypnotic. Like *Silbury Air*, *Pulse Sampler* involves the superimposition of different rates of pulse, but this time they are non-coinciding pulses rather than closely related ones. This is just one of many strategies that ensure the piece is more about the *absence* of unambiguous pulse than its presence. The basic idea of the piece is simple: both claves and oboe proceed through the same succession of different tempos, but the claves are constantly a step ahead of the oboe, setting the tempo for it in advance, as it were. The two instruments' tempos coincide only briefly before the claves move on to the next speed. This creates a sort of 'temporal stratification' – a textural ploy found in different forms in much of Birtwistle's music.[31] Still greater complexity arises from the fact that the claves, rather than playing a regular pulse, play from a 'pulse mobile' which gives rise to distortions of the pulse *within* a particular speed (see Example 4.4). In struggling to perceive the continuity of pulse between claves and oboe in successive sections, or to accommodate the unpredictable shifts in attack provided for in the pulse mobile, a listener will be made uncommonly aware of just how strong and 'bodily' the urge for the establishment of regular pulse can be. Through means rather more complex than those

Ex. 4.3. *Silbury Air*: wind at [38]

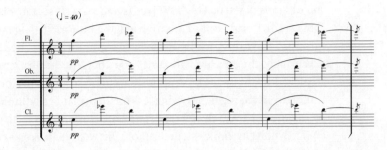

Ex. 4.4. *Pulse Sampler*: pulse mobile

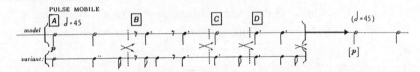

used in *Pulse Field*, this piece nevertheless makes a similar claim for the essential corporeality of pulse.

It is indicative of Birtwistle's general preference for the disrupted pulse over the ominously regular ones found in *Chronometer* that his only other piece to allude explicitly to timepieces should go out of its way to avoid regular metrication. *Harrison's Clocks*, a set of five short pieces for piano, was inspired by Dava Sobel's book *Longitude*, which tells the story of the eighteenth-century clockmaker John Harrison and his struggle to perfect a clock that would keep accurate time at sea. Ironically, John Harrison's clocks were important precisely for the chronometric exactitude that Birtwistle's music has frequently sought to avoid. As Stephen Pruslin has pointed out, the connection of Sobel's book to the piece in large part takes the form of the opportunity it provided for a punning title; that title should not be taken to imply 'any one-to-one correspondence between Birtwistle's musical "clocks" and John Harrison's real ones'.[32] A better comparison for Birtwistle's clocks would be the 'recalcitrant machinery'[33] of György Ligeti's recent sets of piano Études: Birtwistle's repetitive musical mechanisms, for all their intricacy, consistently shun complete regularity. In the first piece this irregularity is articulated by a single repeating figure, which comprises interlocking pairs of notes in each hand. The third piece is more complex. Six different mechanisms, each registrally as well as rhythmically defined, sporadically kick into action – as if one coils a spring that then suddenly activates another. The prevailing irregularity remains, however, for the succession of mechanisms follows no obvious pattern. The last piece is a toccata. It sustains fast, even semi-quavers for practically its entire length, but, as in *Silbury Air*, they are grouped asymmetrically by a succession of larger repetitive figures. Eventually the mechanism jams, and the semiquavers are progressively replaced in the score by empty stems. The second and fourth pieces are different in character, focusing less on identifiable rhythmic patterns than on a note (E) and a chord-type (ten-note clusters) respectively.

The polyrhythmic structure of Birtwistle's pieces strengthens the resemblance to the Ligeti Études. In the scores of both composers, vertical bar lines are overshadowed by the horizontal beams that join the stems of each rhythmic stratum, and which repeatedly defy the authority of the bar line – visually symbolising, as it were, the resistance of both composers' music to containment within a regular pulse.

Journeys

Grimethorpe Aria (45) • *Gawain's Journey* (83) • *The Cry of Anubis* (93) • *Still Movement* (64) • *Endless Parade* (71) • *Exody '23:59:59'* (103)

Birtwistle's treatment of pulse tends to distance his music from prevailing social constructions of time. Another of Birtwistle's compositional preoc-cupations, however, would seem to *strengthen* the connection between his music and time, rather than undermine it. This is the idea – developed in the metaphors of commentators upon Birtwistle's music, as well as in the titles and descriptions of the composer himself – that his music traces some sort of journey. Given that musical sound is not itself capable of undertaking a journey (it does not in any literal sense 'go' anywhere), such a conception is largely dependent upon the understanding that music is capable of articulating *time's* journey-like qualities. Certain sorts of music may bring into sharp relief time's seamless and unidirectional progress, a progress that is permanently ongoing even if it is not necessarily noticed as such.[34] In other words, to perceive music as a journey is to assume the underlying reality of a journey-like time – just the sort of time that Birtwistle's treatment of pulse throws into doubt.

Actually, the situation is not quite as cut and dried as this. Not all jour-neys possess the seamlessness and unidirectionality of Newtonian time. Birtwistle's music supports comparisons with different sorts of journeys; and, as I will suggest in what follows, the stronger comparisons, at least from a listener's point of view, tend to be with the types of journey *least* like the confident onward progress of linear time. Something of this has already been hinted at in relation to *The Triumph of Time*. While some commentators have striven to explain the piece solely in relation to the procession that appears in the foreground of Brueghel's etching, Birtwistle's note is careful to point out that the music corresponds as much to the elements 'in the background, recurrent procedures that are continuously there . . . – the maypole, a weather-vane, the tides'.[35] The piece's distinctive successions cannot adequately be explained simply by reference to Brueghel's linear procession.

Birtwistle's music has not always been likened to journeys. Rather, it was a conception that emerged with the stylistic shift that took place in his music in the early 1970s, away from the overtly disruptive forms of *Tragœdia* and *Verses for Ensembles*, towards a style that is 'predominantly quiet, slow, and [characterised by a] homogeneity of timbre'.[36] Encouraged perhaps by the way in which the Brueghel etching suggested an interpretation for *The Triumph of Time*, other works of the period which shared broadly similar musical characteristics also came to be thought of as 'processionals'. Michael Hall, for instance, describes seven works dating from 1970 to 1973 in these terms.[37] It was a description that seemed to encapsulate a shift in Birtwistle's attitude to musical time; as Stephen Walsh put it, 'Having struggled [in earlier works] so violently to restructure musical time through forms which tended to work against it, Birtwistle now appears to step outside it altogether and consider it from a purely objective position'.[38] The processional, after all, is the type of journey that is most directly analogous to Newtonian time. Processionals are straight rather than circular; they move determinedly in one direction only; and they proceed at an unchanging pace. They also involve not a handful of people but a multitude – which reflects the idea that time's movement is all-containing, and that only part of it can be perceived at any one time. Brueghel was, of course, playing upon the strength of the analogy when he portrayed time as a procession in his own *The Triumph of Time*.

In *The Triumph of Time*, as we have seen, prominent recurring elements complicate the impression of an irreversible progression. Other works from the early to mid-seventies contain no such audible recurrence. Even so, they only really support the comparison with a processional in the sense that, as Birtwistle himself has noted, 'we could say all music is a processional', simply by virtue of its continuous unfolding.[39] *Grimethorpe Aria*, for brass band, is wholly representative of these so-called 'processional' works, in that the description more accurately reflects the music's sombre mood than a particular property of its form. The musical form is comparably sectionalised to that of *The Triumph of Time*, proceeding cleanly and without attempted transition from one section to the next; this dissipates any sense of common purpose, just as it did in the earlier piece. Indeed, the work's predominantly stark, glacial textures give, if anything, *less* of an impression of forward motion than was the case in the orchestral piece, where small-scale ostinati figure more prominently, giving textures a vaguely motoric undertow.

Grimethorpe Aria's 'processional' character arises instead from the work's grim demeanour, and its suppression of soloistic antics in favour of a sombre form of *collective* action. It is consistent with this severe collectivity that, in spite of the work's title, no 'aria' ever unambiguously emerges – in contradistinction to the stereotypical treatment in *Silbury Air*. A residual song-like element is perhaps identifiable in the brief flugelhorn solos and tutti chorales that occur throughout the piece; but it is only in the gentle epilogue that melody is allowed real space, solo euphoniums and horns tentatively threading their way between austere chordal columns erected by the rest of the ensemble. Even here, the melodic soloists proceed extremely cautiously. It would seem that the work's title is intended to refer less to song and more to the element of *staticity* that aria brings to operatic narration. The music foregrounds aria as a moment of frozen activity, rather than as an emblem of melodic linearity.

To question the usefulness of the linear processional as a metaphor for the effect of Birtwistle's music is, of course, not to imply that the theme of journeying has no importance for Birtwistle. Birtwistle has often enough encouraged the comparison with journeying himself, not least in his operas. The scenarios of *Punch and Judy*, *The Mask of Orpheus*, and *Gawain* all give a prominent place to journeys, for instance. Two orchestral offshoots from the operas, *Gawain's Journey* and *The Cry of Anubis*, moreover, take it as their central theme. The former is something of a curiosity, being nothing more than a patchwork amalgam of short excerpts from *Gawain* itself, assembled by Elgar Howarth;[40] as a result, there is little sense of an overall likeness to the business of journeying. The suite does contain the music that, at the beginning of Act II in the opera, accompanies Gawain's treacherous voyage to the Green Chapel, but its simple succession of abruptly contrasting sections, each vaguely characterised by a sense of effortful endeavour, will evoke an impression of journeying only to a listener familiar with the plot of the opera.

The Cry of Anubis, which is scored for bass tuba and orchestra, is a rather different case. For a start, the music is not drawn directly from the opera with which the piece is associated, meaning that there is no specific dramatic action upon which any impression of journeying might prop itself.

Instead, certain of its musical devices are themselves strongly connotative of Anubis' travels back and forth across the waters separating living and dead. The piece makes special efforts to highlight those aspects of Birtwistle's later idiom that, rather than loosely evoking a processional through a sombre musical succession, give a more literal sense of journeying. These devices seem not so much to portray a journey from the outside, as to put the listener in the position of the journeyer. The periodic, verse-like recurrences that characteristically form the audible substructure of individual formal sections are a crucial aspect to this. Once established, they give the immediate musical future a degree of predictability, and allow the construction of an organised musical past. In other words, they open out a traversable temporal terrain for the listener, both ahead and behind. The smaller-scale ostinati that are so often the basis of Birtwistle's invention take on the responsibility of creating an impression of motion through this terrain. They effectively assure as to the ongoing nature of the journey – measuring out the traveller's progress, as it were. In many pieces these ostinati are layered and repeated at different rates (Birtwistle refers to 'contrapuntal ostinatos'[41]), and this device can bring heightened realism to the journey, suggesting a certain perspectival depth, in which objects at varying distances appear to move at different speeds.

Birtwistle's recent music thus has the capacity to convey the impression of movement through a space. It is presumably no accident that *The Cry of Anubis* is both particularly rich in periodic verse structures and sufficiently transparent texturally (with its small, classical orchestra) for the motivating local ostinati to be clearly heard: a strong sense of journeying is an exemplary characteristic of the work. The journeying evoked in Birtwistle's recent music is, however, *not* of a particularly assured sort – in sharp contrast to the sort of movement characteristic of a processional. This is because it is constantly disrupted by Birtwistle's sectional forms. While Birtwistle's local repetition schemes, once grasped, provide a *degree* of assuredness about the journey, there are also recurrent moments of blindness at the onset of new formal sections – terror, almost, in the face of new material for which no mental map has yet been established. These moments of dazed disorientation, frequently signalled in the recent music by flurries of scalic activity, give way only gradually to a predictive grasp of a new stretch of terrain. The journeying of this music is far removed from the certainties of the processional; rather, in its limited forward view, its sudden changes of perspective and its frustration of any longer-term goal or aim, it closely resembles the unpredictabilities of the *labyrinth*. This is surely appropriate to the imagined murkiness of the waters travelled by Anubis' boat, at least as experienced by his fated passengers. It is their journey, specifically, of which the music of *The Cry of Anubis* is representative.

Birtwistle has likened his musical forms to labyrinthine journeys on a number of occasions. Part of its appropriateness as a metaphor, especially in comparison with that of the processional, lies in the way in which it accommodates the combination of cyclical and linear temporal processes that is so characteristic of Birtwistle's music. Travelling through a labyrinth involves both an ongoing progressivity, in that one is always steadily moving through it, but also the possibility of retracing and return – one sometimes stumbles across familiar places. In discussing *The Triumph of Time* it was suggested that an analogy for Birtwistle's play with process and repetition was provided by the two opposing models of time, linear and cyclical, presented in Brueghel's etching. But in some ways the labyrinth is a better analogy. *The Triumph of Time* is characterised not so much by the stark opposition of 'no change' (cyclical time) and 'perpetual change' (linear time), as by a continuum of 'degrees of change'.[42] This continuum (which is also a feature of *Silbury Air*[43]) is more readily accommodated by the idea of the labyrinth, in which we may come across previous locations directly (exact repetition), but also may glimpse them from a variety of altered perspectives (varied repetition).

The idea of the labyrinth is in an obvious sense appropriate to the unpredictable continuities and aspects of circularity of Birtwistle's forms, but it also points to something less immediately evident about the relationship of Birtwistle's music to time. As a metaphor for musical experience, the labyrinth reminds us of the possibility of an experience of change that is underpinned by no larger certainty as to form or shape – that makes no recourse to the assurance of an underlying 'time'. The limited view afforded within a labyrinth, and the complexity of the route taken through it, mean that the traveller is likely to accumulate little in the way of a larger impression of the configuration of the labyrinth, for all that the moment-to-moment progress may be vividly eventful. In a labyrinth, one tends to experience passage rather than *the* passage. In resembling the experience of journeying through a labyrinth, then, Birtwistle's music serves as a reminder of the possibility of transient experience that takes no concretisable form. It alerts us to the fact that existence can be changing but 'time'-less.

Still Movement, a short piece for string orchestra, serves as a good example of this. It has its origin in *Yan Tan Tethera*, and is one of the earliest products of Birtwistle's growing interest in musical context and the influence it has upon compositional invention.[44] Although its title suggests that the connection with the opera is less intimate than in the case of *Gawain's Journey* and *The Cry of Anubis*, in certain respects it is the most literal 'offshoot' of the three. Birtwistle describes the string piece as 'a spin-off from the pastorals in *Yan Tan Tethera*',[45] and its existence is wholly due to his feeling that, at these moments in the opera, the music

> offered two alternative continuations. The dramatic context of the work demanded that [Birtwistle] choose one path, and that is the music with which *Yan Tan Tethera* proceeds . . . What became *Still Movement* not only set out from the music for the pastoral but returned to it, so that effectively it offers an alternative musical path between two fixed points in the parent work.[46]

The very conception of the piece, then, is testament to the new priority given to the demands exerted by every individual musical situation. To judge from this description by Andrew Clements, Birtwistle's conception was in fact as much to do with the *shape* of the route between the 'fixed points' in the opera – viewed synoptically as it were – as with the experience of actually travelling through it. A listener does not necessarily have the benefit of such a bird's-eye view, however. And aspects of Birtwistle's context-aware style actually appear to work *against* a strong impression of the route taken. The music's continuous exposition (which is to say, its shirking of any kind of identifiable repetition) and its complementary focus on the persuasiveness of local sectional contrast (its desire to maintain the music's momentum through its putative discontinuities) make it tempting as a listener to live wholly *in* the moment. There is little encouragement to develop the sort of ambitious mental mappings to which we resort in order to make sense of more jarring musical non-sequiturs and juxtapositions, and which give a stronger impression of 'ground covered'. Instead, the piece is full of busy but rather aimless activity: 'sure', but not of its route, only that it must *keep going*. If the music does 'pursue a path' in any strong sense, it is a path of compositional decision-making wholly private to Birtwistle himself.[47]

I have dwelt upon the ways in which the idea of the labyrinthine journey is contrasted to that of the processional, and have argued that the former is a stronger analogy for Birtwistle's more recent music than the latter is for some earlier works. Two of the more recent works, however, strive to *combine* the two types of journey – the experience (from inside) of the labyrinthine journey *and* the portrayal (from outside) of the processional. Such a combination is made explicit in the revealing explanatory programme note that Birtwistle provided for *Endless Parade*, a twenty-minute piece for trumpet, vibraphone and strings:

A way to explain this piece is through metaphor. One summer I was in the Italian town of Lucca, a Medieval labyrinth of streets encircled by impressive walls . . . My visit coincided with 'Festa', and a long procession of *tableaux vivants* snaked its way through the narrow streets. I became interested in the number of ways you could observe this event: as a bystander, watching each float pass by, each strikingly individual yet part of a whole; or you could wander through side alleys, hearing the parade a street away, glimpsing it at a corner, meeting head on what a moment before you saw from behind.[48]

Birtwistle does not intend the piece to be an illustrative evocation of this scene. But its musical processes correspond in a general way both to the long procession as viewed by the static bystander, and to the labyrinthine experience of the observer wandering through the side alleys of the town. This invests every passage of the piece[49] with an intriguing ambiguity. A passage may be held to correspond to one of the passing elements in the procession, as successive sections were deemed to in *The Triumph of Time*. Or it may correspond to a particular stretch of labyrinthine locomotion, with its limited forward and backward view, as in *The Cry of Anubis*. The situation is analogous to Wittgenstein's famous duck-rabbit: a listener may construe a stretch of musical activity in terms of the sight of the procession, or in terms of the experience of wandering, but logically speaking musical activity cannot support *both* impressions at the same time. It is left to the listener to flit back and forth between them – duck and rabbit, procession and wandering, being entertained alternately.

Birtwistle's most recent orchestral work, *Exody*, involves similar tensions. The original title for the piece was 'Maze',[50] and Birtwistle states that the later change of title did not imply a change of structure: 'the piece is still about journeying through a maze, a journey that ends at the place where it started from'.[51] In another description, he likens the piece even more explicitly to the labyrinth:

> It's very much a journey into a labyrinth and out again. Where you enter therefore has to be where you leave, and the piece begins and ends with the music that ended my last orchestral piece *Antiphonies*: the widest C possible on the orchestra. There are also points where it comes back to a place where it's been before.[52]

This 'journey into a labyrinth' is reflected in different ways in the piece. Birtwistle resorts again to an essentially through-composed structure that contains sporadically recurring elements, reflecting the essentially unplanned progress and occasional familiarity of the journey through a labyrinth. The piece's recurring elements are relatively few and far between. The very first wind melody of the work occurs three times in quick succession, on each occasion re-rhythmed (b. 16, b. 34, b. 38); towards the end a prominent solo trumpet motive appears twice (b. 382 and b. 427), as does a brief figure in the orchestra's two saxophones (b. 479 and b. 494). Longer-term recurrences are limited to two dramatic unison arrivals at the G below middle C (b. 47 and b. 481), and the very beginning and end of the piece which, as Birtwistle mentions, form the single door leading into and out of the labyrinth. In addition to these moments of recognisability, *Exody*'s journey is punctuated by other distinctive features. Throughout the score, very brief passages of contrasting music interject upon the music's prevailing continuities. These moments of interruption are particularly evident towards the end, where they take the form of soft, high murmurings in solo strings, harps, xylophone and piccolos, contrasting dramatically with the noisy tuttis that surround them. At one level, these interruptions, which Birtwistle calls 'windows', create obvious discontinuities, forming 'framed and self-contained glimpses, like a curtain opening for a moment and then closing again'.[53] At another level, though, they are intended to be continuous with the journey, akin to sideways glances in the context of a prevailing forward view. In glancing left or right in this manner, one momentarily loses one's view of the direction of travel, yet what one sees remains integrally related to one's progress. The result is, as Birtwistle puts it, 'discontinuities that in another way add up to a continuity'.[54]

All of this suggests that, as in *The Cry of Anubis*, the listener is cast in the role of the traveller in *Exody*. The music simulates the experience of travelling through the labyrinth, rather as a remote-control camera might. But this picture is complicated by Birtwistle's inclusion of a musical element that is itself connotative of the journey. This takes the form of a heterophonic melodic line, whose progress can be traced through most of the piece. It appears in different registers and different instruments, and lends an unusually lyrical quality to the piece. Its evocation of a journeying individual can be effective indeed – as in the passage that immediately follows the first dramatic unison G, where it inhabits a tenor register and unfolds against a simple backdrop of a periodic, repeating figure in harp and percussion and distant piping on the flute and piccolo. At the same time, though, this melodic line gives rise to a tension, similar to that found in *Endless Parade*, as to whether listeners are to understand *themselves* as travelling through the labyrinth, or merely as observing someone or something else doing so. Rather as in the case of Birtwistle's instrumental roles, it appears that the music offers a variety of possibilities for conceptualisation, possibilities that may be redrawn in the process of listening without apparent incongruity.

An important element of Birtwistle's conception has not yet been addressed. This concerns the work's subtitle, '23:59:59'. For Birtwistle, the last second of the day is a 'moment of leaving', a sort of frozen, 'final moment when the changeover comes'[55] – at once signifying the imminent start of a new daily cycle, and yet also wholly continuous with that new start. It is also a moment that brings a temporal illusion familiar to anyone watching a digital watch. The last second before midnight appears to linger, to be a moment of 'unreality' suspended apart from the relentless flow of clock time. On such occasions, a clock paradoxically gives rise to a type of experience that cannot be explained in terms of clock time.

Birtwistle has not elaborated at any length upon the significance of his subtitle for *Exody*, beyond the general parallel between the final second of the day and the theme of 'departure' suggested by the work's title. There is, though, a resonance of the idea of the frozen moment in the way that Birtwistle talks about his 'sideways glances'. He contrasts them with the more purposeful, forward-looking aspects of travelling – describing them as 'the moment where you are *within* the journey',[56] as opposed to being focused upon an ultimate destination. In other words, the sideways glances represent a different, de-linearised perspective on the transient experience, just as the frozen moment before midnight does. One is aware of ongoing existence in these moments, but that awareness takes no quantity, and no shape. If Birtwistle's subtitle performs any wider function relative to the piece, it is surely precisely as a reminder that there is much about changing existence that resists reduction to the time-bound realm. In so doing, it is symbolic of the presence in *all* Birtwistle's music of elements that are more akin to the frozen moment or the sideways glance than a determinate route or an objectified time.

5   Sections

In an assessment of Birtwistle's approach to musical form, Stephen Walsh has remarked upon how his titles have reflected 'his enthusiasm for verse-refrain forms . . . whereas titles associated with the traditional developing forms of classical music are scrupulously avoided'.[1] Two decades have passed since Walsh made this observation, but it remains as true now as it did then. Birtwistle's stance on this matter is in sharp contrast to his contemporary Peter Maxwell Davies, for whom the forms of symphony and concerto have become primary compositional vehicles during the last twenty years. By and large Birtwistle has, of late, avoided *all* generic formal titles, those referring to sectional structures included. But the continued absence of traditional, developmental genres from his œuvre is accurate reflection of an approach to form that has consistently privileged sectional contrast over integration, juxtaposition over through-composition.

In this regard Birtwistle positions himself within a robust modern tradition of 'sectional' or 'block form' composition, amongst whose earlier principal exponents are Stravinsky, Messiaen and Stockhausen.[2] Sectional form involves the construction of musical works from relatively discrete blocks of material, their juxtaposition determined as much by their mutual contrast as by their consistency with one another. Individual approaches to this broad structural principle differ. For instance, formal blocks may recur, as in many of Stravinsky's and Messiaen's works; or they may appear only once, as in Stockhausen's 'moment-form' works. They may be self-contained, closed entities; or they may be fragmentary, each rudely interrupted by succeeding sections.

Where Birtwistle is concerned, attention has tended to focus on his use of interlocking cycles of recurring material – the 'verse-refrain forms' to which Stephen Walsh alludes. This is where the present discussion will also begin. The principle of sectional form finds other manifestations in Birtwistle's music, however. The verse and refrain model does not properly explain the forms of many of the works from the 1970s, for instance, which although defiantly sectional involve little repetition. Later still, in the mid 1980s, a new approach to sectional form emerged from Birtwistle's growing concern with local continuity, a concern that tended to temper precompositional, abstract formal schemes. The second and third sections of this chapter trace, respectively, each of these developments. Taken together, these discussions aim to articulate a more rounded picture of Birtwistle's multifaceted approach to musical form.

Verse

Tombeau in Memoriam Igor Stravinsky (40) •*Refrains and Choruses* (1) • *Three Movements with Fanfares* (10) • *Verses* (15) • *Three Lessons in a Frame* (21) • *Music for Sleep* (9) • *Verses for Ensembles* (25) • *Some Petals from my Twickenham Herbarium* (26)

As Walsh indicates, the principle of verse and refrain figures prominently in Birtwistle's music. Pre-eminent amongst Birtwistle's explorations of verse forms are the three works that allude explicitly to the principle in their titles – *Refrains and Choruses*, *Verses* for clarinet and piano and *Verses for Ensembles*. The terms 'verse', 'chorus' or 'refrain' also appear in other works, usually to describe various subsections or movements. In *The World is Discovered*, for instance, each section is called, alternately, 'Verse' or 'Chorus'; *Cantata* is built around a recurrent 'Refrain'; and Punch's 'Lullaby', towards the beginning of *Punch and Judy*, is divided into 'verses' and 'refrains'. In still more pieces, verse-like repetition schemes of varying strictness may be identified which receive no explicit labelling of any sort.

Repetition is, of course, central to the principle of verse and refrain. Whichever type of verse form is entertained – whether both refrain and verse are repeated, or only the refrain, separating changing verses – some sort of repetition is always involved. This perhaps makes verse structure an unlikely candidate for the avant-garde composer contemplating different formal options. The structural 'redundancy' of repetitive verse schemes – indeed their very clarity and simplicity – is at odds with an aesthetic that favours uniqueness and complexity. Verse structure *can* be made more intellectually satisfying, however. One way to do this is to emphasise the 'ritualistic' associations of formal repetition. This gives verse structure the necessary air of ahistorical abstraction, thus making it more appropriate for use in an avant-garde context. Birtwistle's European contemporaries have variously taken this route, from Stockhausen's *Refrain* (1959) with its chiming, bell-like sonorities (Paul Griffiths says that the piece has 'the aura of a ritual enactment'[3]), to Boulez's *Rituel* (1975), an act of commemoration projected through an alternating block structure of monumental simplicity (Boulez himself has described it as 'a sort of verse and response for an imaginary ceremony'[4]). The ritualistic connotations of formal repetition may largely explain its attraction to Birtwistle. His *Tombeau in Memoriam Igor Stravinsky*, a tiny work for flute, clarinet, harp and string quartet, makes explicit the connection. In this piece, a three-chord refrain in the harp is repeated identically between five short, more melodic 'verses', which are played alternately by the two winds and the four strings. In the process, elegant homage is paid to Stravinsky's own use of repetition and sectional form to evoke sacred or pagan ritual.

By and large, though, Birtwistle pursues strategies that serve to complicate, rather than underline, the formal simplicity of traditional verse structure – to deprive it of some of its clarity and predictability. This is particularly apparent at the outset of his career, when he was most under the influence of the Darmstadt generation of composers. Birtwistle's first published work, *Refrains and Choruses*, undermines many of the conventional expectations that may be aroused by the title. Birtwistle explains its title as follows:

> [The piece's] compositional scheme is simple, having five sections, each section consisting of two elements: a constant one called 'chorus', and a recurring one called 'refrain'. The refrain, through repetition, becomes a predominant entity, and so the chorus material of the following section.[5]

Birtwistle thus makes it clear that the work's form is fundamentally *sectional*. However, he also hints at an evolutionary element in his design that is not typically associated with verse and refrain; and, indeed, the work's form is far less bold and obvious than the title would suggest. Successive 'sections', for instance, are not clearly offset. Instead, the music flows continuously from beginning to end, so that, as Michael Hall has noted, the piece 'gives the impression of being entirely through-composed' rather than sectional and repetitive.[6] Nor do the music's main sections coincide with statements of chorus or refrain. Rather, the exchanges of chorus and refrain occur *within* each formal section. As Birtwistle's note explains, the repeated, 'refrain' element of one section is used as the basis of the constant, 'chorus' element of the next. So the relation between the work's sections is defined primarily in terms of a section's *evolutionary* connection with the previous one, rather than in terms of repetition.

In fact, the work's sections are disguised to such a degree that their identity is far from immediately apparent. Birtwistle's note refers to the existence of five sections. Andrew Clements, on the other hand, has suggested that there are not five but *seven* main sections,[7] while the score's rehearsal letters, reinforced by double bar lines, divide the music into *eight* parts, the second of which is itself split by a double bar line without rehearsal letter (b. 45). Similar ambiguities exist at the level of refrain and chorus. Rather than alternating his two types of material, Birtwistle allows the two to proceed concurrently. And, despite Birtwistle's description of the 'refrain'

Fig. 5.1. *Refrains and Choruses*: formal chart

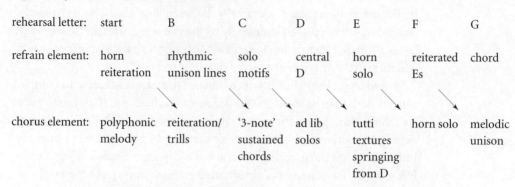

rehearsal letter:	start	B	C	D	E	F	G
refrain element:	horn reiteration	rhythmic unison lines	solo motifs	central D	horn solo	reiterated Es	chord
chorus element:	polyphonic melody	reiteration/ trills	'3-note' sustained chords	ad lib solos	tutti textures springing from D	horn solo	melodic unison

as the 'recurring' element, the music actually contains very little in the way of identifiable repetition – until the work's closing section, where a chord comprising five pitches reappears in a successively narrower register.[8] To distinguish between refrain and chorus for the bulk of the piece, it is necessary to resort to the evolutionary relationship between the refrain of one section and the chorus of the next (see Figure 5.1 for a rough and ready account along these lines). Each element has an identity of only the loosest sort, defined as much by the contrast it makes with its surroundings as by concrete or stable characteristics of its own.

In various ways, then, Birtwistle works to disguise the simple formal plan he outlines in his note. Interestingly, Birtwistle's note makes no reference to the instrumental role-play, discussed in Chapter 2, between the horn and the rest of the ensemble. It is possible that this instrumental drama involved some degree of compromise to Birtwistle's initial formal scheme: the latter arguably exists not as the primary focus of the work but as a loose frame within which the instruments play out their antipathies and affinities. That the piece is concerned with matters beyond the purely formal is also hinted at by its title. It opposes 'refrain' and 'chorus', while failing to make any mention of the 'verse' to which each is traditionally opposed. In other words, it combines musical elements frequently regarded as having entirely synonymous formal functions. One effect of this is to highlight the slightly different connotations of each term. Where 'refrain' suggests simply a recurring element, 'chorus' has a number of different meanings. Birtwistle's interest in ancient Greek theatre immediately suggests one way in which to interpret this part of the title: by reference to the sorts of formalised interactions characteristic of Greek tragedy. More generally, the contrast presented by refrain and chorus is one of abstract form against enacted drama. Birtwistle's title reminds us that the verse and refrain principle can never be treated as a wholly abstract mould for musical material. Rather, it carries strong associations with certain sorts of dramatic interaction, largely on account of its importance to different sorts of song. These have historically dictated that the verse is essentially soloistic, the refrain communal, as David Lindley explains:

> To a group of singing people the arrival of 'the chorus' generates a sense of release into the known and shared, and symbolizes community. This is true of the leader-chorus pattern of work songs, or of the sung responses in a liturgical litany, as it is of the invitation a music-hall singer offers to his audience to join in with a well-known chorus. In many musical forms – music-hall songs, theatrical 'musicals' and 'pop' songs – the distinction between verse and chorus is heavily marked by the subordination of a quasi-recitative verse to the 'big tune' of the chorus which we as audience are invited to know.[9]

Birtwistle follows this pattern explicitly in the slightly later work, *The World is Discovered*: each 'Verse' is scored for just two instruments, while each 'Chorus' features the whole ensemble. In *Refrains and Choruses*, the total absence of 'verses' makes the drawing of a straightforward connection between the work's formal elements and its instrumental role-play more difficult; and, as Figure 5.1 indicates, the horn is not consistently assigned to either 'refrain' or 'chorus'. This is not to say that there is no such connection, however. A more detailed analysis would strive to establish precisely how the distinct levels of the work – the formal and the dramatic – interrelate.

The World is Discovered marks an important stage in the development of Birtwistle's use of verse structure, for it is here that entire formal sections are first treated as single verses or refrains.[10] This becomes standard practice for Birtwistle in the remaining verse and refrain pieces of the 1960s. *Three Movements with Fanfares*, a little-known but substantial piece for chamber orchestra written three years after *The World is Discovered*, makes no explicit reference to verse structure, but it follows a broadly similar formal pattern. Each 'Movement' is preceded by a 'Fanfare', and the whole is prefaced by a short 'Introduction'; accordingly, the Movements may be likened to three verses, with the Fanfares forming the refrains.[11] As Michael Hall has pointed out, the analogy is supported by aspects of the work's scoring. The Movements give greater prominence to soloistic textures, while the Fanfares predictably present mostly tutti (or 'choral') textures – though, in the case of the third Fanfare, exceedingly quiet ones! The solo-tutti distinction is not as rigidly maintained as in *The World is Discovered*, however, and it is perhaps better to view the work's proximity to verse structure in slightly different terms. David Lindley points to the fact that the chorus symbolises 'the known and shared'. The same can be said of Birtwistle's Fanfares: their title is specific, indicating the sort of material likely to be found there, and thus in an important sense they acquire the familiarity – the 'shared ownership' – of a refrain. The Movements, on the hand, give nothing away through their title. They are the moments when we are unable to predict or participate, but must instead attend to the unforeseen course of events unfolded by the composer. They are more akin to sung verses, traditionally the responsibility of a single soloist or leader. The Movements' widely contrasting content lives up to this analogy. The first is manic and dance-like, remaining for much of the time in 3/8. The second is slow and delicate, gradually spawning polyphony out of finely spun unisons. The last is more volatile, and moves towards a series of unison octaves that suggest a kinship with Birtwistle's later orchestral work, *Chorales.*

The verse and refrain structures in *The World is Discovered* and *Three Movements with Fanfares* emerge, then, not so much from the repetition of specific musical material as from patterns of 'functional' similarity. The refrains involve 'shared' material, while the verses are more the preserve of single individuals. In this way Birtwistle is able to avoid the more literal repetition that was such a bête noire for the post-Webern school. But *Three Movements* was followed in Birtwistle's output by *Entr'actes and Sappho Fragments*, a work whose very premise (the expansion of an earlier work using rewritten versions of movements from it) implied far more literal and audible musical recapitulation. *Entr'actes and Sappho Fragments* thus prepared the way for the composition of *Tragœdia* a year later, with its mimicking of Aristotle's description of the repetitive structure of Greek tragedy.

As was seen in Chapter 2, the instrumental role-play in *Tragœdia* involves some recognition of the centrality of alternating soloistic and choral statements to ancient Greek tragedy (see Figure 2.1 on p. 41). But it is Birtwistle's next work, baldly titled *Verses*, that most manifestly seizes upon the verse-like component of tragedy. This short work for clarinet and piano is the first in Birtwistle's output to unite an explicit reference to verse structure with the musical repetition that is traditionally its counterpart. It comprises eight brief sections, each numbered and closed by a double bar. So, as in *The World is Discovered* and *Three Movements with Fanfares* (but in contrast to *Refrains and Choruses*) primary formal sections are clearly distinguished. Indeed there is nothing to prevent a player selecting individual 'Verses' from the cycle: the score presents them as if they were self-contained miniatures. The work's repetition scheme is also clearly apparent. In essence, two contrasting types of material are alternated (see Figure 5.2).[12] Verse 1 presents soft, sustained repeated notes in the clarinet

Fig. 5.2. *Verses*: formal chart

verse:	1	2	3	4	5	6	7	8
material:	A	(note) B	A	(note) B	A	(note) B	(B)?	(note) A

against a gentle, filigree piano accompaniment. Similar material then recurs in Verse 3, while Verses 5 and 8 simply reverse roles so that the repeated notes appear in the piano and the angular melodic material in the clarinet. Verse 2, on the other hand, presents a solo melodic line in the clarinet, which is reprised with embellishments and contrasting piano accompaniments in Verses 4 and 6. Verse 7 stands somewhat apart: it begins with a version of the opening material from Verse 2 but thereafter its connection to earlier verses is less obvious. A sustained single note in the clarinet, included after the piano's double bar, ends every odd-numbered verse, strengthening the piece's division into groups of two verses.

As is clear from this description, Birtwistle's 'repetition' is inexact. In fact, Birtwistle has often stated his opposition to verbatim repetition. In the interview at the end of Michael Hall's first book, for instance, Birtwistle argues that Messiaen's music suffers from too much exact repetition, and claims that he, on the other hand, 'would never copy something out again from another page'.[13] This last assertion needs to be taken with a pinch of salt: Birtwistle's music contains several instances of exact repetitions of lengthy and complex passages, and it is unlikely that they were all written out from memory. Nevertheless, verbatim repetition is undeniably the exception rather than the rule, and in this Birtwistle remains true to his avant-garde heritage. Recurring material is consistently subjected to varying degrees of transformation, thereby denying the music complete predictability. This applies to local-level ostinati as much as to the global level of form.

Birtwistle's suspicion of more literal strophic form, where verses recur unchanged, is indicated by the fact that he avoids it even in the genre with which it is most closely associated – namely, song. As we have seen, song features prominently in Birtwistle's output, but only one setting is strophic: the unpublished *The Wine Merchant Robin of Mere*, for male voice and piano, which appeared in the twentieth anniversary wine list of Yapp Brothers Wine Merchants.[14] Beyond that, acknowledgement of the tradition of strophic song is confined to a few of the songs that occur in the operas, and to the wholly instrumental *Dinah and Nick's Love Song*. Even in this last piece, the instrumentalists' three-fold progression through 'the same music' is disguised by the inclusion of alternative routes for each of the work's melody instruments.[15] The absence of strophic forms in the other songs is, of course, in large part a reflection of Birtwistle's choice of texts. His preference for the contorted imagery and syntax of Logue and Celan, or the fragments of Sappho, largely prevents strophic settings.

Yet the traditional conjunction of strophic musical form and song serves certain purposes; and once these are properly grasped it becomes clear that, even if Birtwistle's own songs are remote from the tradition of strophic song, there remain intriguing parallels with his instrumental works. Musical repetition serves the purpose of song in two important respects. Firstly, it throws attention onto and makes additionally memorable the *words* that are being sung. Music that is repeated is easily remembered: thus memorised, it can assist the comprehension and memorisation of the words to which it is attached. (This ability of music to embed verbal information in the mind of a listener has not been lost on the makers of radio and television commercials.) Secondly, musical repetition minimises the demands made on a listener by musical structure, and thus allows attention to focus instead on the very act of *singing*. A repeated verse foregrounds the activity of the performer, highlighting his or her distinctive embellishments and idiosyncratic vocal inflections. In these two significant respects, the repetitiveness of the music is simply a substructure that enables the emphasis of other sorts of communicative and expressive *change*.

This sort of 'change in repetition' remains central to the contemporary pop song.[16] It is, in fact, arguably a more prominent feature of pop than of strophic classical song, where the changing text is traditionally ascribed less importance relative to the music, and where the degree of performative variation characteristic of pop or jazz is not usually permitted. Viewed in this light, Birtwistle's incorporation of change into the very musical material of his verses (see, for instance, the two examples from *Verses* given in Example 5.1) can be understood as an attempt to forge a classical equivalent to the heightened dynamism of strophic song in other, non-classical traditions. It is a strategy that, far from standing in opposition to 'simple' strophic song, provides a form of compensation for those very vital aspects of strophic song that the classical tradition marginalises. In so doing, it humanises Birtwistle's repetition schemes, much as strophic song, in highlighting the verbal text and the person relating it, places humanity centre stage. Birtwistle's testiness about pop risks obscuring the real similarities his music sometimes has with it.

Birtwistle himself, on the other hand, has preferred to explain the principle of altered repetition in rather different terms, likening it to viewing the same object from slightly different perspectives:

Ex. 5.1. *Verses*: clarinet line in Verses 2 and 4

Essentially I'm concerned with repetition, with going over and over the same event from different angles so that a multi-dimensional musical object is created, an object which contains a number of contradictions as well as a number of perspectives.[17]

[I'm interested in] the notion that this piece of music exists, just like an object, and what you can do is perform certain facets of it, examine it in different ways . . . There are things that keep repeating, but if you listen to them or look at them closely, they're not repeating . . . The total object is never sounded, but through time you build up a memory picture of what it is.[18]

The idea that music may successively represent different planes of a physical object, so that 'one links together separate impressions . . . into an idea of a whole which one has never seen as a totality',[19] has remained one of the most durable of Birtwistle's obsessions. It bears a striking resemblance to statements by Edgard Varèse, who as early as 1936 spoke of 'the movement of sound-masses, of shifting planes . . . Certain transmutations taking place on certain planes will seem to be projected onto other planes, moving at different speeds and at different angles.'[20] Birtwistle's explorations of the idea are in some respects more literal than Varèse's. This is clear from a withdrawn work, *Three Lessons in a Frame* for piano solo and five instruments. According to Michael Hall, this piece 'explores the visual

Fig. 5.3. *Verses for Ensembles*: formal chart

b.1	A						Introduction
[6]-1		B					Wind (3 'lines')
[8]			C				Low brass canon (with perc.)
[10]		B					Wind, with perc. (3 'lines')
[13]				D			Horn solo (start)
[16]					E		Brass ritornello
[17]				D			Horn solo (conclusion)
[18]						G	Alternating ensembles
[30]			C				High wind canon (with perc.)
[33]					E		Brass ritornello
[34]						F	Bassoon solo
[37]					E		Brass ritornello
[38]						F	B♭ clarinet solo
[41]					E		Brass ritornello
[42]						F	Oboe solo
[45]					E		Brass ritornello
[46]						F	E♭ clarinet solo
[49]					E		Brass ritornello
[50]						F	Piccolo solo
[53]					E		Brass ritornello
[54]		B					Wind, with brass and perc. (3 verses)
[57]				D			Horn solo (abbreviated)
[58]						G	Alternating ensembles
[70]			C				Low brass and high wind canons combined (with perc.)
[73]	A						Conclusion

image of a mould and its copy. The first two lessons, for piano alone and instruments alone respectively, are really the same work twice, except that whatever is implied but missing in one of them is to be found in its complement. In the third lesson the two interlock.'[21] Lesson I and Lesson II, then, each represent views of the same object from different perspectives. The rhythmic structure of each is identical, and the pitches of Lesson II are only modestly transformed – transposed by the interval of a fourth, up or down, with additional octave displacements. Both perspectives return, mostly unchanged, in Lesson III, where they alternate and occasionally play together to create a more multi-perspectival image. These simple transformations are embedded in a 'Frame' of refrains and ostinato-based textures, played by the percussion and the instrument(s) not reading the Lesson.

By the standards of other works which adopt the idea of multiple perspectives on an object, *Three Lessons in a Frame* takes a remarkably

Fig. 5.4. *Music for Sleep*: formal chart

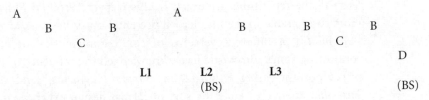

A, B, C, D = Refrains
L1   = 'Lullaby on a Ground' (words by A. P. Graves)
L2   = 'Nocturne' (words by William Wordsworth)
L3   = 'Cradle Song' (words by James, John and Robert Wedderburn)
BS   = Bird Songs 1–3

simplistic approach. Birtwistle withdrew the work after its first performance, maybe because he felt its procedures were too transparent –
though similarly blatant transformations are found in the cyclical elements of *Punch and Judy*.[22] Elsewhere, Birtwistle's approach to altered repetition is less formulaic, and may range over the entire continuum of
degrees of change, from identical repetition to total difference. The bigger
the change, the more the perspective taken on the 'total object' has been
altered. So, in *Verses*, Verses 1 and 3 suggest relatively slight realignment,
while Verses 2 and 7 suggest the adoption of a very different 'viewpoint'.
The occasional similarities between Verses 1 and 2 might be taken as signifying diametrically opposed perspectives on a single object, where only a
few features remain identifiable from each side. (This would be consistent
with Hall's analysis, linking Verse 2 back to Verse 1.)

Verses for Ensembles inflates some of these preoccupations to epic proportions. As Figure 5.3 shows, it intermingles not two but *seven* types of
material, each appearing between two and seven times and subject to a
different degree of alteration on each occasion.[23] The multi-layered ambi-
tion of this verse structure makes it very far removed from the earlier
Verses, but it is not wholly unprecedented in Birtwistle's output. In *Music
for Sleep*, a work intended for performance by children, four instrumental
'Refrains' (labelled A, B, C and D) are interspersed either singly or in combination between three lullabies for children's chorus. An extra layer of
repetition is added by the inclusion of identical woodwind bird songs in
both Refrain D and the second lullaby. The resulting form is summarised
in Figure 5.4. *Verses for Ensembles* plays with a similar formal design,
departing from the children's piece only in its subjection of each type of

repeated material to a different degree of alteration, where in *Music for Sleep* all the repetitions are exact. In this respect *Verses for Ensembles* is more comparable to the interleaved presentation in Boulez's *Le marteau sans maître* of different versions of (or 'commentaries' upon) three contrasting songs. Birtwistle has acknowledged the influence of Boulez's piece upon the earlier *Entr'actes and Sappho Fragments*,[24] and *Verses for Ensembles* merely extends the sort of formal design experimented with there. In Birtwistle's terms, it presents a variety of 'perspectives' on seven distinct 'musical objects'; some are rotated considerably on each appearance (for example, C and F on Figure 5.3), some are rotated slightly (B, D and E), and one is not changed at all (G).

If this would be Birtwistle's preferred way of metaphorically describing *Verses for Ensembles*' structure, there remain aspects of the piece that are more receptive to explanation in terms of the analogy of strophic song that was used in discussing *Verses* for clarinet and piano. In certain respects, *Verses for Ensembles* pushes the analogy even more forcefully than did the earlier work. The internal structure of certain sections takes a decidedly text-like form. The material labelled B in Figure 5.3, for instance, comprises soft music for low winds, split into three segments whose similar length and material create the impression of three scanning lines in a poetic stanza. Additionally, while each appearance of B looks identical on the page, the provision of alternative routes for each player means that each occurrence will sound related but different. (In the note to the score Birtwistle encourages each musician to alter his or her choices on subsequent occasions.) The resulting succession of slightly altered, three-line stanzas is not dissimilar to the succession of verses in a poem where metre and rhymes are retained from verse to verse.

Verses for Ensembles also foregrounds an issue lurking behind *Verses*, but not openly addressed there – namely, the relation between verse and *refrain*. Neither work makes room for refrain in its title; and in *Verses* it appears that there *is* no refrain, and that the two alternating elements simply represent different verses. *Verses for Ensembles*, on the other hand, designates one of its component sections as a 'ritornello'.[25] This is the brass material labelled E in Figure 5.3. At first appearances, the ritornello seems to be a literal refrain – which is to say, it forms an identically repeated formal element, that contrasts with the changing formal elements between which it is interspersed. It separates a succession of highly varied, accompanied solos for the high wind instruments, which are unified only by common horn and percussion material. This further emphasises the sense in which it forms a 'choral' refrain, alternating with 'soloistic' verse. However, Birtwistle complicates matters by requesting in the note to the score that 'each appearance of the brass "ritornello" should sound strikingly different'. This is to be achieved by varying dynamics, phrasing, and mutes. Birtwistle appears intent, both here and elsewhere in his music, upon ambiguating verse and refrain relative to each other. He has observed that, 'When you have a refrain, or something that repeats obviously, it's a question of what's the bread, and what's the filling . . . I like to think that in my music there's an ambiguity about what the bread is and what the filling is.'[26] Despite initial appearances, the brass 'ritornello' does not unambiguously take the function of a refrain.

In part, Birtwistle's exploration of this ambiguity is a product of the paradox that faces any composer contemplating writing an *instrumental* verse and refrain structure. Traditionally, musical strophic structures are found in vocal rather than instrumental music. They typically involve the repetition of both refrain-music *and* verse-music; it is only the words that tell them apart. There are exceptions to this: early sixteenth-century English song, of the sort preserved in the so-called Fayrfax Manuscript,[27] provides numerous instances of forms where a repeated refrain or 'burden' separates verses with different *music* as well as different texts. But Birtwistle is also intrigued by the more traditional model, which seems so difficult to replicate in purely instrumental music. His tiny birthday tribute to Universal Edition's Bill Colleran, *Some Petals from my Twickenham Herbarium*, plays the same game as the central passage of *Verses for Ensembles*. It alternates high, shrill, decidedly hortatory statements for piano and piccolo with shorter, gentler, 'choral' contributions for glockenspiel, clarinet, violin and cello. The refrain-like character of the latter is reinforced by the fact that the glockenspiel's six chords are identical on each occasion. Yet this is deceptive, for the other 'choral' instruments are subtly altered on each occasion. Birtwistle at once connotes a refrain function and questions it – and in the process he enriches the associative content of his instrumental forms.

Fragment

Verses for Ensembles (25) • *An Imaginary Landscape* (38) • *Carmen Arcadiae Mechanicae Perpetuum* (53)

One of the consequences of Birtwistle's multi-levelled scheme in *Verses for Ensembles* is that related 'verses' are rarely adjacent. One is obliged to wait for the next verse at a given level to appear. This dramatically diminishes the formal predictability that is so central to simple strophic structures. In this important respect, *Verses for Ensembles* fights, contradictorily, against the very nature of strophic form, supplanting regularity and predictability with uncertainty and tension. Michael Nyman has suggested that the piece's extremely forceful, aggressive character may be explained by the need to project to a listener this complex formal interweaving:

> The architecture makes itself perceptible by asymmetrical balancing over an extended period of time, relying for its effect on the art of suggestion by sledge-hammer. The sledge-hammer is necessary for Birtwistle because music as it passes in time tends to flatten out the sharp outlines one might 'see' with a frontal elevation/cross section-type analysis on paper.[28]

But 'the art of suggestion by sledge-hammer' serves a second purpose. It emphasises the rudeness of Birtwistle's contrasts – and thereby also the music's indebtedness to the abrupt disjunctions of Stravinsky or Messiaen, as much as to the accumulating formal homogeneity of traditional verse and refrain. A few years before the composition of *Verses for Ensembles*, Edward Cone's classic theoretical formulation of Stravinsky's aesthetic of disjunction appeared in *Perspectives of New Music*.[29] Birtwistle spent most of 1966 at Princeton University where Cone had been teaching for two decades, and this makes it particularly likely that he was acquainted with Cone's writings at the time of composing *Verses for Ensembles*. Cone's central concepts, most famously developed in relation to Stravinsky's *Symphonies of Wind Instruments*, may be fruitfully applied to Birtwistle's piece. Principal amongst these concepts is the idea of 'interlock'. This refers to the juxtaposition of contrasting sections of music, each of which arouses the expectation of some sort of eventual resumption or completion, thus generating a sense of accumulating tension as the music proceeds. *Verses for Ensembles* very obviously involves interlocking sections of contrasting music. Abrupt contrasts 'affecting almost every musical dimension: instrumental and registral, rhythmic and dynamic'[30] are at least as important to the work as the exploration of possible analogies to texted strophic form. (It is significant, in this connection, that the work's title was originally not 'Verses' at all, but 'Signals'.[31]) This affinity with Cone's theory is strengthened by the visual resemblance that parts of *Verses for Ensembles* have, in the score, to Cone's notational analysis of Stravinsky's *Symphonies*. At the section labelled G in Figure 5.3, for instance, the music proceeds in an abrupt succession of fragmentary statements from each of the different ensembles. In Birtwistle's notation, the dialoguing ensembles each occupy their own layer of a page, and the absence of staves for bars when they are silent strengthens the impression of material prematurely suspended.

This notational resemblance to Cone's famous analysis is not just a coincidental one-off. It occurs again in the work that eventually received the title Birtwistle rejected for *Verses for Ensembles*. *Signals*, for clarinet and electronic sounds, with its intricate options for realisation,[32] makes particularly imaginative use of the notated page. The work's fourth 'Trace' could almost be lifted from Cone's Stravinsky analysis (see Example 5.2). Its four distinct strata of contrasted material are segmented and interweaved, and connected by lines and arrows suggesting possible routes for the clarinettist. Beyond the purely visual resemblance, the brevity of segments and the distinctive identity of individual strata in this part of *Signals* bespeak a compositional process of interruption and fragmentation very similar to that identified in the *Symphonies of Winds* by Cone.

If there are important areas of similarity between *Verses for Ensembles* and Cone's analysis of Stravinsky, there are also points of difference. Cone claims that, in Stravinsky, contrasting 'strata' of material are marked out by 'interruption'; as a result, 'the ideas thus presented are usually incomplete and often apparently fragmented'.[33] But a *verse* typically comprises a passage of music that is self-contained, not interrupted or fragmentary. *Verses for Ensembles* concerns itself not so much with fragmentation and interruption as with the unpredictable juxtaposition of self-contained units. In fact, it might be argued that the same is true for Stravinsky's *Symphonies of Winds*. The work's opening statement, for example, appears to be a complete phrase. It gives rise to none of the expectations associated with, for instance, the 'antecedent' of a classical melody. The contrasting material that immediately follows (Cone's layer 'B') inscribes a miniature ABA form, and so gives a similar impression of local closure. If the work's opening juxtaposition of ideas gives rise to an impression of tension, it is more because of the brevity of the two sections than because each is interrupted or fragmentary. Richard Taruskin's comparison of the *Symphonies of Winds* to the structure of the *panikhida* service, the Russian Orthodox office of the dead,[34] would tend to confirm the impression that many if not all of the work's individual units form self-contained 'verses'.

Cone's intention in his essay is to elaborate upon a method common to all of Stravinsky's music – a consistency of approach that underlies each 'superficially' divergent phase of his compositional career. But in the process he risks smoothing over important differences in technique and effect. Though all of Stravinsky's music surely proceeds according to the principle of 'continuity-by-means-of-discontinuity',[35] literal 'interruption' is only one means to this end. As with Stravinsky, justice is not done to Birtwistle's treatment of sectional form if a range of different possible approaches is not kept in mind when examining the music. *An Imaginary Landscape*, for brass, double-basses and percussion, represents a different

Ex. 5.2. *Signals*: Trace 4

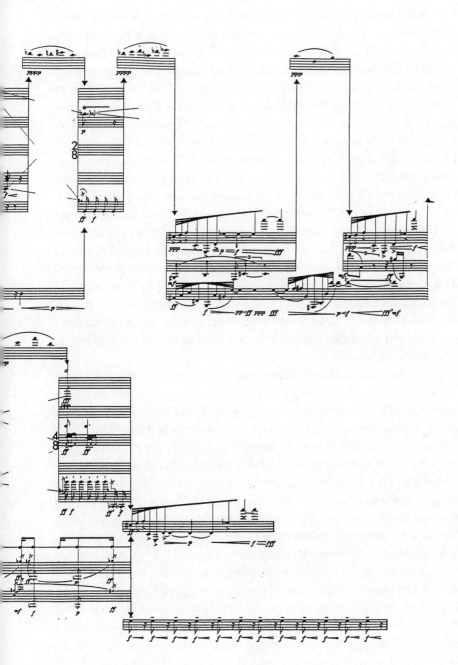

take on the model presented by Cone's analysis of the *Symphonies of Winds*. Like *Verses for Ensembles*, this piece has particular affinities with the Stravinsky: their sombre concluding chorales, for instance, reflect their common function as memorial pieces (*An Imaginary Landscape* is dedicated to the memory of Birtwistle's mother); and the construction of Birtwistle's piece from 'five different musics',[36] freely alternating, is reminiscent of the distinct 'strata' in the Stravinsky.[37] There are also important differences from Stravinsky's work. Firstly, *An Imaginary Landscape* takes the form of a continuous, single movement, with sections slurred and dovetailed rather than separated by silence. Glaring contrasts are generally played down, in favour of a more homogeneous effect. As Nyman states, 'the five musics each have their own recognisable character, but collectively fall within an overall unity of colour and image: they are not over-differentiated (unlike *Verses for Ensembles*)'.[38] Secondly, the music can no longer be understood to comprise a collection of self-contained verses. This is in part due to the relative brevity of individual sections, which in itself suggests a certain partialness or incompletion (at least by comparison with *Verses for Ensembles*); but it is also because successive appearances of the work's constituent 'musics' do not invariably take the form of an exact or varied repetition.

Figure 5.5 gives a rough outline of the piece's form. It shows how the reappearance of a certain kind of material frequently takes the form of a *continuation* of an earlier appearance, rather than a verse-like repetition. Passages of verbatim repetition do occur – primarily in the central section of the work, and also at the end, where the sombre chorales that open the work return in a changed instrumental context. But where in *Verses for Ensembles* literal repetition was combined with various degrees of varied repetition, in *An Imaginary Landscape* it contrasts with continuations of material previously interrupted. What I have described, in Figure 5.5, as 'Chorale 4' presents a good example of this. After only six bars its progress is halted by one of the work's many hushed paused chords, which introduces a brief section of highly contrasting percussive music ([12]). This in turn is halted by a further paused chord, whereupon Chorale 4 returns, beginning with the last bar of its previous appearance and then continuing from that point. That these two appearances of Chorale 4 are to be thought of as a single stretch of music, rudely interrupted by contrasting material, is confirmed when Chorale 4 returns at the end of the piece ([82]): this time the disruption does not occur and the chorale proceeds as a single, continuous passage.

A similar process of fragmentation affects Chorale 5, which is interrupted twice. On each occasion it resumes with the music that just pre-

Fig. 5.5. *An Imaginary Landscape*: formal landmarks

[2]	– [3]	**Chorale 1** (trpt. 4, hrn. 4, tuba)
[5]	– [7]+2	**Chorale 2** (do.)
[6]	– [7]+2	**Chorale 3** (trpt. 3, hrn. 3, trbn. 3)
[11]	– [12]–1	**Chorale 4** (do.)
[12]	– [13]–1	(Xylophones and high brass)
[13]	– [15]	**Chorale 4** continued
[19]–2	– [24]–1	**Chorale 5** (trpts. 2–4, hrns. 2–4, trbns. 2–3, tuba)
[24]	– [27]–1	(Double basses and lower brass)
[27]	– [29]–1	**Chorale 5** continued
		Growing xylophone ostinati
[29]	– [31]–1	(Similar to [12])
[31]	– [32]	**Chorale 5** and xylophone ostinati continued
[32]	– [35]+3	Xylophone ostinati continue
		Brass instruments move to Position B
[36]–1	– [48]	Succession of very short sections separated by soft, tutti, paused chord
[38]–1	– [40]	As at [24]–1 – [27]
[42]–1	– [43]	As at [12]–1 – [13]
[47]–1	– [48]+1	As at [29]–1 – [31]
[48]	– [56]	Succession of very short sections separated by loud, percussive 3/16 attacks
[56]	– [71]–1	Tutti climax
[73]+1	– [74]	**Chorale 1** (repeated identically, different accompaniment)
[74]	– [75]	Growing xylophone ostinati as at [27]
[75]	– [77]–1	**Chorales 2 and 3** (repeated identically, different accompaniment)
[77]	– [87]–2	Growing xylophone ostinati continue, from [80]–3 as at [31]
[82]	– [87]–2	**Chorale 4** (repeated identically; no interruption and different accompaniment)
[87]	– end	Closing tutti chorale

ceded the interruption. At such moments *An Imaginary Landscape* presents a closer analogy to Cone's structural principle of interruption and incompletion than anything in *Verses for Ensembles*, or even in the *Symphonies of Winds*. Birtwistle's notation sometimes graphically illustrates his adherence to this principle. At [31] he reintroduces the xylophones' varied ostinati that first appeared a few bars earlier. The fact that this is a resumption, rather than a repeat, is notationally indicated by a dotted phrase line pointing off into the music's past, as if the ostinato has restarted mid-phrase. The effect that this gives, of Birtwistle 'cutting his cloth' to precisely the dimensions required, is furthered when the varied ostinato material is repeated at [77]. Birtwistle begins his repetition, not at the same point at which the ostinato first commenced, but a few bars 'earlier' – bars that were excised from the ostinato's original appearance.

The prominence of intercutting and interruption in *An Imaginary*

Landscape, relative to *Verses for Ensembles*, has an impact on the overall impression given by the later work. For, as Cone predicts in his essay on Stravinsky, the result of such a structure is the setting up of 'a tension between successive time segments'.[39] If, in Birtwistle, we are less likely to desire the 'completion' or 'synthesis' that Cone strives to identify in Stravinsky,[40] nevertheless the work's sense of temporal deferral – its positive encouragement to the making of long-term formal connections – does give rise to a distinctive structural 'reach'. The musical present tends to be characterised by a sense of incompletion, a lack of immediate reward; instead, one is directed ahead, to seek fulfilment in what is not present. (Birtwistle's austere musical material contributes to this effect.) By comparison, the repetition of sections in *Verses for Ensembles* (and arguably also the *Symphonies of Winds*) is a far less urgent affair temporally. It gives rise to a pleasing patterned succession, but answers no accumulating structural need.

Elements of both *An Imaginary Ensemble* and *Verses for Ensembles* come together in *Carmen Arcadiae Mechanicae Perpetuum*, which was written as a birthday piece for the fourteen musicians of the London Sinfonietta. In his note to the work, Birtwistle explains that it is built around 'six mechanisms which are juxtaposed many times without any form of transition'.[41] This would seem to announce a return to the abrupt contrasts and audible recurrences of *Verses for Ensembles*. In a more recent discussion of *Carmen*, however, Birtwistle has emphasised how the return of a particular 'stratum' of material never takes the form of a repetition. Rather, each section of the piece is only a *partial* manifestation of one of the six mechanisms: 'You move from one mechanism to the other . . . When you go back to them you're not back to where you left off, so something's been going on in the meantime which you couldn't hear . . . It's as if the one block of music has done a journey in silence while another block of music is taking place.'[42] This particular formula, where audibly fragmentary segments from a larger musical object are placed in abrupt and contrasting juxtaposition, borrows from both *An Imaginary Landscape* and *Verses for Ensembles*. It seems to promise that the literal interruption of the former is to be thrown into vivid relief by the stark contrasts associated with the latter.

In the event the picture is rather different, for a number of reasons. For a start, *Carmen*'s mechanisms present 'a music not of process but of state', to borrow Richard Taruskin's formulation of the prevailing compositional principle in *Le sacre du printemps*.[43] Each mechanism is based on multiple, cyclical ostinati,[44] and as a result they are capable of connoting neither directionality nor closure. In principle, they could continue interminably ('mechanicae perpetuum' indeed); no point of termination would be more inappropriate, or interruptive, than any other. The linear chorales and accumulating xylophone ostinati of *An Imaginary Landscape*, by comparison, have far more pronounced temporal 'shapes'; as a result the suspension of an area of activity has a strongly interruptive and premature feel, whereas in *Carmen* it just feels like an arbitrary change of material. A second reason why *Carmen* needs to be distinguished from the procedures of the two earlier works concerns the relationships *between* associated sections. As Birtwistle's description makes clear, each recurring mechanism starts up in a different place from where it left off, having undertaken a 'journey' during its period of absence. Birtwistle's choice of words here is strikingly reminiscent of Cone's observation that each type of material in *Symphonies of Winds* 'continues to exert its influence even when silent'.[45] But the procedure is different from both *Verses for Ensembles*, where the music obsessively returns to earlier starting points, and *An Imaginary Landscape*, where material is frequently picked up from precisely the point where it was suspended. In fact, the mechanisms in *Carmen* sometimes start up in such a different 'place' that their identity is barely recognisable. Some indication of the degree to which material is transformed in the course of the piece is given by the fact that the three writers who have analysed the piece in detail have arrived at different conclusions as to the identity and location of each mechanism.[46]

In the context of *Verses for Ensembles* or *An Imaginary Landscape*, it is the relative *degradation* of the principle of perceivable return that is the significant feature of *Carmen*. Birtwistle's interleaved structure is likely to remain obscure for most listeners; instead, each section sounds more or less autonomous. This aural impression is not wholly inappropriate to Birtwistle's compositional concerns, even if it is inaccurate to the structural premise of this particular piece. The music of Stockhausen was an acknowledged early influence on Birtwistle and it would be surprising if Birtwistle had not, at some stage, contemplated the concept of 'moment form' pioneered by his older contemporary. In moment form, a number of individually characterised passages are juxtaposed, each of which may or may not relate to those around it: 'every present moment counts . . . a given moment is not merely regarded as the consequence of the previous one and the prelude to the coming one, but as something individual, independent, and centred in itself, capable of existing on its own'.[47] For a listener, *Carmen* may well come close to moment form, in which each apparently independent section of the piece comprises 'an experiential unit, a "moment", which can potentially engage the listener's full attention and can do so in exactly the same measure as its neighbours. No single "moment" claims priority, even as a beginning or ending; hence the nature of such a work is essentially "unending" (and, indeed, "unbeginning").'[48]

Moment form assumes complete dissociation between sections – privileging a hedonistic engagement with each individual passage over any obligation to retain an impression of content or structural implications from one section to the next. So *Carmen*, with its real if disguised structural connections between sections, does not comprise an example of moment form in the strongest sense. But it does appear to flirt with the idea of moment form, from the 'safe ground' (as it were) of an initial structural premise that demands an accumulative rather than momentary purview. Birtwistle's more recent music frequently goes even further, retaining a basically sectional approach to form but abandoning all identifiable connection between sections. *Carmen* can be seen to be pointing in this direction, letting the listener decide whether to remember, or to forget.

Context

Clarinet Quintet (58) • *Secret Theatre* (65) • *Endless Parade* (71) • *Berceuse de Jeanne* (67) • *Pulse Shadows* (Nine Movements for String Quartet) (100)

Birtwistle's note to *Carmen Arcadiae Mechanicae Perpetuum* unambiguously announces that the music's constituent sections are juxtaposed 'without any form of transition'. This is in contradistinction to Cone's articulation of Stravinskian 'method', which allows for bridging sections. According to Cone, Stravinsky's bridges are not transitions 'in the conventional sense', but they do serve to 'mitigate the starkness of the opposition between strata'.[49] In *Carmen* Birtwistle avoids any such mitigation. This 'transitionless' state does not, however, bring a complete return to the blank silences separating sections in *Verses for Ensembles*. Instead, paused notes in one or more instruments create a rudimentary join between the work's contrasting mechanisms. Indeed the possibility of a moment of silence is fastidiously insured against by tying over many of these sustained pitches to a grace note at the very start of the next section. Even in this most brusque of sectional forms, then, there is evidence of an overriding concern for sonic continuity.

This concern comes increasingly to the fore in Birtwistle's music in the late seventies and eighties. Birtwistle's approach to form remains an essentially sectional one – manifested in his scores by regular emboldened bar lines, as well as differentiated musical content. This sectionality is tempered, however, by a growing attentiveness to the relationship of adjacent sections, and, specifically, by the sense that a new section has a certain *responsibility* to the musical situation brought about in the immediately preceding one. Birtwistle's Clarinet Quintet represents an interesting stage in this development. The work began as a collection of miniatures, 'like entries in a diary':

> I gave myself one condition: each had to be exactly as long as the paper I was using. It wasn't a question of writing until I came to the end of the sheet, then stopping; each had to fit the page exactly, each had to be complete. And for some reason, when I'd composed about eight of these pieces . . . I couldn't let them be, I had to join them together, I had to write links. But I couldn't leave the links alone either. As well as relating them to the statements I had to relate them to each other. As a result the piece became a long, continuous line and none of the original elements can be distinguished.[50]

Birtwistle's description presents a strikingly different picture from that found in *Carmen Arcadiae Mechanicae Perpetuum*, written only three years earlier. Where, in *Carmen*, mechanisms recur – albeit in transformed guise – giving individual sections a partial or contingent quality, in the Clarinet Quintet the constituent sections originate in distinct, self-contained miniatures. And where *Carmen* highlights sectional boundaries and contrasts, in the Clarinet Quintet Birtwistle appears to have been more concerned to render his sections largely indistinguishable. These novel features have led at least one critic to view the Clarinet Quintet as the product of a creative impasse, following the exhaustive mining of very different structural procedures in *Silbury Air*, *Carmen*, and *...agm...*.[51]

The score, on the other hand, indicates a rather simpler and more recognisable state of affairs than all this might suggest. The entire piece is divided into sections by large brackets – the type usually used to group staffs at the beginning of every system in a printed score. Each opening bracket is marked by a rehearsal number, and each closing bracket is followed by a much briefer passage of music – sometimes only a single sustained pitch – before the next section begins with another opening bracket. On the face of it, we have here precisely the sort of form found in most of Birtwistle's works of the later 1970s: substantial sections of music, marked off by emboldened bar lines, and separated by brief 'transitional' bars.

Such sectionality might appear to be at odds with Birtwistle's claim that the work presents an undifferentiated stream of music in which 'none of the original elements can be distinguished'. But this would be to assume that the numbered sections presented in the score correspond to

Birtwistle's original, page-long pieces. In listening to the piece, it is the *heterogeneous* quality of individual bracketed sections that is most evident, rather than any sense that they each comprise cogent, self-contained units. A few retain an element of consistency for their entire length, thus constituting a distinct formal section after the manner of *Carmen Arcadiae Mechanicae Perpetuum* or *Verses for Ensembles* (examples include the long first section, which is characterised by regular shudders of string activity at every bar line; and the ninth section, where clarinet and first violin sing in rhythmic unison against pulsing string accompaniment). Other sections, however, are highly variegated in their content, making it difficult to distinguish aurally between what lies inside and outside Birtwistle's notated brackets. Such confusion is heightened by the widely varying lengths of each section: section 5, for instance, is only three bars long. Ultimately, the significance of the brackets remains mysterious. They may well not correspond to the original pieces and their links at all, but represent some sort of superstructure that Birtwistle arbitrarily placed on top of his 'long, continuous line' of music.[52] For the listener, meanwhile, the effect of Birtwistle's design is dramatic. The general impression is one of structural 'decomposition'. Lacking any clear distinction between section and transition, Birtwistle's music suddenly comes to be more about its moment-to-moment progress than the articulation of large-scale, modular shapes.

A year after finishing the Clarinet Quintet, Birtwistle was at work once again on *The Mask of Orpheus*. The Quintet is quite different in mood and compositional preoccupations from the opera; it foreshadows instead the developments that were to affect Birtwistle's music in the works immediately following *Orpheus*. These revolve around a concern on Birtwistle's part to reduce his dependence upon precompositional formal schemes. Such schemes had largely determined musical progress in, amongst other works, *Verses for Ensembles*, *An Imaginary Landscape* (which, according to Michael Nyman, was designed in response to computer-processed information[53]), *Carmen Arcadiae Mechanicae Perpetuum*, and, more recently, *The Mask of Orpheus* itself. In the early 1980s Birtwistle increasingly felt that, while schemes of this sort might act as a useful point of departure, there was a stronger obligation to the demands of the musical moment. In a conversation with Michael Hall in 1983, Birtwistle referred to this compositional principle as 'the sanctity of the context'[54]:

> You see, you can create a formal position before the event, an elaborate schemata, and that you can call your idea. That's what you're trying to express. You have a duty to that schemata, a duty to that initial idea. But in the process of composition you make contexts which are not necessarily concerned with it.

Other things are thrown up which have a life of their own and are just as important. You now have a duty to two things . . . The context of the moment is unique and must exert an influence, a strong influence.[55]

It is difficult not to see this position as a direct outcome of the delayed completion of *The Mask of Orpheus*. Birtwistle has described it as 'the worst period of my life. I nearly went out of my mind . . . It was very, very hard.'[56] The effort involved in thinking himself back into the opera's complex structure must have highlighted the degree to which his current compositional concerns – as manifested in works like the Clarinet Quintet – had drifted away from an adherence to rigid formal schemata. The result was an ardent belief in the importance of persuasive local continuity, a belief that has lasted to the present day.

What is particularly intriguing about this sense of responsibility to immediate context is that it has not overridden a continuing commitment to the construction of large-scale forms out of blocks of contrasting material. *Secret Theatre* exemplifies the way in which moment-to-moment continuity and sectional juxtaposition are maintained in delicate balance.[57] As in the Clarinet Quintet, sectional boundaries are indicated notationally by emboldened bar lines passing through all the instrumental staffs. Unlike the earlier work, these bar lines typically demarcate sections of an audibly distinct character. The first few pages of the work give a good idea of this. The opening section of the piece is defined by staccato ostinato patterns in the strings. At the work's first large bar line these give way to accented iambic rhythms in the piano and vibraphone, played in a new tempo. If these two sections were played without the melodic overlay of the 'cantus' instruments, they would resemble the cleanly juxtaposed musical mechanisms of *Carmen Arcadiae Mechanicae Perpetuum*. The third section of *Secret Theatre*, however, rather than presenting a third, different mechanism, *combines* elements of both previous textures. It also serves notice that, unlike most of *Carmen*, the piece's sections may contain musical growth as well as circular repetitiveness. On top of the string and piano textures Birtwistle superimposes brass material whose rhythmic activity and dynamic level increase rapidly: its effect is to generate a sense of impetus towards the conclusion of the section. As a result, the third section-change appears of correspondingly greater significance than the previous two.

Throughout *Secret Theatre*, there is a sense of smaller blocks of material being grouped to form larger dramatic paragraphs. Tempo is one of the most important ways in which smaller blocks of material are bound into a larger conglomerate shape. The music between [15] and [23], for instance (from roughly five and a half to just over seven minutes into the piece), contains at least three successive subsections in the continuum, but the binding force of the single tempo is felt strongly, as is clear when it finally gives way after an impressive crescendo of activity. There are other ways, too, in which the music's continuity is heightened. While the continuum largely defines the music's sectionality, a single textural layer from it may remain in place across a number of sections. At [9], for instance, the cyclically rotating pitch material in piano, contrabassoon and double-bass participates in a number of different sectional textures and thus helps to articulate a larger paragraph. The cantus plays a more prominent role in ensuring a relatively unproblematic flow from section to section, its melodic continuity helping to bind the work together. It is not wholly immune from the section changes taking place around it: its rhythmic qualities or instrumental line-up frequently undergo some alteration at a section boundary, and the conclusion of larger paragraphs in the continuum sometimes brings the cantus to a temporary halt (as at [23] – a moment of melodic hiatus that allows the bassoon to sneak in and take the lead). Almost regardless of the changes it undergoes, however, the cantus retains a singularity of identity denied the non-melodic continuum. The changing sections of the continuum provide little assurance that they all belong to the same compositional endeavour; the cantus, on the other hand, simply by virtue of its sustained linearity, gives the impression of a singularity of purpose through all its various manifestations.

Jonathan Cross has made a connection between the melody of the cantus instruments and the delivering of a narrative.[58] This seems an appropriate analogy, at several levels. To begin with, the continuity and perpetual unfolding of the cantus form a striking contrast to the profoundly anti-narrativistic disruptiveness and circularity of earlier works. Then there is the importance of theatre to the piece: the movement of the musicians, the suggestion of musical roles, the work's title, even its association with Graves's poem, all work to suggest that at some level the work is unfolding a dramatic narrative. Finally, aspects of the piece's 'shape' – its central passage of profound reflection ([42]), its culminatory climax ([73] to [79]) and the elegant epilogue that follows immediately after – suggest a loose conformity with a conventional 'narrrative curve'.

None of these features, however, explains how the work attains the coherence typical of narrative. Narratives are not just continuous streams of events in time: rather they present a delimited perspective that relates interconnected occurrences and actions. Traditionally, music apes the coherence of narrative through repetition – themes or formal sections reappear in order to signify the endurance of protagonists or agents

Ex. 5.3. *Secret Theatre*: motives

through the music's intervening machinations. Birtwistle's principle of the 'sanctity of the context', however, tends to imply a refutation of this sort of large-scale formal repetition. Consequently, to construct a coherent form in the traditional sense, Birtwistle is limited to another option: motivic repetition. It is a technique lightly but effectively deployed in *Secret Theatre*. Recurring motives contribute significantly to the piece's impression of overall coherence, compensating, to a degree, for the lack of any larger-scale formal reprise. Most prominent of these motives is a dyad comprising the D and F immediately above middle C (see Example 5.3(a)). This motive seems to have taken on a peculiarly personal significance for Birtwistle during the 1980s, for it features prominently in *Earth Dances*, *Endless Parade*, *Salford Toccata*, *Ritual Fragment* and *Gawain*. (In *Still Movement* and *Words Overheard*, works written immediately before and after *Secret Theatre*, the motive appears in the slightly different form of A-C (at the end and beginning, respectively, of the two works).) In *Secret Theatre* itself, the D-F dyad performs many functions: it begins and ends the piece; it initiates the still music at the work's centre; it emerges softly from the aftermath of the work's climax (in a harmonic context knowingly close to D minor); and throughout it is used to indicate a prevailing and common intent on the part of all those involved, whatever the vagaries of role or musical structure at any given moment.

It is not the only motive to connect separate sections of *Secret Theatre*, as Example 5.3 shows. Motive (c) appears initially as the basis for an entire section ([48] onwards), where it is subjected to varied repetition and eventually conjoined with the D-F dyad; subsequent isolated appearances take the form more of imagined reminiscences than actual returns. Motives (b) and (d) appear to be variant forms of a single figure, and are less readily associated with a single section. Motive (b) initially appears at four separate points in an increasingly hectic cantus passage ([17] – [20]), and is then isolated for varied repetition in the following section ([21] onwards). Its transformed return at [65] coincides with the return of the D-F dyad, which from this point onwards is brought back frequently and insistently. Thereafter (d) acquires a certain prestige 'by association', its three isolated reappearances each seeming more portentous and significant than their

Ex. 5.4. *Endless Parade*: trumpet motive

incidental nature would imply. It seems unlikely that the connections discerned here between the piece's most prominent recurring elements are
wholly coincidental. Rather, Birtwistle appears concerned to forge a web of
associations as compensation for the lack of any more systematic formal
patterning.

Recurring motives play a part in *Secret Theatre*'s companion piece *Earth
Dances*, though their role there is altogether less important. In *Endless
Parade*, on the other hand, motives are particularly important in articulating the work's progress. This is partly because the piece is characterised by
a further breakdown in what might be called 'sectional discipline'. The
notational device of the large bar line remains in use, but its reflection of
musical content is more tenuous than in *Secret Theatre*, with even short
'sections' frequently containing more than one distinct type of material.
Where *Secret Theatre* and *Earth Dances* tend to reserve rapid turnover of
material for the beginning or culmination of a larger paragraph, *Endless
Parade* uses it throughout. Recurring motives help to allay the rather rest-
less impression that results from this strategy. The most prominent of
these is not the D-F dyad (although that does appear several times), but a
four-note figure in the trumpet (see Example 5.4), which occurs identically eight times during the piece, on each occasion played by the trumpet.
This suggests that it serves a role-playing function as much as a formal one
– it 'represents' the trumpet, as it were. This use of motives as 'tags' for particular instruments is found again in *Ritual Fragment*, where each solo
instrument has its own motive, played both during their solo and when
accompanying other soloists.[59]

A second important recurring element of *Endless Parade* is spread more
evenly around the different instruments: the note D. Between the opening
bars, with their octave Ds in the strings, and the piece's flamboyant final
gesture in trumpet and vibraphone, sounding for all the world like a
perfect cadence in D, there are at least fifteen further occasions when D is
emphasised in some way. It may appear as a pedal, underpinning a texture;
as a tutti pizzicato, puncturing textures like an iron rivet; or as a point of
departure or termination for a cascading scale (a good example being the
scale in trumpet and strings at [3]). Such unapologetic highlighting of a
single pitch-class is an unorthodox thing to find in an otherwise fully chro-

matic idiom, but emphasised pitches have long been an element of Birtwistle's atonal harmony. In the 1970s, the note E frequently served as a point of departure or a stimulus for renewal, while in a number of works from the mid-1980s onwards (including *Earth Dances*, *Ritual Fragment* and *Gawain*) it is D that increasingly takes on this privileged function.[60] *Endless Parade* is unusual only in the density of appearances of its emphasised pitch, which helps to give the piece a cogency that structurally it might otherwise lack.

Of course, the cohering function of emphasised pitches is not usually seen as 'motivic' in nature. Privileged pitches are typically referred to as tonics, not motives. Their unifying function is understood to be less a matter of the frequency and placing of their appearance (though this is surely significant), than the result of the particular system of relationships they establish between themselves and every other pitch event in a piece. Tonics *govern* other events, in a way that motives do not. Birtwistle himself has suggested that something of the same overarching pull is exerted by his emphasised pitches, which he says 'create centres of gravity'.[61] Taken literally, this would imply the existence of some sort of heightened 'tension' when the pitch is absent – other pitch events representing a measure of resistance to that centre of gravity. But it is precisely the *absence* of such an impression in Birtwistle's music that confirms that his emphasised pitches are better understood as essentially motivic in nature – regardless even of how the composer might see them. Such a conception acknowledges their unifying function, without insisting that all surrounding events be understood in reference to it (that is, existing in a state of tension relative to it). The parallel sometimes made between Birtwistle's recurrent motives and landmarks in a landscape or labyrinth proves helpful here. However familiar such a landmark becomes, chanced upon repeatedly as it were, it creates no necessary tension when it is absent, and compels no return. Its recognisability – reassurance, even – should not be mistaken for some kind of magnetic or gravitational pull.

Intriguingly, the last act of *The Mask of Orpheus* points quite directly to the specifically *motivic* status of its emphasised pitch, E. The act is dominated by the electronic 'Aura of the Tides', which is made up of Es at many different registers. In Birtwistle's conception, each E corresponds to one of the metaphorical objects on the beach that are covered and revealed as the tide rises and falls throughout the act. In other words, the emphasised pitch is here explicitly likened to an object repeatedly chanced upon, rather than a force to which all else must answer.

According to Michael Hall, Birtwistle 'insists over and over again that essentially he is a modal composer'; in his second book, Hall demonstrates how a number of passages in Birtwistle's recent music are built from modes 'containing distinctive patterns of intervals nearly always of a symmetric nature',[62] and argues that certain pitches take on a pseudo-tonal function according to their role within these modes. In only one published piece is the existence of such a pseudo-tonic likely to be felt by a significant number of listeners, however. The brief *Berceuse de Jeanne*, a short piece for the beginner pianist, uses only the white notes of the keyboard: its 'mode' accordingly coincides with the scale that is the basis of most tonal music. The conventional functions of the various notes of that scale are confirmed in a number of ways: by the basis of the piece on A and E, in rocking fifths in the left hand; by the privileging of C and E in the melodic part; and by the three-fold expressive dwelling on the diminished fifth, B-F, each time marked 'poco rall.', and each time 'properly' resolved onto a consonance. These devices all serve to confirm A as the tonic of a modal minor scale. Birtwistle's newly invented modes, on the other hand, cannot call upon the sort of culturally ingrained knowledge of pitch relations that assists the perception of tonics in tonal music. In the absence of an unambiguous diatonicism, the creation of a comparably strong gravitational impression has to be doubted.

In *Endless Parade*, then, the recurrent Ds offer unusually persistent points of reference, but perform no grander cohering function. The motivism that is so prominent in the work extends to the piece's single larger-scale repetition. Towards the end of the work, Birtwistle engineers two wholesale reprisals of the first five bars of the piece (just after [37], and at [41]). The exactness of the repeat, and its relatively modest length, emphasise that this device, too, is in essence motivic – in contrast to, for instance, the altered verse structures typical of earlier works. This approach to sectional repetition demonstrates how far removed Birtwistle's priorities in formal construction have become, in the late 1980s, from those of the late sixties and early seventies. Persuasiveness and eventfulness at the local level are now unambiguously prioritised over the large-scale formal patterning of *Verses for Ensembles* and *An Imaginary Landscape*. The listener is no longer obliged steadily to accumulate a mental picture of Birtwistle's forms; instead, one is borne along on the flow of moment-to-moment incident. Repetition is thus confined to the motivic level. Motives, as incidental features of the musical flow, may be recalled from the past, but the recognition of motives neither implies nor requires any more comprehensive retention of musical structure.

In this connection, it should be noted that Birtwistle's motives do not really guarantee the narrative-like quality that led us initially to seek them out in *Secret Theatre*. Narratives are usually constructed on the assumption that a reasonably complete, accumulating grasp is being kept of their progress – at least, this is important if their various twists and turns, and eventual denouement, are to have their proper effect. *Secret Theatre*'s motives are not sufficient to ensure that we acquire that complete grasp. In this, as in so many other respects (some of them discussed in Chapter 2), *Secret Theatre* constitutes an unusually literal exemplification of a quality discerned by Jean-Jacques Nattiez in music generally: namely, that it is not so much a narrative as 'an incitement to make a narrative'.[63]

Indeed, it might be argued that Birtwistle's more recent music priorit- ises the local over the long term to the extent that it actually *encourages* lis- teners to dispense with the musical past. If formal sections bear little apparent relation to each other, beyond that minimal connectedness that ensures a new section is appropriate to the 'context' established by its pre- decessor, their formal function arguably changes. Each completed section, rather than becoming a component part of a larger, composite form, has minimal consequences for the remainder of the piece and thus does not need to be retained. Section boundaries, therefore, rather than cueing the transferral of retained musical material to longer-term memory stores, are more likely to determine the jettisoning of that material. There is, after all, little incentive to retain the musical past beyond the confines of individual sections.

As Birtwistle's transitions between sections become more elaborate, the idea that they cue a listener's 'forgetting' becomes more plausible. In *Secret Theatre*, although the continuum textures are comparable to the mecha- nisms of *Carmen Arcadiae Mechanicae Perpetuum*, the process of moving between different sections is a site for compositional invention in a way quite foreign to the earlier work, with its rudimentary paused pitches. A particularly characteristic section marker, in *Secret Theatre*, is the rapid scale. This is usually played by the cantus instruments, although occasion- ally (as at 4 bars before [23]) it spills over into the continuum. In its ascending form, this device is reminiscent of the recurring cimbalom flourish in Stravinsky's *Renard*, whose function, similarly, is to bridge contrasting sections. In Birtwistle's music it helps mitigate the abruptness of sectional contrast, dissipating ongoing material and providing cover for the introduction of something different. This enhanced continuity does not bring with it any obligation to carry the impression of the foregoing music through into the new, however. On the contrary, Birtwistle's transi- tional scales seem to wipe the structural slate clean, encouraging a limiting of formal awareness to the processes of the moment. *Earth Dances* and *Endless Parade* make further use of the device, borders between formal blocks becoming swathed in rapid registral sweeps. In *Salford Toccata*, a little-known work for brass band written two years after *Endless Parade*, these scales have become so ornate that they increasingly comprise the music's most distinctive moments, standing out from the relatively swift succession of intricate textures that comprise the bulk of the piece. One virtuosic cascade in *Salford Toccata* encompasses almost the entire twenty-four-strong band, and spans almost four octaves (4 bars after [31]).

Paradoxically, then, Birtwistle's 'context-aware' sectionality, which would appear to imply greater connectedness to the past, actually brings with it a certain structural ephemerality – a focus upon moment-to-moment fantasy rather than some evolving, obligatory larger form. The musical past comes to seem curiously impalpable; larger processes are guessed at rather than unambiguously perceived. This might seem to be a recipe for disaster as far as audiences are concerned: how is a listener to orientate him- or herself if he or she is deprived of a definite, evolving musical past? In fact, experimental work suggests that the approach to form taken in Birtwistle's recent music is consistent with listening psychology, which tends to privilege 'moment-to-moment events' over 'large-scale structure'.[64] Birtwistle's more continuous style naturally foregrounds the music's 'constant flow',[65] the very aspect of musical organisation that appears to be most responsible for sustaining listeners' interest. Thus, the minimising of larger structural aspirations seems likely to have little detrimental impact on most listeners.

If the formal section appears to be undergoing a degree of erosion in *Endless Parade* and *Salford Toccata*, it re-emerges with a vengeance in the huge verse schemes of *Gawain* and the clear-cut instrumental exchanges of *Antiphonies*. More recently, the sectional principle has been channelled through the idea of the musical 'frieze', in works such as *Slow Frieze*, and the Nine Movements for String Quartet that comprise part of *Pulse Shadows*. Birtwistle uses the term partly as a metaphor for his sectional forms, stating that, 'the idea of a frieze in music is something central to my work – that is, it explains itself in blocks of musical material, and these blocks can return in various guises'.[66] The parallel is particularly clear if one thinks of the Doric friezes that adorn the buildings of ancient Greece. These friezes take the form of a succession of enclosed panels, so that 'the visual effect . . . is one of repeated structural modules'.[67] Not all friezes take this modular form, however. Later Greek architecture, for instance, 'employed a frieze filled with a continuous band of figured relief sculpture . . . The visual effect of an Ionic frieze is one of uninterrupted horizontality.'[68] These sorts of friezes lack the sectionality that makes Doric friezes such an apt analogy for Birtwistle's forms. They emphasise instead another aspect of the frieze that appears to interest Birtwistle. This is the tension that they create, between their static, sculptural qualities, and the element of temporality or motion that their form – namely, the horizontal band – implies. In *Slow Frieze*, Birtwistle plays as much on this aspect of the frieze as the modular one, constructing a musical analogy for the frieze's paradoxical mobile staticity in the form of an 'unchanging harmonic backdrop' that appears periodically in the wind instruments. This is created by weaving, melodic lines which, taken together, spell out fixed harmonic fields.

As far as *Pulse Shadows* is concerned, the analogy of the frieze would appear to be most appropriate as a description of the work as a whole, made up as it is of small, constituent pieces or modules which, according to Stephen Pruslin, 'share the same spiritual terrain'.[69] That the piece might be conceived as a single, large, sectional form is emphasised by Birtwistle's own comparison with the verse structures of earlier works. He has suggested that, 'the string quartets and the songs in *Pulse Shadows* . . . are both functioning as the ritornello to the other, simultaneously. . . There's an element [of identical repetition], in that one is being played by a string quartet without a song, and then the other has a voice and it's a different instrumentation.'[70] Nevertheless, the individual pieces' disparate composition dates (the songs and quartets were both written over a period of several years[71]), and the fact that the work is 'flexible in concept' and allows for either songs or quartets to be 'performed as independent cycles, either complete or in part',[72] suggest that there are limits to the cycle's coherence. Birtwistle in fact uses the word 'frieze' not in relation to the cycle as a whole but to describe four of the nine quartet pieces. These four 'Friezes' are interleaved between five 'Fantasias', thus creating a further layer of verselike alternations when the cycle is performed in its entirety. The distinction between the two quartet types is an obvious one: the granitic formality of the frieze is intended to contrast with the greater freedom and fluidity of the fantasia. This is loosely borne out in the individual pieces. The Friezes each adhere to a broadly consistent type of material for their entire duration, culminating in the quasi-fugal structure of Frieze 4, which was written in response to Celan's famous poem 'Todesfuge'. The Fantasias progress more fitfully, and give greater room for individual instruments to make themselves heard – all four instruments speaking out individually in the second halves of Fantasias 1 and 2, and the viola taking a privileged role in Fantasias 3, 4 and 5.

Only one of the Friezes, however, falls into clearly defined sections. This is Frieze 1, the earliest of the quartet movements, which was written in 1991 as a self-contained birthday tribute to Alfred Schlee. It remains at one

Ex. 5.5. Nine Movements for String Quartet, Frieze 3: motives

remove from the other pieces. For the other Friezes, the title refers not to a modular form but, more loosely, to the rather impersonal quality of the music's exploration of repetition and change. Each is built from a rapid succession of tiny, recurring motives, scattered amongst the instruments and subject to different degrees of change (Example 5.5 shows some of the principal motives in Frieze 3). These recurring motives are, additionally, often offset by a more continuous element – an ostinato or a pulse – although these too are usually short-lived, constantly reinventing themselves. Of course, the idea of creating a larger structure by combining a number of recurring smaller elements, each subject to a different degree of change, is far from new in Birtwistle's music. We have seen a number of examples of this process in the works discussed in this chapter. What is new about these quartet movements is the application of the process to such tiny, motivic elements. In *Verses for Ensembles* and *Carmen Arcadiae Mechanicae Perpetuum*, the basic units are larger sections of a number of bars each. In Friezes 2, 3 and 4, they are, at most, a handful of notes.

This development, though initially startling to those accustomed to the more homogeneous local progress of Birtwistle's recent music, is in an important sense a logical one. The principle of the 'sanctity of the context' dictated that verse-like repetition was no longer to be found at the large scale in Birtwistle's music. Instead, verse structure has retreated to the local level, manifesting itself in the varied ostinati and small-scale exchanges from which individual sections are still typically built. (This characteristic of Birtwistle's recent music was discussed in the previous chapter, in relation to *The Cry of Anubis*.) However, just as, in Birtwistle's earlier music, the construction of *large-scale form* from a simple succession of related verses was eventually superseded by more complex and unpredictable multi-layered structures, so in the 1990s it appears as if the periodic repetitivity of Birtwistle's *microstructures* has given way to a far more complex, though still not unverse-like, patterning. The 'fugue' of Frieze 4 emphasises the parallels that can be made between these quartet pieces and the multi-layered structure of a piece like *Verses for Ensembles*. Birtwistle's 'subject' is not a single, fixed idea but a collection of five distinct motives. These motives are initially presented (by the viola) quite separately, one to a bar. The 'answer' (in the second violin) repeats the same motives, but in a

Fig. 5.6. Nine Movements for String Quartet, Frieze 4 – 'Todesfuge': order of
motives in bb. 1–20

A B C D E | C D A E B | D A C B E | B D E A C

different order, and in slightly altered versions. The remaining two entries
follow exactly the same procedure. Figure 5.6 shows the resulting structure. In this piece the regularity provided by the fugal structure gives an
extra layer of formalisation to the recurrence of motives, making the parallel with Birtwistle's earlier treatment of verse forms particularly marked.
It is a revealing comment on Birtwistle's changing attitudes to form that,
firstly, the fugue – the most thoroughly integrated and anti-sectional of all
musical forms – should find a place in his œuvre at all; and secondly, that
he should still be able to reconcile it with his enduring attachment to the
constructional principle of the juxtaposition of contrasting units.

6 Layers

Melody

Monody for Corpus Christi (2) • *Linoi* (23) • *Duets for Storab* (61) •
Hector's Dawn (70) • *An Interrupted Endless Melody* (85)

One of the more dramatic of the generalising claims made by Michael Hall
in his first book on Birtwistle is that, 'all his music, no matter how dense
and rich it may be, is essentially monody'.[1] Hall asserts that all of the
material in a piece springs from an underlying, single line; this line is 'filled
out by other lines moving in parallel motion with it, or by heterophony,
the presentation of differing versions of the same line simultaneously'.[2] Of
course, Birtwistle's complex textures frequently give little indication of
their simple origins, and it might consequently be wondered whether there
is anything to be gained from trying to understand the final product in
such 'monodic' terms. If nothing else, though, Hall's assertion reflects the
importance to Birtwistle's music both of melody and (more generally) of
clearly delineated textures. As early as Birtwistle's second published work,
Monody for Corpus Christi, melody was unashamedly brought centre stage
– and this at a time when many of Birtwistle's contemporaries in continental Europe were shunning it in favour of a focus upon the various parameters affecting the individual note. Since then, a number of other pieces
have taken melody as their specific, principal concern; and melody has
become a staple element of Birtwistle's style generally[3] – to the extent that
the sustained, unison wind melody is now something of a trademark,
readily and gratefully borrowed by younger composers.

One of the reasons why melody should be so prominent in Birtwistle's
music was suggested in Chapter 2. Melody, the 'traditional vehicle of bourgeois subjectivity' in music,[4] has an important part to play in the articulation of Birtwistle's instrumental theatre. It is suited to the musical
representation of dramatic characters both through its proximity to
speech and through its symbolisation of the maintaining of a coherent
identity or character through time.

There is another way of explaining Birtwistle's proclivity for melody,
however, and that is as an analogy to line in visual art. Birtwistle's fondness
for visual art is well documented, and he has claimed that he frequently

turns to painting for 'inspiration' or 'a way forward'.[5] Conceptualising melody as a drawn or painted line implies a rather different understanding of the effect it has on a listener. Under this conception, the function of melody is to inscribe its own, notated shape in the mind of a listener, rather than to act as a sign for something beyond itself (such as a dramatic character). It was noted in Chapter 5 that Birtwistle frequently conceives of his musical forms in three-dimensional terms, relating successive sections of a work to different facets of a material object. He has also claimed that *textural* ideas frequently form the point of departure for pieces, and speaks of being able to 'see the textures' before he starts work. [6] The conception of melody as line is consistent with this urge to invent music that possesses a tangible physicality, that can almost be seen and handled by a listener.

Birtwistle has singled out Paul Klee as having a particular significance for his thinking about melody. His statement, for instance, that his melodic ideas 'come from things like Paul Klee – that sort of way of thinking about melody, not in a nineteenth-century way',[7] if rather elliptical, seems to be struggling to articulate the 'contour versus sign' opposition just outlined. Where nineteenth-century melody is stereotypically 'expressive' of something else, Klee's lines are (for Birtwistle) just that: abstract shapes. Klee's influence on Birtwistle's melodic writing is just part of a wider influence that the Swiss artist has had on Birtwistle's music. According to Michael Hall, Birtwistle is attracted by Klee's 'combination of rigour and fantasy', and his ideas about formal juxtaposition and balance.[8] This influence is openly acknowledged in the titles of two works: *An Imaginary Landscape*, which Birtwistle borrowed from Klee rather than John Cage, and *Carmen Arcadiae Mechanicae Perpetuum*, which Birtwistle describes as 'a title [Klee] could have invented'.[9] *Carmen* is in fact intended as a homage to Klee. That Klee's work should be attractive to a composer is hardly surprising, for Klee was himself a musician and his theoretical writings are full of comparisons between painting and music. For instance, Klee frequently uses musical terms such as 'melody', 'polyphony' and 'rhythm' to describe different sorts of line and form. More dramatically, he argues that visual art possesses a temporal dimension. The unfolding perception of a painting can be guided and structured by the artist, just as the composer leads a listener through a piece of music: 'There are paths laid out in an art work for the eye to follow as it scans the ground rather like a grazing animal . . . The image is created from movement, is itself fixed movement and is recorded in movement (eye muscle).'[10] Klee's titles, too, are often musical in orientation; some – such as *Pastoral (Rhythms)* and *A Garden for Orpheus*[11] – might even have been thought up by Birtwistle himself.

Both Birtwistle and Klee thus seem drawn to the qualities of the other's medium. Just as Birtwistle likens his melodies to lines in a painting, so Klee, in his writings, compares his lines to melodies. Klee's analogies for line are not limited to melody, however, and his alternative metaphors reveal further points of comparison with Birtwistle. In particular, Klee attributes to some of his lines a form of *agency*. In a famous passage from his Notebooks, Klee compares three basic types of line: two of these (the 'medial' and the 'passive' lines) create closed shapes or planes; but the third (the 'active' line) does not loop back on itself in this way. Rather, it 'develops freely. It goes out for a walk, so to speak, aimlessly for the sake of the walk.'[12] This imagery in itself seems to encapsulate the qualities of many of Birtwistle's melodies, with their apparently spontaneous generation – unencumbered by loyalties to musical context or gravitational pitch, and moving 'without goal'.[13] Underpinning this similarity is a shared conception of line and melody in terms of the actions of an individual. A passage in Klee's Notebooks that assesses four possible ways of combining two contrasting lines gives a further example of this. It consistently refers to both lines as 'characters'. Two of the possible combinations are analogous to 'solo voice and accompaniment'; a third 'lets the two types of articulation fight for equality; in music you would call this thematic treatment'; while in the fourth, 'both types of articulation [are treated] equally, so that they do not conflict but complement each other in a friendly way, each in turn letting the other gain the upper hand'.[14] In this way, Klee's lines are able to connote the interaction of dramatic characters in much the same way as Birtwistle's textures do.

Given the similarities between Klee's and Birtwistle's ideas, it is easy to overlook the differences. These come about principally as an unavoidable consequence of the different medium in which each is working. In painting, line is the basic medium, which may then be used to symbolise dramatic action. In music, sound is the basic medium. A listener can choose to convert a melody into a visualised line (just as they can choose to convert it into a representation of dramatic action), but such a conceptualisation is neither essential nor inevitable, for all that our notational system may suggest to the contrary. Melody frequently communicates while leaving little impression of its notated contour or shape. So where in Klee line and agency exist in a direct relationship, no such relationship can be assumed in music. Birtwistle's explicit interest in *both* ways of comprehending melody – as symbol of a dramatic agent, and as an unfolding shape – leads to something of a tension. The two options for conceptualisation audibly vie for supremacy. One option may be most plausible at one moment, another at the next, depending on the form that the melody takes.

Monody for Corpus Christi illustrates these contrary tendencies. It is a three-movement work for soprano, flute, violin and horn: the outer movements set, respectively, a medieval English carol and a sixteenth-century devotional poem, while the central movement is a purely instrumental 'Fanfare'. Monody is the term conventionally applied to music consisting of a single line, and at first it is not clear how the rather elaborate four-part counterpoint of most of Birtwistle's work relates to its title. However, Birtwistle's note to the piece explains that, in the first movement at least, one line does have primacy – namely, the vocal part, 'to which all other parts are embellishments and from which they may be said to stem'.[15] While rhythm and articulation suggest that the four voices are independent from each other, closer scrutiny reveals that each is merely an elaboration of a more basic, common melodic contour. Example 6.1 illustrates this process of melodic embellishment. *Monody for Corpus Christi* thus establishes a precedent for the heterophonic treatment of melody that has been followed in much of Birtwistle's subsequent music, down to the present day. In more recent works the primary line is less hidden and Birtwistle's ornamentation comes closer to a genuine heterophony – which is to say, 'the simultaneous variation of a single melody'.[16] In Example 6.2, which comes from the earliest of Birtwistle's settings of Celan, the differences between individual instruments are not sufficient to obscure the underlying monody that they are together articulating. A direct parallel to this sort of heterophonic melody can be found in Klee's Notebooks, at the point where Klee envisages the possibility of 'two secondary lines, moving round an imaginary main line'.[17] The diagram that Klee draws to illustrate this configuration serves to emphasise how the sorts of musical situation presented in Examples 6.1 and 6.2 suggest an essentially *visual* image, individual parts being assessed in terms of their relative spatial proximity to the 'imaginary main line', rather than interpreted as autonomous agents.

The relative obscurity of the underlying melodic line in the first movement of *Monody for Corpus Christi* may be explained by the fact that the music is simultaneously responding to a number of other demands. Not the least of these are its allusions to some evocative songs for voice and violin by Holst, which Michael Hall claims were the direct inspiration for Birtwistle's work.[18] The Holst songs make much use of the violin's open strings; these same four pitches are, fascinatingly, made prominent in all four parts throughout Birtwistle's setting. More pertinent to the present discussion is the way in which the piece also responds to a second connotation of 'monody' – one that concerns the activity of an individual, as much as a particular textural quality. Specifically, the term monody is associated

Ex. 6.1. *Monody for Corpus Christi*: bb. 48–56, showing hidden monody

Ex. 6.2. Nine Settings of Celan, 'White and Light': heterophony in clarinets and voice, bb. 6–13

with a repertoire of solo song from early seventeenth-century Italy, a repertoire that developed largely as a vehicle for vocal virtuosity. The extreme agility and stamina that Birtwistle requires of his soprano underlines his piece's connection to this tradition. It would, therefore, be inappropriate to treat Birtwistle's 'monody' simply as an exercise in lines and contours, despite the similarities with Klee's drawings: it is just as much about the activity of singing and the dramatic persona of the singer. This work's melody strives both to trace an abstract geometric configuration *and* to represent the mental states and actions of an individual.

In later works, one or other of these competing tendencies sometimes comes to the fore. For instance, Birtwistle's melodic lines occasionally follow such a clear registral course that the visual impulse is unambiguously foregrounded. This is the case in another essentially monodic work, *Linoi* for basset clarinet and piano. Here compass and contour are so carefully and methodically treated that the listener is compelled to visualise the clarinet's melody. The clarinet unfolds five phrases. The first three gradually ascend through one, two and three octaves respectively, while the fifth descends the entire four-octave range of the instrument. Between each phrase, the piano provides a brief interpolation in the form of a few pianissimo pitches, on each occasion lower in register. The result is a heightened focus on the 'spatial' deployment of the musical material. It is left to the title to suggest how the music might be interpreted dramatically, as opposed to geometrically. Linus was a character in Greek mythology about whom there exists a number of different stories, each involving his violent murder. Once this information has been established, a purely abstract, 'spatial' hearing becomes more difficult. The clarinet's extremely savage fourth phrase, and the subsequent descent to the clarinet's lowest note, seem to ring with the myths' terrible common outcomes.

In sharp contrast to the patient expansiveness of *Linoi*, the melodies in *Duets for Storab* (a set of six short pieces for two flutes) are circular and restricted – suggesting, in the second piece especially, not so much an extending line as an obsessive scribble. Where the earlier work highlighted the shape of its melody, *Duets for Storab* provides little encouragement for such a visualist conceptualisation. Instead, the work's instrumentation – two identical melody instruments – seems to have prompted a particularly distinctive exploration of melody's potential to symbolise agency. Birtwistle revels in the ambiguities that arise when lines are not given in their entirety to one or other of the flutes. The work abounds in lines shared between both instruments, a device that is visually reinforced in the score by beams connecting the alternating notes of the two parts. And, rather than rest content with the generation of one line by two instruments, Birtwistle plays up the tension that arises when two musical protagonists are given material connotative of only one. The second section of the first piece, for instance, comprises a circular, 'scribbled' melody filling the chromatic space D – G, played in even quavers and shared between the two flutes. But Birtwistle transposes one of the flutes down an octave, and sustains every note of each part, so that the illusion of a single line can never be fully entered into (Example 6.3). The 'single' melody sounds decidedly frayed at the edges. (Such registral displacement is common in Birtwistle's music, representing a basic means of disguising the origins of melodic material. Michael Hall has demonstrated how the opening of the cantus line in *Secret Theatre*, for instance, is arrived at through registral alteration of a wedge-shaped melody.[19] The tiny *Hector's Dawn*, a piano piece written for the first birthday of Birtwistle's godson, is essentially an essay in octave displacement, its 'twining double melody'[20] expressively distorted by transpositions of one and two octaves.) A different strategy of melodic deconstruction is taken in the fifth of the *Duets for Storab*. Here

Ex. 6.3. *Duets for Storab*, 'Urlar': bb. 13–17

Birtwistle again strings a single line between the two instruments, but then proceeds to undo the aural illusion by gradually increasing the incidence of pitches to the point where both flutes play notes at the same time. The chattering doubled line that eventually results then becomes the backdrop for a repetition of the same process. At moments such as these, the convention that equates line with a single instrumental role is ruthlessly unpicked.

In Birtwistle's music, the potential of melody to symbolise some form of human agency is enhanced by the fact that his melodies are frequently contrasted against rather brusque ostinato patterns. The mechanical cast of these ostinati almost inevitably means that melody will take on a humane quality by comparison – whether Birtwistle intended it or not. In the case of *An Interrupted Endless Melody* for oboe and piano, which was written in memory of the oboist Janet Craxton, the melody (in the oboe) is offset from its mechanical surroundings (provided by the piano) to a particularly extreme extent. Exactly as the title suggests, the melody of this piece has no logical end: the oboist is instructed to begin at any one of three points on the melody and is free to observe or ignore a number of *al segno* repeat marks, meaning that the melody could theoretically continue for ever. The pianist, meanwhile, chooses one of three alternative piano parts, each of which proceeds unidirectionally from beginning to end, but remains temporally wholly independent of the oboe. The impression that this arrangement gives, of an individual discoursing against a distinct and largely anonymous backdrop, is strengthened by the slightly oratorical character of the oboe's line. Regular pauses parse the melody into sentences and paragraphs, and the line itself appears intent on expressivity rather than the articulation of any particular registral contour. Yet even here, where in so many respects Birtwistle's melody appears to be performing the largely conventional function of symbolising the states and actions of an individual, there remains an element of kinship with Klee's 'aimless', 'freely developing' line. The absence of a determinate beginning or end means that the melody never sounds particularly assured of its purpose – an impression of aimlessness strengthened by the likelihood (because of the numerous options for repetition) that it will come across the same material more than once. Birtwistle's melodic lines rarely achieve the rhetorical certainty of nineteenth-century melody: the pleasure in doodling, in inscribing shapes, is never far away, touching the melodic invention with a reticence and a hesitancy that is one of its most endearing features.

Polyphony

Medusa (31) • Five Chorale Preludes (47) • *Bach Measures* (102) • *Chorales for Orchestra* (7) • *Chorale from a Toy Shop* (19) • *Hoquetus David* (30) • *Ut heremita solus* (29) • *Machaut à ma manière* (76) • *Mercure – poses plastiques* (56) • *Hoquetus Petrus* (94) • *The World is Discovered* (5) • *Nomos* (22) • *Secret Theatre* (65)

All the pieces discussed in the previous section focus upon melody, yet none of them allows it to exist completely unadorned. The 'monody' of *Monody for Corpus Christi* is dressed in elaborate heterophonic clothing; the 'line' and 'melody' of, respectively, *Linoi* and *An Interrupted Endless Melody* are accompanied by non-melodic piano parts; and the two flutes in *Duets for Storab* tantalise us with single melody, only to contaminate it by failing ever to convincingly carry off the illusion that they comprise a singular persona. Nor is there genuine monody anywhere in Birtwistle's output: his other 'soloistic' pieces variously feature piano, claves or tape in addition to the melody instrument. In the larger-scale works, melody may be a prominent ingredient but only as part of a more complex, polyphonic texture.

It was noted earlier how Birtwistle's interest in melody distinguished his music from that of much of the continental avant-garde. All the same, his treatment of melody shows a wary suspicion of the sort of textural priority it unquestioningly receives in most tonal music. In Birtwistle's music, melody is not accorded an importance over and above other types of musical configuration; instead it competes with them for prominence. In this respect, Birtwistle's textural strategies owe more to archaic compositional practices than to anything from the more recent musical past. Rather than opt for the complete dissolution of melody, Birtwistle looks back to polyphonic styles that either predate or challenge the privileging of treble-register melody in tonal music.

Some indication of which earlier music has been important to Birtwistle in this respect is given by the arrangements and reworkings he has made, at various times in his career, of music by other composers. J. S. Bach features prominently on this list. Birtwistle has made two sets of instrumental arrangements of Bach's settings of chorale melodies (Five Chorale Preludes and *Bach Measures*), while in *Medusa* chorale settings by Bach are treated to a rather less reverent dissection. In this last piece, the inclusion of Bach's music appears to serve primarily parodic purposes, rather than acting as an exemplar for questions of technique. The impression of ironic parody is emboldened by the stridently distorted sound of amplified saxophone and cello. Nevertheless, Birtwistle's treatment of the Bach material is as much technical analysis as it is an exercise in nose-thumbing – especially in the second version of the piece, which involves, firstly, all manner of manipulations of one of Bach's four-part chorale harmonisations,[21] including the separation of its pitch and rhythmic structure,[22] extreme acceleration, and juxtaposition against thoroughly Birtwistlian xylophone ostinati and banshee-like cantus lines; and, secondly, a truly bizarre rewriting, for piano, of the chorale prelude on 'Meine Seele erhebt den Herren' (from the so-called 'Schübler' chorales). The latter retains the rhythmic skeleton of Bach's cleverly imitative structure, but alters the notes: the result sounds for all the world like Hindemith. All this, plus Birtwistle's own *Eight Lessons for Keyboard*, which the pianist is instructed to insert at a specified stage in the second version of the work, is contained within *Medusa*'s central section. It is the outer sections of the work's ternary form, however, that contain its most eloquent music, in the form of hypnotic, partly aleatoric assemblages of small repeated motives; in the second version these are set against an electronic 'aura'. The end of the piece, in which the multiple motives from the opening are once more set in motion and then allowed gradually to run out of steam, foreshadows (in technique if not sound) the music that Birtwistle was to write thirty years later to conclude *The Second Mrs Kong*. Birtwistle clearly felt that these passages were insufficient to redeem the rather ramshackle nature of the rest of his conception, however, and, following a single revival in the mid-1970s, the score was withdrawn.

Birtwistle's other dealings with Bach take the form of more straightforward arrangements, following in the line of earlier musical homages by prominent twentieth-century composers. Webern's famous orchestral transformation of the six-part 'Ricercar' from *The Musical Offering* is a well-known example. Webern, however, chose a fugal work, rich in motivic content; as he himself stated, 'My instrumentation is intended ... to reveal the [work's] motivic coherence'.[23] Birtwistle, in contrast, repeatedly turns to Bach's chorale settings, reflecting an interest not so much in Bach's motivic and imitative technique as in his treatment of melody. The more apt comparison is with Stravinsky, rather than Webern. Stravinsky's respects to his illustrious predecessor were most visibly paid in the

Variations on the Chorale 'Vom Himmel Hoch', an elaborated arrangement for chorus and orchestra of a set of chorale variations that Bach wrote for organ. Where Webern's arrangement of the 'Ricercar' largely dissipates Bach's melodic structure, distributing single parts among many instruments in a 'prismatic splintering' of Bach's six-voice texture,[24] Stravinsky and Birtwistle leave Bach's lines largely intact. Rather than obliterate melody, they are concerned to examine Bach's negotiations with it.

In fact, Birtwistle's Five Chorale Preludes are nothing more than literal transcriptions. The set consists of three four-part chorale preludes from the *Orgel-Büchlein*, arranged for soprano (who sings the original chorale text to Bach's embellished rendering of the chorale melody), clarinet in A, basset horn and bass clarinet; between these are interspersed two three-part chorale preludes, drawn from other sources and arranged for clarinets alone.[25] The first and last preludes are, additionally, each preceded by a simpler, four-part harmonisation of their respective chorale melodies. *Bach Measures* also draws from the *Orgel-Büchlein*,[26] but its musical treatment is rather more interventionist. This is in part due to the use of a much larger (thirteen-strong) ensemble, which provides the opportunity for plenty of doubling at the octave or (in imitation of the organ's *Quintatön* stop) the fifth. The larger ensemble also allows Bach's contrapuntal lines to be passed between instruments. Occasionally this fragmentation is disruptive, in the manner of the Webern 'Ricercar'; but more generally the impression is of a gradual, smooth transition in colour rather than a thorough disassembling. The chorale melodies themselves are kept notably intact. Birtwistle's presence is felt most strongly in the first and last pieces, where the original structure of the preludes – retained untouched in the other six – is altered. In the case of the first piece (BWV 599), this alteration takes the form of a lengthy introduction, which works its way through the whole chorale melody, alternating from phrase to phrase between the elaborate decoration of the *Orgel-Büchlein* and a far more austere four-part harmonisation. The final prelude of the set is Bach's famous setting of 'Durch Adam's Fall', and here Birtwistle seizes on the falling sevenths of Bach's pedal line to create a brief, thoroughly Birtwistlian refrain. This is used to separate three different arrangements of the whole prelude. In the first and second of these arrangements, the bass line is highlighted in a further respect: the sevenths are inverted into seconds and the whole line is raised by two or more octaves, to form a new treble counterpoint to Bach's own elaborations.

It may seem surprising that Birtwistle should prefer the baroque floridities of the chorale prelude to Bach's more austere, four-part harmonisations. As we shall see, Birtwistle's own 'chorales' are very far from florid, placing a premium instead on rhythmic unison and simplicity of texture. The explanation lies in the way in which the chorale preludes make ambiguous the roles of melody and accompaniment. In the four-part harmonisations, for all the contrapuntal elegance of Bach's subsidiary voices, there is little doubt as to the privileged status of the upper voice. This is determined as much as anything simply by the fact that it *is* the upper voice: even when the other parts are comparably eventful, registral privileging tends to determine its heightened textural status. The result is a singularity and predictability of textural focus that Birtwistle finds uncongenial. The chorale preludes, on the other hand, are more active in their undermining of the distinction between principal and subsidiary melody. They do this in a number of ways: by heightening the contrapuntal independence and prominence of the 'free' voices; by embellishing the chorale melody so that its original identity is disguised; or, most extremely, by treating it canonically, as in BWV 619 and 620 (which appear in *Bach Measures* and Five Chorale Preludes respectively). Through means such as these, the usual textural priorities become blurred.

In 1969 Michael Nyman observed that 'Harrison Birtwistle is partial to chorales',[27] a comment that reflects the fact that their appearance in his output is far from confined to his arrangements of Bach. Nowhere is Birtwistle's 'partiality' more apparent than in his first orchestral work, *Chorales for Orchestra*. The relationship between the title and the music is, however, characteristically oblique. Only in the last of the work's four sections does a chorale unambiguously appear, helpfully labelled as such in the score. It exhibits the principal characteristics by which all Birtwistle's subsequent chorales may be identified: a number of voices, moving in similar rhythm, at a steady speed. In this particular case, Birtwistle doubles both outer parts at the octave, making the material stand out even more keenly from the textural complexities that have preceded it. The knotty sonorities of this first chorale are followed by further, more refined chordal passages – firstly using three-part parallel fifths and then simple octave doublings. These passages are not explicitly labelled, but they presumably account for the plural of the work's title. They finally provide the textural clarity towards which the scraps of unison melody in the work's earlier, predominantly contrapuntal sections seem to have been striving.

For Birtwistle, a chorale is a type of polyphonic doubling in which no single line obviously holds pre-eminence. This causes difficulties for anyone who seeks to establish a firm connection between the rather tardy, labelled 'Chorale' in *Chorales* and the work's earlier stages. For it is not immediately evident *which* of the chorale's constituent parts is most likely to have been anticipated. Birtwistle's intention appears to be to

Ex. 6.4. *Punch and Judy*: harmonic summary of Passion Chorale

achieve complete parity between the different voices, and so it cannot be assumed that thematic connections will be located in the chorale's upper voice. In this respect Birtwistle's chorale technique again invites a comparison with Stravinsky. Stravinsky's chorales are as indebted to Russian Orthodox chant as to Bach, something that may be felt even in the mock-Lutheran 'Great Chorale' in *Histoire du soldat*. This movement begins with an allusion to the Lutheran melody 'Ein' feste Burg', no less;[28] but thereafter the treble voice loses its nerve – sometimes rotating listlessly between two pitches (at [2] and [4] in the Chester score), and at one point grinding to a halt altogether (just before [4]). The relative stasis of the uppermost part in Orthodox choral chant receives rather more eloquent testimony in Stravinsky's 'Russian' chorales, examples of which can be found in the last of the Three Pieces for String Quartet and at the end of the *Symphonies of Wind Instruments*. The rather glacial austerity of these movements makes them solemn rather than celebratory affairs, and Birtwistle maintains this expressive character in his own chorales. Chorales play an important role in *An Imaginary Landscape*, which is dedicated to the memory of the composer's mother, and in *The Mask of Orpheus* and *Gawain*, where they appear to be associated with themes of destiny or statements of intent.

Two of Birtwistle's chorales make particularly explicit reference to Stravinsky. The 'Passion Chorale' that appears in three slightly altered versions in *Punch and Judy* clearly points in name and function to Bach rather than Stravinsky. Musically, however, there is no more Stravinskian moment in the whole of Birtwistle's output. Birtwistle's chorale contains a host of diatonic collections and a number of characteristically Stravinskian false relations (see Example 6.4). An orienting presence is also exerted by the pitch-class D, which is sounded in twenty-five of the chorale's twenty-nine four-part chords. This note – so often a significant

Ex. 6.5. *Chorale from a Toy Shop* (first version)

pitch in Birtwistle – goes some way to mitigating the focal pull of the upper line, which in this one instance *is* considerably more 'melodic' than any of the other parts.

That Birtwistle associated chorales with Stravinsky at this period was confirmed in the tiny *Chorale from a Toy Shop*. This miniature was written immediately after *Punch and Judy* to mark Stravinsky's eighty-fifth birthday, in response to a commission from the music journal *Tempo* (Example 6.5).[29] Once again it has striking tonal resonances. The title possibly refers to the piece's curious intermingling of tonally referential harmonies and far more harshly chromatic collections (the latter seeming to suggest that some of the tonal 'cogs' are not functioning properly), as well as the brusque, almost automated manner in which the piece's material is despatched. Birtwistle later revised the work for publication by Universal Edition, proceeding not once but twice through the original sequence of chords, and altering rhythms and octave transpositions: the new voicing brings the Stravinskian quality of the harmonies into particularly high relief.

A more startling reincarnation of the *Chorale from a Toy Shop* is that found in the middle of *The Triumph of Time* (shortly after [15]). Birtwistle embarked on the latter piece only a few weeks after Stravinsky's death, and it seems reasonable to assume that he was prompted to incorporate the earlier tribute as a memorial homage – giving the larger work's title an extra (if not often recognised) resonance in the process. The pitches of the original version are mostly retained in individual wind parts, but they are thoroughly submerged by wind and brass doublings of massive density. Birtwistle's outward expansion of his chorale serves to confirm that the upper line of the original has no particular melodic pre-eminence: the identity of the chorale is not radically affected, Birtwistle seems to be saying, by the addition of further parts above it. Indeed, Birtwistle's readiness to proliferate his material in this way might lead one to question whether the five voices of the *original* piece have a genuine independence, or whether they, too, are the product of an earlier process of melodic embellishment. No such relationship is readily apparent – not even a canonic one, despite the fact that the great majority of the other pieces written for the *Tempo* tribute are canons of one sort or another. Michael Hall and Brian Robison have, however, documented several instances in Birtwistle's music where organum-like proliferation of a single line gives rise to a complex polyphonic texture in which little trace of the original doublings remains.[30] This is achieved by a largely randomised process of filtering and crossing between doubled lines in order to create real parts. In these structures, importantly, 'the composer's generating melodic structure isn't necessarily privileged over the derived voices. The pitches of the original monody are just as susceptible to filtering as any of the other pitches, and even if all monody pitches are preserved, they're not necessarily prominent in the texture.'[31] Birtwistle's chorales, if they are generated in such a way, occupy an ambiguous position, for they are the expression neither clearly of a single line nor of many independent ones. In this respect they are closer to organum, in which an added part doubles an existing chant at a higher register, but also occasionally strays from its contour and makes decorative additions, so that it is neither clearly dependent nor independent.

Of course, the chorale is only one means to the complication of traditional textural hierarchies in Birtwistle's music. In many pieces – including those discussed in the first section of this chapter – line is counterpointed against non-line and thus retains its distinctive qualities, rather than having them neutralised in a multiple, organum-like doubling. As was seen in the case of *An Interrupted Endless Melody*, Birtwistle's polyphonic treatment of melody may actively reinforce the very polarity between melody and its 'other' that is so effectively suspended in his chorales. What remains similar, however, is Birtwistle's refusal automatically to accord the melody pre-eminence. For Birtwistle, a play with relative prominence is essential to the creation of real complexity:

> Once you have a foreground, then you have a middle ground and a background – you have a depth, you have something you can go into. That way you can have complexity. I don't think you can have complexity in a situation where it's all complex, or all thick, because then it's all of the same order, and it's not complex then.[32]

Birtwistle has made a parallel with early renaissance paintings, such as Piero della Francesca's *The Flagellation* and Brueghel the Elder's *The*

Martyrdom of St Catherine. In each of these the putative subject is represented off-centre, in the background; as Birtwistle says, 'the essence of the painting lies beyond its subject'.[33] Birtwistle is not the first to make a connection between textural prioritising in music and the figure-ground relationship in art. Philip Tagg, for instance, has suggested that the 'advent of the figure/ground dualism in European visual art, and . . . that of the melody/accompaniment dualism in European music' are related, and that both developments 'prefigure and/or accompany the rise of the bourgeois notion of the individual'.[34] Tagg then assesses the implications of the apparent suspension, in contemporary dance music, of the figure-ground relationship. Birtwistle's approach is different. He *maintains* the distinction between figure and ground, but refuses automatic priority of the one over the other. It has already been seen that, even in as stark an arrangement as is presented by *An Interrupted Endless Melody*, the coherence and self-certainty of the music's 'figure' cannot be taken for granted.

Once again, Birtwistle's arrangements of the music of other composers suggest how, in pursuing this idea, certain earlier musical techniques have formed useful models. Medieval music, and particularly the music of the fourteenth-century composer Guillaume de Machaut, has been revisited on a number of occasions. Birtwistle's interest in medieval music is well known, Michael Hall going so far as to claim that 'his music is a combination of medieval techniques . . . and twentieth-century interests'.[35] Medieval music frequently incorporates melody, yet uses various means that prevent it from becoming an automatic textural focus. Machaut's mass and motets, for instance, like much sacred music of the medieval period, are built around a structural melody in the tenor – either a section of plain-chant, or an invented melody. They have, in other words, a melodic basis. At the same time, a number of aspects of Machaut's idiom serve to challenge melodic coherence and prominence. Most obvious amongst these is the placing of the structural melody in a registrally submerged position, supporting one or more upper parts. This feature can be traced back to organum; there, though, the higher, added part would have followed the original plain-chant fairly closely and thus obscured it relatively little. As sacred polyphony developed, the added parts became more elaborate and thus increasingly distant from the original chant. For a modern listener to Machaut's sacred polyphony, it is correspondingly difficult to be certain about where the music's melodic focus is located.

The melodic integrity of Machaut's tenor parts is further compromised by the technique of isorhythm, which arbitrarily segments the original melody into short, rhythmically identical phrases. Again, to the modern ear, this repetitive rhythmic structure is more connotative of a supportive than a leading function. Even the upper voices in Machaut's polyphony are prevented from taking on an unproblematically focal role. This is in large part because of the technique of hocket. Hocket – derived from the Latin or French for 'hiccup' – involves the distribution of successive notes of a melody between different voices. Machaut's tendency to alternate between hocketing textures and more sustained counterpoint means that two voices consistently present neither two lines nor one – and as a result their melodic profile is blurred.

These techniques are exemplified by Machaut's *Hoquetus David*, which Birtwistle has arranged several times. The piece has been described as 'a textless isorhythmic motet for three voices'.[36] Its tenor part is derived from the plain-chant melisma on the word 'David' that completes the verse of the Marian chant 'Alleluia Nativitas'. Machaut's isorhythmic structuring thoroughly dismantles the chant's melodic integrity, dividing it into rhythmic phrases of twelve notes. In itself this is an arbitrary segmentation; but additionally, because the melody only has thirty-two notes, its subsequent repetition does not even coincide with the start of a rhythmic pattern. As a result, an entirely new sequence of twelve-note phrases is generated. Meanwhile, the two upper parts oscillate between two-part counterpoint and single-line hocket. Birtwistle's first published setting of the *Hoquetus David*, written in 1969 for the Pierrot Players,[37] retains these features exactly, and limits its alterations largely to matters of register and doubling. Even so, Birtwistle manages to emphasise the ways in which Machaut's music accommodates melody only to problematise it. The registral submersion of the tenor part, for instance, is brought into dramatic relief. In the original, the difference in register between the tenor line and the other two parts is relatively small. Birtwistle's arrangement, on the other hand, begins with the upper parts an octave higher than in the original; and as the piece progresses this extra registral separation gradually widens to two octaves (b. 34), and then three (b. 88). Machaut's isorhythmic fragmentation of the borrowed chant receives no special attention in Birtwistle's arrangement, but Birtwistle is not averse to superimposing a further layer of patterned structuring of his own. In the work's opening section, for instance, Birtwistle's setting of the upper, 'triplum' part alternates between different instrumentations, carving Machaut's line into short, arbitrary phrases just as Machaut carved up the borrowed plain-chant. Later, the element of inherent fragmentariness in Machaut's upper voices is emphasised when the tenor suddenly rises an octave and, simultaneously, the second part plummets two octaves (b. 71). This forces duplum and triplum apart, with the tenor stranded in between, making the stammering discontinuity of the two hocketing voices vividly apparent.

Birtwistle's concern to underline the ways in which medieval technique brought melodic integrity into question is evident again in his arrangement (also written in 1969 for the Pierrot Players) of the four-part motet 'Ut heremita solus' by the fifteenth-century composer Johannes Ockeghem.[38] Ockeghem's piece 'uses a complex puzzle canon in the formation and manipulation of [its] tenor';[39] but despite this the tenor line itself is rhythmically plain and lacks the clear, repetitive segmentation of Machaut's *Hoquetus*. Revealingly, Birtwistle seems to have felt an urge to compensate for this, for throughout his otherwise fairly literal arrangement the tenor line is treated as a succession of individual notes rather than a coherent melody. Each note in the tenor is articulated separately, as if played on a set of bells: cohesion between notes is actively avoided.

Birtwistle returned to Machaut's *Hoquetus* in 1987, when he used it as the linchpin for a series of concerts at the South Bank Centre in London, for which the programmes were devised by himself and Bayan Northcott. Ten composers were invited to make their own arrangements as preludes to each concert, and Birtwistle wrote a new, orchestral version of his own, giving it the fanciful title *Les Hoquets du Gardien de la Lune*. Birtwistle described this new version as 'really an arrangement of my second [i.e. 1969] arrangement, a sort of second stage Chinese whisper'.[40] As this description suggests, *Les Hoquets* is more a reworking than a transcription. All the pitches of Machaut's *Hoquetus* are retained; Machaut's rhythmic structure, on the other hand, is refracted through a Birtwistlian prism, the rhythmic hesitancies and asymmetries of the original becoming greatly exaggerated. And in place of the modest fifth and octave doublings of the earlier version Birtwistle constructs an enriched polyphonic elaboration of Machaut's pitch structure, in which lines frequently take independent flight from those they are putatively doubling.

Les Hoquets was not published separately, but became instead the second half of *Machaut à ma manière* (literally, 'Machaut in my own way'), in which the new version of *Hoquetus David* is preceded by an arrangement of another work by Machaut, the three-voice motet 'Fons tocius/O livoris feritas/Fera pessima', and followed by a reworking of an 'Amen' from Machaut's *Messe de Nostre Dame*. The motet arrangement is characterised by much the same Birtwistlian modifications. At the very outset, for instance, Birtwistle makes clear his intention not to be confined by Machaut's registral arrangements: the short monophonic introduction that begins Machaut's motet is split by Birtwistle into three phrases, each of which is delivered at a different register (by bassoon, oboe and cor anglais respectively). Elsewhere the upper voices venture into bass regions, or, conversely, the tenor line is found soaring above the other voices in the soprano register (as at [15]). More dramatically still, the tenor occasionally departs from its original pitch level by an interval *other* than an octave or its multiples – in the case of the five bars after [7], for instance, down a major seventh. Transpositions of this sort boldly assert the relative independence of each line in Machaut's polyphony, which even at their original pitch level give rise to high levels of vertical dissonance. When lines are more concerned in pursuing their own ends than in conforming to their surroundings (Birtwistle seems to be saying), it really makes little difference how they are transposed.

Birtwistle's obsessive manoeuvring of material between instruments and through registral space is a logical consequence of Machaut's technique in a further, stronger sense. Machaut's motet, like much other medieval vocal music, is multi-texted. Each voice has its own text, and although each text shares some thematic link with the others, in all other respects they are completely different. This situation works against Machaut's polyphonic texture being perceived as a homogeneous whole. Instead, a listener is likely to be drawn to just one of the three parts at any one time, attempting to comprehend its text until distracted by one of the other, conflicting texts. The motet's multi-textedness thus ensures a continual fluctuation of focus from one part to another. Birtwistle's procedure, in his arrangement, of bringing different lines into registral relief is merely a natural extension of the same process.

Registral play of this sort is an important feature of other works to be discussed later in this chapter, such as *Nomos* and *Earth Dances*; it is one significant way in which medieval melodic strategies have proved suggestive for Birtwistle's own music. It even makes an appearance in Birtwistle's arrangement of Satie's ballet *Mercure*. Here Birtwistle largely adheres to the piano reduction of Satie's score, his stated intention being to preserve the 'quirkiness' of the music which he felt was ironed out by Satie's own orchestration.[41] Birtwistle's kaleidoscopic succession of chamber textures is indeed more colourful than the rather drab homogeneity of Satie's full orchestral scoring, but sometimes this is achieved by wholesale registral recomposition – as at just after [C] in the 'Danse de Tendresse', where trumpet and glockenspiel 'take possession' of a subsidiary, tenor-register voice in order to extend their own high treble melody.

Other aspects of the medieval techniques discussed above also make a more general appearance in Birtwistle's music. According to Michael Hall, isorhythmic processes lie behind the construction of all Birtwistle's melodies;[42] a claim he demonstrates in relation to *Verses* for clarinet and piano.[43] However, literal isorhythms are rare in Birtwistle's music, and Brian Robison has argued that the role of isorhythm in his music is best understood if 'we generalize from the strict medieval practice . . . to a broader concept which embraces traditional isorhythm as a special case'.[44] This 'broader concept' concerns the generation of a large amount of ever-changing material from the combination of small repeating cells, and studies of Birtwistle's sketches are beginning to reveal the full extent of the importance of such processes to his music.[45] Hocket also plays an important role in Birtwistle's music. It is often central, for instance, to Birtwistle's ticking ostinati, where a composite rhythmic pattern may be created from the contributions of a number of instruments: *Carmen Arcadiae Mechanicae Perpetuum* provides countless examples. More Machaut-like instances have already been identified in *Duets for Storab*, where the hocketing parts consistently form neither one nor two melodic lines. *Hoquetus Petrus*, a brief piece for two flutes (one doubling piccolo) and piccolo trumpet, written for Pierre Boulez's seventieth birthday, is a concentrated exercise in the distribution of single streams of material between a number of instruments. In contrast to Machaut's three-part writing in the motets, Birtwistle's piece has no sustained tenor to moderate the impact of the quick-fire exchanges: instead, a single pedal note (the E a tenth above middle C), fleetingly but frequently referred to by all three instruments, helps anchor their busy interplay.

Birtwistle's arrangements of Machaut and Ockeghem point to his interest in cantus firmus as one means of incorporating melody into a polyphonic context without allowing it an automatic textural pre-eminence. His interest in early music is by no means confined to cantus-firmus compositions, however. In his early work *The World is Discovered*, which is scored for twelve instrumentalists, Birtwistle turned to a rather different polyphonic style from the early Renaissance. The piece is subtitled 'Six Instrumental Movements after Heinrich Isaac (1450–1517)', and takes its title from Isaac's canzona 'Der welte fundt'. According to Michael Hall, it 'amplifies facets' of five of Isaac's canzonas, arrangements of which he had earlier made for the pupils of the schools at which he was teaching at the time.[46] Isaac's canzonas, like the works of Machaut and Ockeghem discussed above, incorporate borrowed melodies into their tenor parts – in this case usually popular tunes, rather than plain-chant.[47] They do not, however, treat the melodies as a cantus firmus. Instead, the melodies are elaborated and altered, delivered at a comparable speed to the other parts, and allowed (through imitation) to permeate the entire four-part texture. Isaac's works thus present a different model for the polyphonic treatment of melody. Melody, instead of being treated as a discrete linear element around which a more complex and largely independent texture is elaborated, becomes a resource for the generation of a carefully mediated vertical and horizontal unity.[48] Birtwistle's piece betrays no sign of the Isaac originals, but it adheres to the spirit of Isaac's approach to texture, with its disintegration of vertical and horizontal autonomy. The web-like heterophony that features prominently in the three tutti 'Choruses' represents just such a disintegration; and the virtuosic rhythmic unisons between the two solo instruments in each of the three 'Verses' similarly suggest the polyphonic coagulation of a single line. Most striking of all is the very end of the work. The music settles on a single complex chord, which is subjected to kaleidoscopic variations of timbre and attack. The result, according to a commentator writing shortly after the first performance, 'is a musical intensification of both polyphony and homophony – which might [also] be said of Isaak's technique – here paradoxically operating at the same time'.[49]

If neither Isaac nor (in this piece) Birtwistle makes literal use of cantus firmus, the underlying influence of the technique may nevertheless be identified in Birtwistle's treatment of Isaac's works. According to Michael Hall, Birtwistle's procedure in writing the piece was to magnify 'inconspicuous details' of the canzonas. He was influenced in this regard by a series of paintings by Picasso, which similarly 'expand or exploit certain obscure details discovered in Velazquez's *Las Meninas*'.[50] The idea of 'magnification' suggests one way of making sense of the idiosyncratic textures of *The World is Discovered*. Birtwistle's unfamiliar configurations can be understood as corresponding to the atomic granularity of Isaac's musical materials when hugely magnified. Under microscopic analysis, Isaac's lines and verticalities are transformed into complex, two dimensional planes. In treating Isaac's materials in this way, cantus firmus may have been as important a model as the paintings of Picasso. Cantus firmus is, in many of its manifestations, essentially a form of *temporal magnification* – that is to say, the expansion of found musical material into unlikely dimensions, the 'creation of co-existent time layers'.[51] For English composers in the late 1950s, the sort of time-stretching of sound being pioneered in electronic music studios in continental Europe had been anticipated by several centuries in the music of medieval and renaissance composers. Birtwistle's incorporation and magnification of facets of Isaac's music essentially merely continues the procedure of much earlier composers, who similarly borrowed and magnified pre-existing musical material to create a cantus firmus.

Even in works by Birtwistle that are essentially 'about' sustained melody, the influence of cantus-firmus technique, with its tendency to melodic relegation and disassemblage, may be felt. *Nomos*, for orchestra without violins, gives prominence to a sustained melody played by four solo wind instruments. The winds are seated apart from the rest of the orchestra, and are amplified – facts that suggest that the piece is dramatically conceived, and that the winds' melody is an expression of their dramatic identity. Given this, it would be unlikely to find the wind melody subjected to the extremes of fragmentation and manipulation accorded the plain-chant in Machaut's *cantus firmi*: the articulation of the work's musical drama depends to no small extent on the melody's coherence. (It is presumably not accidental that the work should take a title that evokes ancient Greece rather than medieval Europe.) As the piece progresses, the solo winds' melody becomes steadily more mobile and adventurous. After a rather hesitant start, it is soon coaxed into greater activity by four winds from the orchestra; thereafter, the orchestra appears threatened by, rather than encouraging of, the solo group, expressing its anxiety at the soloists' increasingly ambitious melodic profile in two massive tuttis. Before the second of these, the orchestra makes its own attempt at a conciliatory melody, beguilingly garlanded with fragmentary decoration from percussion and orchestral soloists. But this fails to prevent the soloists' ultimate pre-eminence, which is announced by the very material that was originally played by the orchestral wind to spur the soloists into action. As Michael Nyman has observed, it is as if the whole process is then 'ready to begin again, a few inches off the ground, perhaps with the orchestra amplified, with an electronic tape taking the place of the amplified quartet, till meta-musical solutions suggest themselves'.[52] This cyclic drama of initiation and eventual succession plays on one of the two meanings of the ancient Greek word 'nomos': namely, the laws of the state (moral, political and social). Such laws are, after all, aimed at ensuring the state's survival down through the generations. However, 'nomos' also refers to melody – as Anton Webern delightedly noted in one of his letters to Hildegard Jone and Josef Humplik.[53] Specifically, 'the "nomos" of the title is a reference to the "nomoi", or traditional melodic formulae on which the music of the Ancient Greek aulos (reed-pipe) was based'.[54] Birtwistle's amplified wind thus effectively meet both connotations of the work's title.

In spite of the rather assertive nature of the winds' melody in this piece, its prominence is neither continuous nor wholly assured. Its wide registral range, especially in the later stages of the work, means that it tends to dip in and out of view; the winds' amplification, meanwhile, is intended to allow the melody 'to complement the orchestral sound rather than to appear as the main feature'.[55] As in cantus-firmus composition, melody provides the work's underpinning, but it is not allowed to dominate throughout. After the first performance Roger Smalley expressed doubts about the intermittent audibility of the solo group,[56] and the more recent recording has confirmed that the density of the orchestral writing frequently renders the soloists' contribution purely theoretical. Arguably though, the threatening quality of the line is enhanced rather than diminished by its partly hidden nature.

The opposition, in *Nomos*, of a wind-based, semi-independent melodic element to a larger and *not* predominantly melodic ensemble clearly foreshadows *Secret Theatre*. And if relative prominence became an issue in *Nomos* partly because of shortcomings of orchestral balance, in *Secret Theatre* it was a central compositional issue from the very start. Birtwistle's 'basic idea' for the piece – namely, 'music which is divided into two of its most basic elements: vertical/horizontal'[57] – necessitated some consideration as to how to avoid a rigid hierarchisation of the horizontal over the vertical. Birtwistle makes this explicit in the notes he made prior to composing the work: 'MELODY/ACCOMPANIMENT ... bad analogy, suggesting one more important than the other . . . FOREGROUND must not always be assigned to CANTUS.'[58] Birtwistle's choice of the term 'cantus' to describe his 'horizontal music' clearly alludes to cantus firmus and its complex textural status – at once the melodic basis of a polyphonic texture, yet also often texturally recessive.

A further analogy for *Secret Theatre*'s play with relative prominence is found, however, not in any specifically musical precedent, but in the writings of Paul Klee. Klee, like Birtwistle, was sensitive to the focal pull exerted by certain sorts of line, and he chose to illustrate this phenomenon in a remarkable comparison with music. This takes the form of a graphical analysis of the opening of Bach's Sonata for Violin and Harpsichord, BWV 1019.[59] Klee's analysis, which charts Bach's textures according to a vertical 'chromatic pitch' axis and a horizontal 'time' axis, anticipates the analytical methods of Jonathan Bernard by some sixty years,[60] and has the additional subtlety of indicating dynamic or metric stress by thickness of line. Having displayed the music in this manner, Klee is able to show how the bass part and the upper line correspond, respectively, to what he terms a 'structural' (or 'dividual') line, and an 'individual' line. The first of these is characterised by repetitive features; the second, conversely, is a line where 'nothing is repeated, every unit is different from every other'.[61] All other things being equal, the individual line tends to dominate over the structural line – in painting as much as in music. The individual, non-repetitive line is, in Klee's words, 'purely melodic, for certain', while the structural, repetitive line has the function of 'pure accompaniment'.[62] Yet Klee, like Birtwistle, is interested in investigating the possibility of a pairing of individual and structural lines that places emphasis not on the former, but on the latter. Klee's diagram illustrating this configuration precisely captures the char-

Fig. 6.1. Paul Klee, *Notebooks: The Thinking Eye*: Diagram [1], p. 300

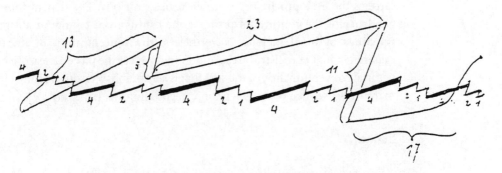

acteristic binary texture of *Secret Theatre* (Figure 6.1). His accompanying description underlines the similarities with Birtwistle's work. In contrast to the Bach Sonata, Klee explains, here

> the structural theme [= *Secret Theatre*'s continuum] has a certain indepen-
> dence. It is aware of this and takes on a dynamic character in the drawing. The
> individual [= cantus] feels exalted by its higher nature, requires no special bol-
> stering of its ego, and runs along flute-like in quantitative silence, despite the
> companionship of the heavy structural instrumentation.[63]

Birtwistle highlights the 'independence' of his 'structural theme' by a number of means. One is referred to in his compositional notes: namely, allowing 'individual *single* voices' to strike up from the continuum. A good example of this can be found about ten minutes into the work (two bars before [35]), where the trumpet suddenly introduces a loud, nervous line, out of synch with the conductor, and which is later continued by the horn. The held notes of the cantus form little more than a backdrop to the heightened activity of the continuum at this point. Alternatively, the cantus may itself allow the continuum to advance texturally, simply by slowing down and thus creating the necessary rhythmic space for the con-tinuum to make its presence felt (as at [9]). It is at moments like these that *Secret Theatre*'s cantus is most 'cantus firmus'-like.

One factor works powerfully against the analogy of *Secret Theatre*'s cantus with cantus firmus. Birtwistle's decision that the cantus should comprise portable instruments means that, registrally, it is unable to leave the treble register. One of the defining characteristics of medieval or ren-aissance cantus firmus is its registral submersion. For all its resistance to the conventional hierarchical relationship of melody and accompaniment, *Secret Theatre*'s melodic component remains firmly entrenched in its most traditional location: at the top of the texture. Indeed the piece has surely found relative popular favour in large part precisely because it so readily satisfies the ear's proclivity for treble-register melody. The defiant independence of the continuum prevents the cantus from taking on all the trappings of tonal melody. Nevertheless, the concentration of linear material in higher registral areas undoubtedly gives the piece a measure of textural conventionality, of the sort that is scrupulously ensured against in many of Birtwistle's other polyphonic negotiations with melody.

Strata

Earth Dances (69) • *Salford Toccata* (77) • *Dinah and Nick's Love Song* (35) • *Slow Frieze* (97)

Secret Theatre's distinctive deployment of two constituent ensembles has tended to deflect attention away from the continuum's own textural complexity. It frequently comprises not one but a number of layers of material, each rhythmically differentiated. Given that melody and rhythmic ostinato are far from wholly confined to cantus and continuum respectively, there are good reasons to understand the relation of cantus to continuum as one of unison to counterpoint, rather than horizontal music to vertical music. The prominence of melody in the piece tends to work against a proper appreciation of the continuum's contrapuntal aspect, however. Instead, it is tempting simply to parse the music texturally into melody and non-melody, regardless of who is playing what.

Earth Dances takes up the principal concern of *Secret Theatre*: namely, the combination of different musics.[64] In *Earth Dances*, however, the different musics are defined by their intervallic properties, rather than in terms of the bold binarism of melody and non-melody. This shift has several important consequences. Firstly, it means that melody loses the prominence it had in *Secret Theatre*. The 'specific interval or set of intervals'[65] that defines a level of activity *can* be expressed melodically, but this is not essential to its identity. Nor are any particular instruments identified with the work's melodic element. This enables melody to undergo a greater degree of registral migration than was possible in *Secret Theatre*. In *Earth Dances*, melody dips out of view and then surfaces again rather as it did in *Nomos*. Or it can vanish altogether, as at the work's tumultuous culminating tutti ([74]).

The lessened dependence on melody in *Earth Dances* in turn allows Birtwistle's ostinato patterns to acquire a heightened profile. In the past these patterns frequently constituted a largely disguised constructive method for generating complex mass textures. Here, however, they are

Ex. 6.6. *Earth Dances*: (a) rhythmic structure of one stratum, [18]; (b) rhythmic structure of whole texture, [18]

a = Piccs., Picc Trpt.   b = Hrns., Harps., Vln.1   c = Tubas, Vlcs., D.b.s   d = Percussion   e = Vln. 2   f = Vlas.

heard in sharp relief, etching out distinct, autonomous musical 'strata' as defiantly as any of the work's melodic lines. Birtwistle's decision to move to an intervallic basis for his layered textures also means he is no longer confined to two basic layers of material (melody and non-melody). Instead, up to six layers may proceed concurrently, each assigned to a particular register in order to keep them distinct. Great rhythmic complexity can ensue: Example 6.6 shows, firstly, the rhythmic structure of a single layer of material, which is made up from a combination of ostinati in different instruments; and, secondly, how that single layer fits into the multi-layered texture articulated by the whole orchestra. There is, however considerable ebb and flow in the music's textural complexity: one of the work's most startling moments is when the multiple layers of material are pared away to leave just a single, stark line in the violins and xylophone ([55]). Birtwistle likens his multi-layered texture to 'the several strata of the earth, constantly interacting, and in continual metamorphosis, living and dying'.[66]

The idea of superimposing a number of independent musical processes is not new to twentieth-century music.[67] Where classical tonality demands a basic vertical homogeneity – all parts, however apparently independent, have to be ultimately reconcilable to a single succession of syntactically-related harmonies – post-tonal musical idioms impose no such demands. Experiments with superimposition have taken many forms: Debussy and Stravinsky constructed sonorities from superimposed tonal harmonies, or wrote counterpoint that implied 'conflicting' keys; Ives combined diatonic melodies with chromatic ostinati in an attempt to forge a transcendental unity of musical material; and Stockhausen and Carter theatrically emphasised the idea of simultaneous multiplicity by writing pieces for three orchestras. Contemporary dance music is assembled along similar lines, technology making possible the ready superimposition of diverse layers of sampled sound. *Earth Dances* is the product of the same, post-tonal obsession with the possibilities of vertical combination.

The motivations behind these examples differ, however, and *Earth Dances* is closer to some than others. It is less inclined than either Ives or dance music to accommodate other musics and their associations, for instance. In both Ives and dance, textural superimposition symbolises the bringing together of different realms of the world around us. Nor should Birtwistle's stubbornly non-coinciding strata be confused with the tonally referential games of Debussy and Stravinsky. These frequently strive after an ultimately unitary effect, despite their multiplicitous origins: the opening chord of Debussy's Prélude 'Feuilles mortes', for instance, is built from conflicting tonal harmonies (a diminished seventh on G and an F♯ major triad) but Debussy treats it as a singular sonority; the more self-consciously modern 'bitonality' of parts of Stravinsky's *Histoire du soldat*, meanwhile, frequently orientates itself around focal pivot pitches that are shared by both scales (as in the middle of the 'Tango', where the C♯ of the clarinet's A major triad nestles happily against the D♭ of the violin's B♭ minor melody). The dramatic interplay involved in Stockhausen's and Carter's pieces for three orchestras is obviously closer to some of Birtwistle's concerns; in *Secret Theatre* at least, it seems clear that the combination of different musics has explicitly theatrical ends. Even this, though, is less apparent in *Earth Dances*, where individual instruments

Fig. 6.2. *Earth Dances*: (a) registral partitioning, five after [39] to one after [40];
(b) registral partitioning, two after [40] to sixteen after [40]

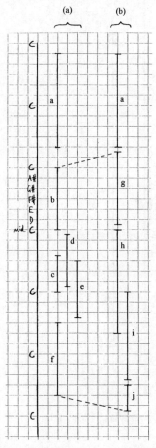

a = Vlns. 1-20, Tutti Wind   b = Vlns. 21-30, Vlcs. 1-4   c = Trbns.   d = Vlas.   e = D.b.s 6-9,
Vcls. 5-9   f = D.b.s 1-5   g = Upper Strings, Tutti Wind, Perc.   h = Middle Strings   i = Brass
j = 'savage' interruptions   k = D.b.s, Tubas

have far less of a direct stake in the proceedings, being instead neutral
vessels for the expression of Birtwistle's intervallic material.

Earth Dances' strata invite instead a primarily *visual*, diagrammatic conceptualisation. They are less concerned with articulating a drama than
with elaborating a spatial configuration. As was the case in *Linoi*, the way
in which the material is deployed tends to enforce this spatialised response.
Firstly, Birtwistle's articulation of registral areas is often meticulously
precise. Layers of activity frequently inhabit snugly adjacent pitch spans.
Figure 6.2 shows the registral partitioning of two consecutive sections in
the piece, and illustrates the way in which the second is related to the first

Fig. 6.3. *Earth Dances*: registral partitioning, [37] to six after [37]

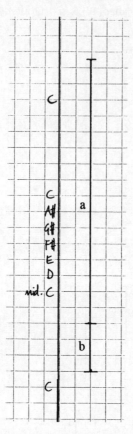

a = Vlns., Wind   b = Vlas., Vlcs., Trbns.

by a process of slight registral expansion.[68] A more audible instance of registral adjacency occurs slightly earlier, where the music briefly reduces to
two strata, situated either side of a shared boundary pitch (Figure 6.3).
Sometimes Birtwistle's registral partitioning additionally appears to be
governed by principles of vertical symmetry (Figure 6.4). These are
unusually exact instances of a situation that prevails more imprecisely
elsewhere, and that also informs textural construction in Birtwistle's next
major piece, *Endless Parade*. That such exactitude is part of Birtwistle's
reckoning, rather than just coincidental, is nicely confirmed by a published sketch page relating to a dense, ten–part string passage in *Endless
Parade*, where Birtwistle's initial move appears to be a precise partitioning
of register.[69]

Fig. 6.4. *Earth Dances*: (a) registral partitioning, five after [39] to one after [40]; (b) registral partitioning, two after [44] to nine after [46]

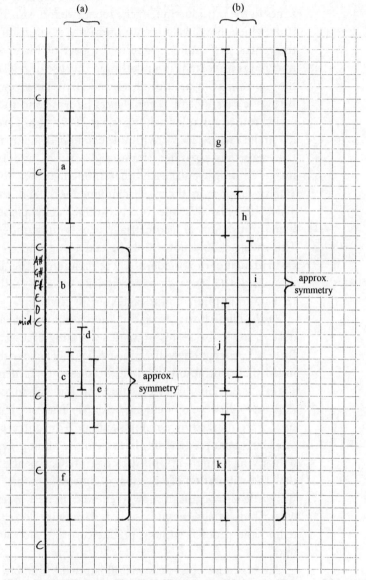

a = Vlns. 1-20, Tutti Wind   b = Vlns. 21-30, Vlcs. 1-4   c = Trbns.   d = Vlas.   e = D.b.s 6-9, Vlcs. 5-9   f = D.b.s 1-5   g = Trpts., Hrns.   h = Vlns., Vlas., Vlcs.   i = Trbns., Tubas   j = D.b.s

By no means all of *Earth Dances* is so neatly regimented registrally. But crucial passages of the piece seem intent on imparting an essentially 'spatial', textural image – be it the abrasive rending of disparate registral zones in the introduction, or the repetitive four- or five-note scales in the coda, which move in contrary motion at varying distances on either side of the central D-F motive. A second aspect of Birtwistle's deployment of material is important in underlining this use of registral space – namely, the *non-coinciding* nature of his strata. In his interview with Paul Griffiths, Birtwistle says that in *Earth Dances* he was concerned to embolden the asynchronicity that lay behind *Secret Theatre* but never really made itself felt in the earlier piece.[70] Without such non-coincidence, there is a danger that registrally separated strata might merge, undoing the vivid spatial image. Grating against each other, though, as they do, the strata of *Earth Dances* emphasise their self-containedness, and thus unambiguously articulate a play of shapes in a two-dimensional plane. The work's title, a literal translation of 'geometria',[71] is only fully understood in this light. This music should not simply be taken as a sonic representation of the earth 'dancing', or a modern-day re-creation of the 'Danse de la terre' of Stravinsky's *Le sacre du printemps*; it concerns, rather, in very precise terms, a conception of musical texture *as geometry*.

Earth Dances brings to culmination a number of earlier compositional obsessions. It also seems to mark something of a watershed, after which Birtwistle pursued new directions. Michael Hall, writing in 1988, astutely noted that contrapuntal ostinati become unprecedentedly important in *Earth Dances*, only to recede once more in the following work, *Endless Parade*.[72] This development has held true in subsequent works, which texturally are marked by developments in two contrary directions. On the one hand, textures generally become more homogeneous, their complexity deriving from their sophisticated embellishment of shared lines rather than the elaboration of a number of independent processes. On the other, Birtwistle also begins to show a renewed interest in textural aleatoricism, where individuals or groups of instruments depart from a prevailing tempo and proceed without precise co-ordination with their surroundings.

The first development is well illustrated by *Salford Toccata*, which was written only a couple of years after *Earth Dances*. The work's title, and its Blake epigraph, mark it out as a sequel to *Grimethorpe Aria*; but its breezy, noisy exuberance could hardly be further removed from its dour companion. The work exhibits a bold bravura in its textural handling, and there is a sense that compositional mastery here becomes an end as much as a means. This showmanship manifests itself in frequent tutti unisons, emerging unexpectedly from more contrapuntal textures, as well as a high turnover of textural alliances, so that the music gives the impression of constant 're-coagulation'. In stark contrast to the non-coincident multiplicity conveyed by *Earth Dances'* textures, *Salford Toccata* gives the overriding impression of confident homogeneity. The urgent sweep of its lines and toccatas give a feeling of common cause to all the music's textural layers, regardless of their putative distinctness as constructive elements. In all these respects, the piece is strongly anticipative of *Gawain* – for which it perhaps acted as something of a study, at least if the unbuttoned brass writing of the opera is anything to go by.

It is interesting, in this light, that *Gawain* should be followed in Birtwistle's output by the piece that most obviously symbolises a renewal of interest in the idea of metrically independent musics. The original version of *An Interrupted Endless Melody*, as mentioned earlier in this chapter, pits a fixed piano part against a melodic matrix for oboe which may be realised in a great number of ways. The oboe melody proceeds completely independently of the piano part, and, as if to emphasise this independence, Birtwistle later wrote a couple of additional, alternative piano parts. One imagines that there *is*, in fact, some subterranean connection between the two instruments' material, but it is their complete temporal independence that is the most striking aspect of the piece. This is not to say that such independence is wholly new to Birtwistle's music. Since the late 1960s, small-scale aleatoric 'mobiles' – little cells of repeated material that may be realised in a variety of ways and which proceed at a different tempo from the other instruments – have been a regular feature of his works: *Meridian* and *Silbury Air* contain particularly plentiful examples. More imposingly, the idea of combining two different tempos is dramatically evident in those parts of *The Mask of Orpheus* that use two conductors. A related but slightly different case is the miniature *Dinah and Nick's Love Song*, for three identical melody instruments and harp. This piece contains within its brief frame countless modest temporal and melodic indeterminacies. But, as Michael Hall observes, what is most unusual about the piece 'is the harmonic relation between the harp and the melody instruments, for any three identical instruments can play regardless of whether they transpose of not. The pitch of the harp is always constant, but that of the melody instruments differs according to whether, say, cors anglais or soprano saxophones are playing.'[73] In certain respects, then, the piece is a forerunner to *An Interrupted Endless Melody*. It brings melody and rhythm together in only the loosest of alignments, the variable pitch of the melody here taking the place of the indeterminacies of form in the later work.

If the temporal independence of the piano part in *An Interrupted Endless Melody* is not new, its relative assertiveness certainly is. In earlier works, aleatoric mobiles typically conjured up gently pulsating 'auras' – backdrops of shimmering sound against which the more rhythmically determined parts would be starkly offset. This is the role played by the harp in *Dinah and Nick's Love Song*. The nervously permutated patterns of the various piano parts to *An Interrupted Endless Melody*, on the other hand, seem reluctant to be consigned to such a status; and the same is true of the temporally independent material in other recent pieces, such as *Five Distances* and *Pulse Shadows*. In these works, in place of the contextualising environment created by the aleatoric mobile Birtwistle devises a more conventionally modernist aural challenge: both temporally conflicting components are equally demanding of attention. They no longer relate as figure to ground. And, unlike the concurrent layers of activity of *Earth Dances*, they also typically provide scant basis for a unitary perception – be it in terms of a clearly delineated registral plane, or the multiple cogs of a complex machine.

Slow Frieze, scored for a fourteen-strong ensemble with a prominent piano part, is Birtwistle's most concentrated exploration of simultaneous independent tempos. Elements of this work link it directly to *An Interrupted Endless Melody*, despite its much larger forces. Each of the four wind instruments plays from melodic matrices similar in style and layout to the oboist's in the earlier piece; they freely select their melodic paths (within certain constraints) for extensive stretches of the score. Unlike the earlier work, however, the melodic matrices in *Slow Frieze* articulate a fixed scale. This is intended to provide an 'underlying harmonic backdrop to the dialogue between the piano and the rest of the ensemble'.[74] Birtwistle labels the two matrices of each of the wind instruments 'Mode I' and 'Mode II' respectively; and the four matrices for each mode, when taken together, do indeed articulate a single scale, overlapping between instruments. As Example 6.7 shows, Birtwistle adopts the conventional signifier of harmonic staticity, the whole-tone scale, for his modes, swapping between the two whole-tone collections at every seventh tone. The musical autonomy of this layer of material is dramatised by its complete independence of the conductor; instead, the modal wind melodies are triggered and terminated by the percussion, which sets its own tempos. Still further complexity is provided by the piano, which frequently strikes out at its own speed. The whole is held together by a complex system of cues of the sort used on a smaller scale in *Five Distances*.

On the page, it is the ingenuity of Birtwistle's manoeuvring of these temporally independent components that is more immediately evident than either their compatibility or their individual distinctiveness. Even in the context of an œuvre that is hardly lacking in arcane and impersonal

Ex. 6.7. *Slow Frieze*: Modes I and II

qualities, *Slow Frieze* leaves an impression of startling anonymity. The surface similarity with *Secret Theatre*, with melodic wind counterpointed against more percussive strings and brass, is annulled by the absence of unisons – the essence of the earlier piece's characteristic texture. Instead, the wind appear caught between two stools. They at once exert a focal pull (for they have the only melodic material in the work) and yet also appear cast adrift from, and often submerged by, the main proceedings. They are unified neither amongst themselves nor with the bulk of the instruments they sit amongst. Similarly, the piano's prominence suggests soloistic status, yet the short-windedness of most of its material is expressive of its failure ever to take the leading role.

Although their expressive world could hardly be more different, *Slow Frieze* and *Panic* take a similar stance on matters of texture. The idea of allowing a percussionist to dictate the speeds of certain instruments, for instance, had already been tried out in *Panic*; there, the solo drum kit occasionally extends its sphere of influence to the orchestral brass, cueing a number of savage brass interjections at a speed independent from the conductor. Both pieces contain music that defies established schemes for the conceptualisation of Birtwistle's layered textures, presenting instead situations that are both meticulously constructed and yet susceptible to no single, coherent hearing. The controversy caused by *Panic* was in no small part due to its apparently self-defeating textural complexity. The next chapter will give further consideration to this aspect of *Panic*, this time approached from the perspective of Birtwistle's relationship with his audiences. The argument to emerge there – that Birtwistle has increasingly courted obscurity as a defensive reaction to the reification of techniques and preoccupations concomitant with public acclaim – applies to questions of texture as much as anything else. It also signals the danger of assumptions of inertia, in this or any other area of Birtwistle's compositional concerns.

7 Audiences

Today, Harrison Birtwistle is the recipient of a steady stream of high-profile national and international commissions. At the time of writing, forthcoming plans include pieces for Glyndebourne and Covent Garden, and a period as composer-in-residence with the Berlin Philharmonic Orchestra. This rise in fame makes for an extraordinary contrast with Birtwistle's earlier career. In the 1960s and 1970s, Birtwistle's rather reluctant public persona – cemented in the minds of many by Meirion Bowen's comparison with Isaiah Berlin's hedgehog[1] – seemed emblematic of an output that was secretive in its methods and prone to introversion and understatedness. This image dates back to his period as a student at the Royal Manchester College of Music (1952–5) and then, after his National Service, at the Royal Academy of Music in London (1957–8), where he studied principally as a clarinettist. Birtwistle's reputation as a composer eventually grew in the 1960s, but his later, long period of service as music director at the National Theatre (1975–83), though clearly a reflection of his proclivity for the theatre, also suggests a continued compositional reticence – after all, theatre music, rightly or wrongly, has traditionally been deemed a marginal genre, where the composer's role is relatively recessed rather than highlighted. The wish to avoid the public eye and public life at this time was more obviously manifested by Birtwistle's decision to set up home in, first, Raasay, a remote island in the Inner Hebrides, and then, from 1983, Lunegarde in the central French region of Lot.

During the 1980s, however, Birtwistle's music gained an increasingly public profile. The first performance of *Secret Theatre*, at the composer's fiftieth birthday concert in October 1984, was an important catalyst in this development: the occasion predictably prompted a degree of critical stocktaking in the daily and musical press, and *Secret Theatre* itself met with great acclaim. 1986 was an even more important year, for by a strange set of circumstances it brought the premieres of three very substantial works: *Earth Dances*, which was brand new; *Yan Tan Tethera*, which was completed two years earlier and whose original television production had never come about; and, most imposingly of all, *The Mask of Orpheus*, the English National Opera production of which finally enabled a work begun eleven years previously to see the light of day. For many critics, the combination of these three pieces provided all the evidence necessary for

Birtwistle to be accorded the status of Britain's most significant living composer. This newly burnished reputation was recognised by a four-day festival of Birtwistle's music at London's Barbican Centre in January 1988; three years later, the Royal Opera House gave the first performances of *Gawain* and each performance sold out. In between, Birtwistle received a knighthood.

Even in 1991, however, few would have imagined that Birtwistle's music would one day feature in the Last Night of the Proms – one of the world's most high-profile classical musical events, broadcast on radio and television networks around the world. The Last Night had rarely featured new music before, let alone the sort of uncompromising modernism for which Birtwistle was renowned. Sir John Drummond, the Director of the Proms and Controller of Music at the BBC since the late eighties, was a long-time supporter of Birtwistle's music, and he used his last year in the post as an excuse to commission a work from Birtwistle for the 1995 Last Night. The resulting piece, *Panic*, was seen or heard by an audience of 100 million people.[2] It thus brought to culmination the process that, over the previous decade, saw Birtwistle's music take a central position, not just in the mainstream of contemporary classical music, but in the musical establishment at large.

In an obvious sense, the music of *Panic* reflects the extreme confidence of a composer 'at the peak of his profession'.[3] Faced with the prospect of writing for the flag-wavers, giddy revellers and large general television audience of the Last Night, Birtwistle devised the most unremittingly ferocious eighteen minutes of music in his entire output – a sustained assault, with brazen alto saxophone and drum kit leading an equally strident stringless orchestra. In a review of the first performance, Jonathan Cross described the piece as 'aggressively single-minded', and noted how 'the overtly lyrical side to Birtwistle's musical language is here underplayed, preference being given to the violent, rhythmic, urgently repetitive aspects of his style'.[4] The prominent parts given to saxophone and drum kit only served to heighten the uncompromising nature of the musical material, for they raised expectations for something more familiar or 'popular' – expectations that were then brutally dispelled. The work's title suggests that the piece, far from disregarding the nature of the event for which it was written, was devised as an act of deliberate, snubbing provocation. Robert Maycock, reviewing the piece in *The Independent*, called it 'the ultimate up-yours piece',[5] a description that captures the way it functioned, at its first performance, principally as a statement of resistance to cultural populism – a forceful expression of the sort of uncompromising stance that has, on many occasions, led Birtwistle to state, 'I can't be responsible for the audience.'[6] This impression is strengthened by the involvement of John Drummond, whose championing of high modernism and concert-hall etiquette became legendary during his time as Controller of Radio 3. Birtwistle dedicated the piece to Drummond, 'in friendship and for services to music above and beyond the call of duty'.[7] In many ways, the piece is Drummond's own arrogant farewell gesture.

Michael Hall says of the piece that, for all its unprecedentedly controversial reception, there was no 'difficulty in relating [it] to what Birtwistle had been doing in the past'.[8] This is consistent with the idea that *Panic* is the expression of a veritable surfeit of compositional certainty and confidence. Rarely, though, have the particularities of a piece of music been so thoroughly obscured by immediate reactions. If we put the circumstances surrounding the piece's creation and realisation to one side for a moment, it is easier to see how the detail of the music suggests an alternative argument: namely, that the piece brings to the fore precisely those aspects of Birtwistle's earlier music that are *least* connotative of certainty, assurance or singularity of vision. In particular, Birtwistle's distinctive approaches to both sectional form and layered textures here turn in on themselves. The persistent risk run by the former, of drifting into an inconsequential short-termism, and the danger, for the latter, of clotting into an incomprehensible multiplicity, are dramatised in *Panic*. The pretence of cogency is dropped; instead, parameters of formal or textural plausibility that might normally be assessed *prior* to composition are here explored in the very course of the piece.

So formal sections appear to be juxtaposed almost randomly – each generally following smoothly upon its predecessor in the characteristic manner of Birtwistle's recent music, but leaving the articulation of any larger formal shape largely to chance. The heady forcefulness of one passage may seem intended to signal a decisive stage in the music's larger form (a point of climax), only for further waves of noisy tutti thoroughly to dissipate any distinctive formal function it might have served. (The keening lament that starts up about thirteen minutes into the piece (b. 432), with saxophone soloist for once working in co-operation with soloists from the orchestra, is one such example of a 'false' structural marker.) At times the piece seems to be in a permanent state of culmination. Similarly, Birtwistle's textural organisation presents an enthralling picture on the page, but appears to be wholly unconstrained by the pragmatics of sonic realisation. As a result, fastidious orchestral textures are fashioned only to be frequently submerged beneath the onslaught of saxophone and drums. (The music at [M] (four and a quarter minutes) and [V] (eight and a quarter minutes) provides good instances of this sort of self-defeating

Ex. 7.1. *Panic:* bb. 542–7

strategy.) Textural complexity dissolves into textural chaos, and the distinction – rather than being built into the piece – is an unpredictable, emergent property of the music's realisation.

That these are not simply the products of a deliberate abandonment of formal and textural lucidity, in imitation of the chaos wreaked by Pan himself, is suggested by the strong elements of design that, for all the work's perplexing content, remain an important feature of the work. An interesting article on *Panic* by David Bruce details some of these.[9] It demonstrates that the piece does *not* totally abandon aspirations of textural and formal clarity. An alternative explanation, namely that certain passages are simply lapses on Birtwistle's part, is also awkward to sustain. There are moments in *Panic* that achieve their intended effect so precisely that one is obliged to hesitate before accusing Birtwistle of miscalculation elsewhere. One of the work's few quiet passages (b. 417, twelve minutes in), for instance, combines soloist and orchestra with great delicacy; and, for all the unrelenting tumultuousness of earlier passages, Birtwistle still holds in reserve his most irrefutably climactic music for the very end of the work (Example 7.1). But such clarity of purpose is only intermittently present. The possibility of falling short of lucidity – of failing conventional criteria for 'success' – is one of the things delineated by the music.

This uncertainty about its own goals – the failure to be completely sure of itself – is not unique to *Panic*. It can be identified in much of Birtwistle's music. Indeed, there have been periods during his compositional career when it has been particularly characteristic. The overstatedness of *Panic* paradoxically returns us, after a fashion, to the *under*statedness of many of the works from the early and mid 1970s, including *An Imaginary Landscape*, *The Triumph of Time*, *Grimethorpe Aria*, the first act of *The Mask of Orpheus* and *Melencolia I*. These works appear similarly reluctant to make their raison d'être – or, more accurately, their 'raison de devenir' – apparent at every moment. They seem more questioning of themselves than critical of the world outside. The growing renown of Birtwistle's music in the 1980s, outlined at the start of this chapter, and the new self-confidence on Birtwistle's part to which it gave rise,[10] is musically reflected in a greater compositional decisiveness – both formally (in the bold dramatic 'curves' traced by *Secret Theatre*, *Earth Dances* and *Endless Parade*; or the clear-cut sectional exchanges that motivate *Antiphonies*), and texturally (in the binary articulation of textures in terms of melody and non-melody that is apparent in many works of the time; and the reduced textural complexity of *Salford Toccata* and *Gawain*). Recent years, however, have seen a reversion to a more hermit-like exploration of compositional possibilities, with half an eye blind to its comprehensibility to the listener. The rather detached examinations of musical allegiances in *Five Distances* and *Slow Frieze*; the exclusive focus on microcosmic workings in the 'Friezes' of the Nine Movements for String Quartet and *Harrison's Clocks*; and the sprawling, hit-and-miss successions of *Panic* and *Exody* – these all suggest a return to the idea of music as a testing-ground for ideas, rather than as a medium for the presentation of honed statements. It may well be that, in the early 1990s, Birtwistle sensed the danger that faces all fêted artists, of succumbing to the slogans that hype and celebrity inevitably bring, and attempting to replicate stylistic clichés in order to perpetuate success. This fate has befallen younger talents before now. It is easy to see why someone might want to return to basics, as a sort of defensive reaction to fame.

Regardless of these particular phases of fame and fortune, however, an element of the same attitude – of the desire to keep at one remove from the music, to treat it with a degree of circumspection – has been perceptible in Birtwistle's approach to composition throughout his career. Birtwistle has been consistent in his embarrassment at the concepts of expression and inspiration in music, responding to one enquiring interviewer, 'Do I look as if I've ever been inspired?'[11] In interview with Michael Hall, Birtwistle says: 'I don't think creative people think about intuition. You take it for granted you're expressing yourself. It's a nineteenth-century, romantic idea that creative artists are people who are preoccupied with self-expression. What really preoccupies artists is simply how the hell you do it.'[12] Birtwistle has tended to emphasise instead the ways in which he *yields* his own intentionality in the process of composing, through the use of random processes. According to Michael Hall, random numbers 'constitute his prime method of messing things up',[13] of disturbing a logic that might otherwise become predictable. Birtwistle says that random numbers 'create the life of my music, the spontaneity',[14] but his use of them is also strictly controlled: Brian Robison has rightly spoken of 'Birtwistle's penchant for the *methodical* application of disorder'.[15] In recent years Birtwistle has compared his use of an element of chance to that of Francis Bacon, for whom chance procedures acted as a means to the realisation of 'something much more profound than what you really wanted', or even as a way of 'coming nearer to the way that my visual instincts feel about the image I am trying to trap'.[16]

At one level, Birtwistle's awkwardness with regard to expression, and his focus upon depersonalised, abstract material, can be seen as simply an extension of the fear of 'pandering to ordinary people'[17] that some have seen as characteristic of the musical avant-garde – a fear of engaging in the sort of 'generic association and automatically communicable meaning' that makes most music meaningful.[18] It was this refusal of ready communicability that was most apparent to *Panic*'s television audience, if not also to the majority of those in the Albert Hall. However, Birtwistle's intention needs to be distinguished from that of composers who have invented novel organisational principles in order to create a more rarefied *musical language*, the subtlety, sophistication and 'difficulty' of whose statements is only accessible to initiates. In Birtwistle's case, there is a stronger sense of the novelty of the idiom being driven not by a view as to the inadequacy of existing musical languages but by the desire to escape the idea of a musical language altogether. To put it more directly, Birtwistle's constructional procedures are driven not so much by the desire to say things of a new refinement and complexity, as by the wish 'to make things in ignorance of what they are'.[19] This stance implies no necessary exclusivity. The value of such music is not dependent upon understanding its codes or techniques; it resides in its *resistance* to such modes of understanding. Admittedly, this picture is complicated by situating such music in the concert hall. Placed in an environment that brings expectations of artistic communication, the semantically inscrutable elements of the music tend to be absorbed as part of a larger expressive statement – and are usually interpreted in terms of the 'tortuous complexities' and 'generous self-laceration'[20] lampooned by Birtwistle's critics. Strangeness becomes 'difficulty', because the reverential atmosphere that constructs everything presented in the course of a classical concert as 'high art' can tolerate the latter (art is sometimes difficult) but not the former (art possesses characteristics that enable us to distinguish it from other made things, and these characteristics are *recognisable* even if they may be difficult to pin down in words). The tendency of a performance environment to work against an element of Birtwistle's music is not sufficient to extinguish it altogether, however. And the resistance of that element of the music to coherent interpretation – its propensity to baffle – is felt as much by 'those friends of art' who undertake the 'clerical services' of analytical dissemblage and sketch study as it is by the 'unconverted', whose open incomprehension is in some respects a more appropriate response.[21] An important part of Birtwistle's music refuses to 'strive for acceptance'.[22]

In this there lies the ingredient of a possible response to those who would lump Birtwistle with a homogeneous avant-garde – a member of that self-sustaining group whose principal concern is with spiralling out of most people's communicative orbit, leaving behind nothing but hectoring reminders of a world of exalted communication to which the great majority will never have access. Unlike the music of many of Birtwistle's contemporaries, which is intended in the last analysis to be completely comprehensible (if only to that minority that possesses the tools to decode it), there is an important element of Birtwistle's music that falls altogether outside the realm of the communicative and the meant. As I have suggested, this is not confined simply to the element of his musical material that is the product of chance procedures, but is in an important respect intrinsic (at least as a tendency) to the primary compositional resources of sectional form and layered textures. Each is prone to give rise to situations that are reducible to no single governing rationale or agenda – that defeat what David Bruce terms 'the sovereignty of logic'.[23] This defeat is felt as much by Birtwistle's advocates as by his opponents, for all that the former may try to overlook it in their efforts to make the music seem intelligible.

Of course, all this only accounts for an element of Birtwistle's music, albeit an important one. In the course of this book, I have elaborated some of the ways in which Birtwistle's music engages with the 'known' – some of the ways in which it is highly susceptible to explanation by reference to things outside itself. Its multi-referentiality – which is to say, the ease with which it reaches out into 'extra-musical' realms – is one of its most distinctive characteristics, and in no small degree accounts for Birtwistle's present-day prominence and (at least by comparison with many other contemporary classical composers) relative public success. But the persistent presence of an element of the self-questioning and self-contradictory

– an element more obvious in the most recent music than at other times in Birtwistle's compositional career – acts as a counterbalance to the music's meaningfulness. It touches the interpretations that would establish its meanings (meanings to do with, for instance, violence, ceremony, the female voice, time, verse form, and melody; meanings about which we may feel approving or disapproving) with contingency. It holds something in reserve that prevents the complete grasp, the containing interpretation, be it a hostile or favourable one. In so doing, it keeps us on the move with regard to our own certainty of what we want from music – in which cause it guarantees itself no necessary future, but, rather, exists in the present as a vivid and formidable stimulant.

Notes

Introduction

1 Nicholas Cook, *Music: A Very Short Introduction* (Oxford University Press, 1998), p. 78.
2 Susan McClary, 'Terminal prestige: the case of avant-garde music composition', *Cultural Critique*, 12 (Spring 1989), p. 73.
3 Lawrence Kramer, *Classical Music and Postmodern Knowledge* (Berkeley: University of California Press, 1995), pp. 3–5. For Kramer, classical music 'is in trouble' because of the victory of 'esoteric' conceptions of music in the twentieth century, meaning that, by the mid-twentieth century, 'classical music had passed out of the public sphere'.
4 Cook, *Music*, 47.
5 Dai Griffiths, 'The high analysis of low music', *Music Analysis*, 18/3 (October 1999)
6 Richard Taruskin, cited on back cover of Cook, *Music*.

1 Theatres

1 Nicholas Snowman, 'Birtwistle the dramatist', essay included in programme booklets for 'Secret Theatres: The Harrison Birtwistle Retrospective', a festival of Birtwistle's music at London's South Bank Centre, April–May 1996.
2 A consequence of this is that the category of 'stage work' is less than usually distinct in Birtwistle's case; several of his purely instrumental works involve particular stage placements or movement. My discussion will continue to use the term 'stage work' in its conventional sense, referring to works that bring together music and types of staged dramatic representation.
3 *HB*, p. 171.
4 See *HB*, p. 23.
5 Excellent synopses of the major stage works may be found in Stanley Sadie, ed., *The New Grove Dictionary of Opera*, four volumes (London: Macmillan, 1992) and Amanda Holden, ed., *The Penguin Opera Guide* (Harmondsworth: Viking, 1995).
6 Paul Griffiths, *Modern Music and After: Directions Since 1945* (Oxford University Press, 1995), p. 171.
7 Paul Griffiths, *New Sounds, New Personalities: British Composers of the 1980s* (London: Faber, 1985), p. 189.
8 *HB*, p. 30; Jonathan Cross, 'Lines and circles: on Birtwistle's *Punch and Judy* and *Secret Theatre*', *Music Analysis*, 13/2–3 (July–October 1994), p. 203.

9 *HB*, p. 57.

10 Stephen Pruslin, 'Punch and Judy', note to compact-disc recording of *Punch and Judy*, Etcetera KTC 2014.

11 Stephen Pruslin, 'Punch's Précis', programme note for Music Theatre Wales production of *Punch and Judy* at London's Queen Elizabeth Hall, 11 July 1998.

12 Birtwistle, in *HB*, p. 175.

13 See Meirion Bowen, 'Harrison Birtwistle', in Lewis Foreman, ed., *British Music Now: A Guide to the Work of Younger Composers* (London: Elek, 1975), pp. 67–8; and Jonathan Cross, 'Birtwistle's secret theatres', in Craig Ayrey and Mark Everist, eds., *Analytical Strategies and Musical Interpretation: Essays on Nineteenth- and Twentieth-Century Music* (Cambridge University Press, 1996), pp. 209–11.

14 Tony Harrison, in John Haffenden, 'Interview with Tony Harrison', in Neil Astley, ed., *Tony Harrison* (Newcastle upon Tyne: Bloodaxe Books, 1991), p. 235.

15 Gabriel Josipovici, *The Lessons of Modernism and Other Essays* (London: Macmillan, 1977), p. 176.

16 Theodor Adorno, *Philosophy of Modern Music*, trans. Anne G. Mitchell and Wesley V. Blomster (London: Sheed and Ward, 1973), p. 143.

17 Andrew Brown, 'Greece, ancient', in Martin Banham, ed., *The Cambridge Guide to Theatre* (Cambridge University Press, 1992), p. 408.

18 Norman Lebrecht, 'Music that makes a stand: Norman Lebrecht talks to Harrison Birtwistle', *ENO and Friends*, 10 (Summer 1986), p. 10.

19 See Ross Lorraine, 'Territorial rites 2', *Musical Times* (November 1997), p. 15; *HBRY*, pp. xi–xii.

20 Francis Bacon, in David Sylvester, *The Brutality of Fact: Interviews with Francis Bacon*, third, enlarged, edition (London: Thames and Hudson, 1987), p. 82.

21 Francis Bacon, ibid., pp. 58–9; pp. 81–2.

22 Stephen Halliwell, *The* Poetics *of Aristotle: Translation and Commentary* (London: Duckworth, 1987), p. 191.

23 Pruslin borrowed his subtitle from one of the nineteenth-century sources he used in assembling his libretto: John Payne Collier, *Punch and Judy, with Illustrations Drawn and Engraved by George Cruikshank*, second edition (London: S. Prowett, 1828), p. 95.

24 Brown, 'Greece', p. 407.

25 Graham Ley, *A Short Introduction to the Ancient Greek Theater* (University of Chicago Press, 1991), pp. 7–8.

26 Bowen, 'Birtwistle', p. 68.

27 Ibid., p. 67.

28 Birtwistle, in *HB*, p. 175.

29 Gordon Crosse, 'Birtwistle's *Punch and Judy*', *Tempo*, 85 (Summer 1968), p. 25–6.

30 Ibid., p. 26.

31 Aristotle, 'On the art of poetry [Poetics]', trans. T. S. Dorsch, in T. S. Dorsch, ed., *Classical Literary Criticism* (Harmondsworth: Penguin, 1965), p. 33.

32 Brown, 'Greece', p. 410.

33 Michael Nyman, 'Harrison Birtwistle's "Punch and Judy"', *The Listener* (10 October 1968), p. 481.

34 This neutrality is confirmed at the end of the opera, where, according to Pruslin, Punch and Pretty Polly are presented 'as a photographic "double image" with an amoral couple like Nero and Poppea as the "negative" and an ideal couple like Tamino-Pamina or Leonore-Florestan as the "positive"' (Pruslin, 'Punch and Judy').

35 The composer has acknowledged this kinship: see Michael Hall, 'Composer and producer speak', in programme booklet for English National Opera production of *The Mask of Orpheus*, May 1986.

36 Pruslin, 'Punch and Judy'.

37 Nyman, '"Punch and Judy"', p. 481.

38 See Griffiths, *New Sounds*, p. 193; Andrew Ford, *Composer to Composer: Conversations about Contemporary Music* (London: Quartet Books, 1993), p. 57.

39 This aspect of the score has occasionally raised critical hackles: 'Never have I seen so many people sleeping during an opera . . . The Birtwistle score is so maddeningly segmented, the forms so inherently undramatic, that the action rarely comes to life' (Michael Davidson, review of Netherlands Opera production of *Punch and Judy*, *Opera* (April 1993), p. 466.

40 The influential eighteenth-century librettist Metastasio was important in cementing the idea that 'opera belonged to the tragic genre . . . [and that] the aria's function [was comparable] with that of the chorus in Greek tragedy'. Accordingly, many of Metastasio's arias 'might . . . be said to trope the action sententiously or imagistically . . . rather than forming a direct part of it' (Jack Westrup et al., 'Aria', in Stanley Sadie, ed., *The New Grove Dictionary of Music and Musicians*, vol. I (London: Macmillan, 1980), p. 577).

41 Nyman, '"Punch and Judy"', p. 481.

42 Birtwistle, in Hall, 'Composer and producer speak'.

43 Tony Harrison, in Jocelyn Herbert, 'Filling the space: working with Tony Harrison on *The Oresteia* and *The Trackers of Oxyrhynchus*', in Astley, ed., *Tony Harrison*, pp. 282–3.

44 Peter Hall, cited in Peter Lewis, *The National: A Dream Made Concrete* (London: Methuen, 1990), p. 159.

45 Peter Zinovieff, *The Mask of Orpheus: An Opera in Three Acts* (London: Universal Edition, 1986), p. 2. This version of Zinovieff's libretto contains different introductory material to the one included with the compact disc recording of *The Mask of Orpheus* (NMC Recordings: NMC D050, 1997). The following discussion makes use of both versions: they will be referred to as Zinovieff 1986 and Zinovieff 1997 respectively.

46 Phyllis Hartnoll, ed., *The Oxford Companion to the Theatre*, third edition (Oxford University Press, 1967), p. 624.

47 Paul Griffiths' description of *The Mask of Orpheus* as 'a drama of showing rather than action' neatly points up its masque-like qualities (Paul Griffiths, 'The twentieth century: 1945 to the present day', in Roger Parker, ed., *The Oxford History of Opera* (Oxford University Press, 1996), p. 231).

48 Griffiths, 'The twentieth century', p. 218.

49 Lebrecht, 'Music that makes a stand', p. 9.

50 Amanda Holden, 'The Second Mrs Kong', in Holden, et al., eds., *The Penguin Opera Guide*, p. 42.

51 Christopher Wintle, 'A fine and private place', *Musical Times* (November 1996), p. 5.

52 Lebrecht, 'Music that makes a stand', p. 8.

53 Michael Nyman, 'Mr Birtwistle is out', *Music and Musicians* (November 1969), p. 27.

54 Cross, 'Birtwistle's secret theatres', p. 208.

55 Brown, 'Greece', p. 408.

56 From the preface to the score of *The Mark of the Goat*.

57 Stephen Pruslin, programme note for first performance of *The Visions of Francesco Petrarca*, at the York Festival, June 1966.

58 Zinovieff 1997, p. 17; p. 23; p. 26.

59 Zinovieff, in *HB*, p. 126.

60 Zinovieff 1986, p. 2.

61 Zinovieff 1997, p. 6.

62 See *HB*, p. 67.

63 Michael Nyman, 'Harrison Birtwistle', *London Magazine*, 11/4 (October–November 1971), p. 121.

64 Michael Nyman, programme note for performance of *Down by the Greenwood Side* at Festival of the City of London, 10 July 1970.

65 Further discussion of the idea of the multi-dimensional object may be found in Chapters 5 and 6.

66 David Freeman, in Hall, 'Composer and producer speak'.

67 Zinovieff 1997, p. 4.

68 Zinovieff, in *HB*, p. 124.

69 Brown, 'Greece', p. 408.

70 Zinovieff 1997, p. 15; p. 34.

71 Birtwistle, in Hall, 'Composer and producer speak'.

72 Birtwistle, ibid.

73 Zinovieff 1986, p. 2; Zinovieff 1997, p. 6.

74 Zinovieff 1986, p. 2.

75 Birtwistle, in Griffiths, *New Sounds*, p. 192. A similar statement appears in a later interview: Ford, *Composer to Composer*, p. 57.

76 *HB*, p. 111.

77 Andrew Clements, 'Music theatre', in Sadie, ed., *New Grove Dictionary of Opera*, vol. III, p. 530.

78 Cross, 'Birtwistle's secret theatres', p. 208.

79 Bryan Magee, *Aspects of Wagner* (London: Panther, 1972), p. 12.

80 *HB*, p. 15.

81 Tony Harrison, '*The Oresteia* in the making: letters to Peter Hall', in Astley, ed., *Tony Harrison*, p. 279.

82 Ibid., p. 275.

83 Ibid., p. 279; p. 280.

84 Stephen Fay and Philip Oakes, 'Mystery behind the mask', in Astley, ed., *Tony Harrison*, p. 289.

85 Birtwistle, in Fay and Oakes, ibid.

86 Oswyn Murray, 'Tony Harrison: poetry and the theatre', in Astley, ed., *Tony Harrison*, p. 268.

87 Peter Levi, 'Tony Harrison's dramatic verse', in Astley, ed., *Tony Harrison*, p. 163.

88 Herbert, 'Filling the space', p. 283.

89 Nevertheless, *Bow Down* was apparently primarily Harrison's conception (Neil Astley, 'The Wizard of [Uz]: preface', in Astley, ed., *Tony Harrison*, pp. 10–11). Harrison's importance for Birtwistle's conception of theatre at this time has been underestimated.

90 Peter D. Arnott, *Public and Performance in the Greek Theatre* (London: Routledge, 1989), pp. 84–5.

91 Brown, 'Greece', p. 407.

92 Warren D. Anderson, *Music and Musicians in Ancient Greece* (Ithaca: Cornell University Press, 1994), pp. 113–18.

93 *HB*, p. 111. Hall erroneously attributes this interchangeability of roles to Japanese theatre.

94 Birtwistle, in Hall, 'Composer and producer speak'.

95 This libretto is published as part of an anthology of Harrison's stage works, which also includes the text to *Bow Down* and the translation of *The Oresteia* (Tony Harrison, *Theatre Works 1973–1985* (Harmondsworth: Penguin, 1986)).

96 Birtwistle, in *HB*, p. 149.

97 Ibid., p. 146.

98 Anthony Bye, 'Birtwistle's *Gawain*', *Musical Times* (May 1991), p. 233.

99 See Jonathan Cross, *The Stravinsky Legacy* (Cambridge University Press, 1998), pp. 132–69.

100 Griffiths, 'The twentieth century', p. 219.

101 Peter Zinovieff, in *HB*, p. 124.

102 A review of the first performance by Bryan Magee commented that, 'King Arthur and his knights are so under-characterised that the singers can do little with their parts; even François Le Roux in the title role of Gawain makes only a modest impression' (*The Independent on Sunday* (2 June 1991), p. 18).

103 Tom Sutcliffe, review of Royal Opera House production of *Gawain*, *The Guardian* (1 June 1991), p. 21.

104 Birtwistle, in an interview with Mark Pappenheim, *The Independent* (8 April 1994), p. 21.

105 Birtwistle, ibid.

106 This comment was made at a Royal Opera House 'study day' on *Gawain*, held at London's Royal Academy of Music, 19 May 1991.

107 Rhian Samuel, 'Gawain's musical journey', in programme booklet for Royal Opera House production of *Gawain*, April 1994, p. 22.

108 Birtwistle, in *HB*, p. 152.

109 Andrew Clements, review of Royal Opera House production of *Gawain*, *The Guardian* (16 April 1994), p. 28.

110 The term ritual is in fact not easily defined; as Richard Schechner has commented, 'Ritual has been so variously defined . . . that it means very little because it means too much' (Richard Schechner, *The Future of Ritual: Writings on Culture and Performance* (London: Routledge, 1993), p. 228). Schechner provides a diagram that links the various usages of the term. In my discussion, the term 'ritual' is used in the same sense that Clements uses it in attributing a ritual function to Birtwistle's music; namely, to refer to what Schechner calls 'religious ritual'. This involves no necessary connection with an established religion, but instead incorporates all manner of 'observances, celebrations, [and] rites of passage' (ibid., p. 229). Ritual is thus reserved in my discussion for activities that are privileged in some way, rather than being used to describe mundane routines such as brushing one's teeth.

111 Catherine Bell, *Ritual Theory, Ritual Practice* (New York: Oxford University Press, 1992), p. 19.

112 T. S. Eliot, in Ronald Gaskell, *Drama and Reality: The European Theatre since Ibsen* (London: Routledge and Kegan Paul, 1972), p. 69.

113 A. E. Green, 'Ritual', in Banham, ed., *Cambridge Guide*, p. 829.

114 Richard Drain, 'Introduction', in Richard Drain, ed., *Twentieth-Century Theatre: A Sourcebook* (London: Routledge, 1995), p. 231.

115 Birtwistle, in Ross Lorraine, 'Territorial rites 2', *Musical Times* (November 1997), p. 12.

116 Griffiths, 'The twentieth century', p. 225.

117 Adorno, *Philosophy*, pp. 147–8.

118 Up to a point, Stravinsky can be defended from this argument. As Max Paddison has argued, what Adorno perceived as the 'primitivist' elements of Stravinsky's technique are more accurately understood as part and parcel of a Russian tradition of composition (see Max Paddison, in Cross, *The Stravinsky Legacy*, p. 134). The implication of Paddison's argument is that, for Stravinsky, these elements of his music represented no stylised imitation of a foreign culture or throw-back to a previous age; rather, they were integral parts of a culture that was living and real. Richard Taruskin has shown that Stravinsky's 'Russian' works were frequently the product of close ethnographic research and understanding (see Richard Taruskin, *Stravinsky and the Russian Traditions: A Biography of the Works through* Mavra, two volumes (Oxford University Press, 1996)), meaning that presumably his own

musical 'rituals' were anything but arcane and mysterious, at least to himself. The argument cannot be extended to Birtwistle, who (as we have seen) is unambiguous about the importance of mystery to his concept of ritual.

119 Nyman, '"Punch and Judy"', p. 481.

120 Bell, *Ritual Theory*, p. 74.

121 Christopher Small, 'Performance as ritual: sketch for an enquiry into the true nature of a symphony concert', in Avron Levine White, ed., *Lost in Music: Culture, Style and the Musical Event* (London: Routledge, 1987), p. 8.

122 Ibid., p. 6.

123 Unattributed programme note for Pierrot Players concert at London's Queen Elizabeth Hall, 3 March 1970.

124 Pruslin, 'Punch and Judy'.

125 Nyman, '"Punch and Judy"', p. 481.

126 Ivan Hewett, 'The second coming', *Musical Times* (January 1995), p. 47.

127 Russell Hoban, *The Second Mrs Kong: An Original Opera Text* (London: Universal Edition, 1994), p. 2.

128 Tom Sutcliffe, review of Glyndebourne production of *The Second Mrs Kong*, *Musical Times* (July 1995), p. 373.

129 *HBRY*, p. 122.

130 Andrew Porter, 'Another Orpheus sings', *New Yorker* (23 June 1986), p. 87.

131 Francis Bacon, in Sylvester, *The Brutality of Fact*, p. 172.

2 Roles

1 Aristotle, 'On the art of poetry', p. 31.

2 Birtwistle, in an interview with Meirion Bowen, *The Guardian* (13 March 1986), p. 12.

3 Cook, *Music*, p. 111.

4 *HB*, pp. 14–15.

5 See *HB*, p. 173. Further consideration is given to this aspect of *Refrains and Choruses* in Chapter 5.

6 Griffiths, *New Sounds*, p. 188.

7 Theodor Adorno, 'Stravinsky: a dialectical portrait', in *Quasi una Fantasia: Essays on Modern Music*, trans. Rodney Livingstone (London: Verso, 1992), p. 168.

8 Birtwistle, in *HB*, p. 174.

9 Aristotle, 'On the art of poetry', p. 47.

10 Birtwistle, in *HB*, pp. 173–4.

11 Halliwell, *The Poetics of Aristotle*, pp. 121–2.

12 Ley, *A Short Introduction*, p. 49.

13 Halliwell, *The Poetics of Aristotle*, p. 187.

14 Birtwistle, in *HB*, p. 174.

15 Brown, 'Greece', p. 407.

16 Hartnoll, ed., *Oxford Companion*, p. 577.

17 Birtwistle, in *HB*, p. 174.

18 Brown, 'Greece', p. 409; p. 411.

19 Ibid., p. 411.

20 Arnold Whittall, *Music Since the First World War*, second edition (London: Dent, 1988), p. 231.

21 Elliott Carter, in David Schiff, *The Music of Elliott Carter* (London: Eulenberg, 1983), p. 198. Carter's exploration of instrumental role-play is influenced by similar devices in the music of Charles Ives; see Cross, *The Stravinsky Legacy*, p. 152.

22 Birtwistle, in Ford, *Composer to Composer*, p. 58.

23 These include one substantial and uncharacteristic verbatim repetition: three pages of instrumental material following the first verse of the Christopher Logue poem ([18]) are reprised exactly after the fourth verse ([54]).

24 See Arnold Whittall, review of *Meridian* and *Songs by Myself*, *Music and Letters*, 69/3 (1988), pp. 449–50; and Michael Nyman, '*Meridian*', note to compact disc recording of *Meridian*, NMC Recordings NMC D009.

25 See *HB*, p. 80.

26 Andrew Clements, in the programme booklet for 'Endless Parade', a festival of Birtwistle's music at London's Barbican Centre, 10–13 January 1988, p. 11.

27 Birtwistle, programme note for Endymion Ensemble performance of *Five Distances* at London's Queen Elizabeth Hall, 19 April 1996.

28 The origins of this idea lie in the linguistic theories of Ferdinand de Saussure, which argued that 'language is a system not of fixed, unalterable essences but of . . . relations between its constituent units'. Much structuralist and post-structuralist thought has subsequently concerned itself with 'relations between mutually conditioned elements of a system and not between self-contained essences' (John Sturrock, 'Introduction', in John Sturrock, ed., *Structuralism and Since: From Levi-Strauss to Derrida* (Oxford University Press, 1979), p. 10).

29 Birtwistle, programme note for *Five Distances*.

30 See Cross, 'Birtwistle's secret theatres', pp. 210–12. The form of *Verses for Ensembles* is discussed at greater length in Chapter 5.

31 David Osmond-Smith, *Berio* (Oxford University Press, 1991), p. 69.

32 Griffiths, *Modern Music*, p. 111.

33 Whittall, *Music*, p. 255.

34 *HB*, p. 52.

35 Birtwistle, in Lorraine, 'Territorial rites 2', p. 12.

36 Birtwistle, in *The Harrison Birtwistle Site*, http://filament.illumin.co.uk/birtwistle/verses.html.

37 Birtwistle, in Ford, *Composer to Composer*, p. 58.

38 Ibid.

39 Birtwistle, programme note to *For O, For O, the Hobbyhorse is Forgot* (held by Universal Edition).

40 Hans Keller, 'Metrical rhythms', *The Listener* (3 September 1981), p. 252.
41 *HBRY*, pp. 85–6.
42 Fred Everett Maus, 'Music as drama', *Music Theory Spectrum*, 10 (1988), pp. 65–8.
43 Ibid., p. 68.
44 Stephen Pruslin, programme note for the first performance of *Monodrama* at London's Queen Elizabeth Hall, 30 May 1967.
45 Ibid.
46 *HB*, p. 53.
47 Birtwistle, speaking on BBC Radio 3 broadcast of *Four Interludes for a Tragedy*, May 1991.
48 *HB*, p. 161.
49 Ibid., p. 163.
50 Strain 4 is reproduced as Ex. 5.2 in Chapter 5.
51 Aristotle, 'On the art of poetry', p. 41.
52 Michael Nyman, programme note to *Chanson de Geste* (held by Universal Edition).
53 Ibid.
54 David Beard, 'Birtwistle and serialism: *Three Sonatas for Nine Instruments*', paper delivered at a Theory and Analysis Graduate Study Day, Oxford University, 21 May 1998.
55 Nyman, 'Mr Birtwistle is out', p. 27. See *HBRY*, p. 29, for other instances of the two terms in Birtwistle's music.
56 See Lorraine, 'Territorial rites 2', p. 12.
57 This poem may be found in Robert Graves, *Collected Poems 1975* (London: Cassell, 1975), p. 402.
58 Birtwistle, in *The Harrison Birtwistle Site*, http://filament.illumin.co.uk/birtwistle/secrettheatre.html.
59 Birtwistle, on BBC Radio 3 broadcast of *Secret Theatre*, 27 May 1991.
60 The form of *Secret Theatre* is discussed in more detail in Chapter 5.
61 Cross, 'Birtwistle's secret theatres', p. 223; Cross, *The Stravinsky Legacy*, p. 161.
62 Cross, 'Birtwistle's secret theatres', p. 220.
63 'Notes made by Harrison Birtwistle prior to composing *Secret Theatre*', included in the programme booklet for 'Response', a weekend of concerts by the London Sinfonietta at London's Queen Elizabeth Hall, 16–18 January 1987; reprinted in *HBRY*, pp. 26–8. According to Michael Hall, the extracts printed in this programme booklet come from 'some 66 pages of random jottings' (Michael Hall, 'The sanctity of the context: Birtwistle's recent music', *Musical Times* (January 1988), p. 14). Birtwistle added a cautionary note when the extracts were reproduced: 'The ideas set down in these random jottings do not necessarily appear in the finished composition.'
64 'Notes made by Harrison Birtwistle'.
65 Andrew Clements, programme note to London Sinfonietta performance of *Secret Theatre* at London's Queen Elizabeth Hall, 4 May 1996.

66 Philip Tagg, *Kojak – 50 Seconds of Television Music: Towards the Analysis of Affect in Popular Music* (Gothenburg: University of Gothenburg, 1979), p. 142.

67 Cross, 'Birtwistle's secret theatres', p. 224.

68 Günter Grass, *From the Diary of a Snail*, trans. Ralph Manheim (London: Picador, 1989).

69 Arnold Whittall, review of *Melencolia I*, *Music and Letters*, 59/1 (1978), p. 110. See also Arnold Whittall, 'Modernist aesthetics, modernist music: some analytical perspectives', in James M. Baker et al., eds., *Music Theory in Concept and Practice* (New York: University of Rochester Press, 1997), pp. 173–7.

70 Birtwistle, programme note to London Philharmonic Orchestra performance of *Endless Parade* at London's Queen Elizabeth Hall, 16 January 1995.

71 Ibid.

72 Further details on the work's motives are given in Chapter 5.

73 Birtwistle, programme note to *Endless Parade*.

74 Birtwistle, in an interview with Stephen Pettitt, *The Times*, 'Weekend' (8 May 1993), p. 14.

75 Jonathan Cross, 'From opera house to concert hall', *Tempo* (April 1995), p. 37.

76 *Panic* receives further discussion in Chapter 7.

77 Birtwistle misremembers the text slightly. The original poem, 'A Musical Instrument', may be found in *The Poetical Works of Elizabeth Barrett Browning* (London: Smith, Elder, and Co., 1897), pp. 537–8.

78 See *HBRY*, p. 128.

79 J. A. Cuddon, *The Penguin Dictionary of Literary Terms and Literary Theory*, third edition (London: Penguin, 1992), p. 253.

80 Ovid, *Metamorphoses I–IV*, trans. D. E. Hill (Warminster: Aris and Phillips, 1985), p. 43.

3 Texts

1 Lawrence Kramer, *Music and Poetry: The Nineteenth Century and After* (Berkeley: University of California Press, 1984), pp. 129–30.

2 See, for instance, Christopher Wintle, 'Webern's lyric character', in Kathryn Bailey, ed., *Webern Studies* (Cambridge University Press, 1996), pp. 231–2. Wintle elaborates upon the distinction by quoting Hegel and Carl Dahlhaus.

3 David Brackett, *Interpreting Popular Music* (Cambridge University Press, 1995), p. 30.

4 Luciano Berio, *Two Interviews with Rossana Dalmonte and Balint Andras Varga*, trans. David Osmond-Smith (London: Marion Boyars, 1985), p. 114.

5 Alain Robbe-Grillet, 'La Plage', in *Instantanés* (Paris: Les Editions de Minuit, 1962), pp. 61–73.

6 Michael Hall suggests, instead, that the birds are represented by the fast repeating pattern in the marimba in the seventh aria (*HBRY*, p. 18).

7 Helen Waddell, *Mediaeval Latin Lyrics*, fifth edition (London: Constable, 1948).

8 See Edward Levy, 'Text setting', in John Vinton, ed., *Dictionary of Twentieth-Century Music* (London: Thames and Hudson, 1974), pp. 740–1.

9 See Osmond-Smith, *Berio*, pp. 67–70.

10 Kramer, *Music and Poetry*, p. 169. Kramer cites Edward E. Lowinsky.

11 According to Michael Hall, these translations are 'taken from *The Greek Anthology*, with an English translation, Harvard University Press, 1916–18' (*HB*, p. 156).

12 *HB*, p. 162.

13 *HBRY*, p. 136.

14 These songs receive detailed consideration in Jonathan Cross, 'Issues of analysis in Birtwistle's *Four Songs of Autumn*', in Michael Finnissy and Roger Wright, eds., *New Music '89* (Oxford University Press, 1989), pp. 16–23.

15 The vocal line for this song is reproduced in *HBRY*, p. 73.

16 The untitled movement separating the Coda and the first Sappho setting (Cantus I) recalls Entr'acte IV; the end of Cantus I and the middle of Entr'acte III (2nd version) both recall Entr'acte I.

17 *Cantata* will be discussed in the following section of this chapter.

18 Andrew Clements says that Birtwistle chose the title 'for three reasons: that syllable seems to occur in a large number of the fragments; the Greek word for "fragment" is *agma*; and the idea of capturing and holding these fragments . . . reminded him of the image of death's hunting net wielded by Clytemnestra in Aeschylus's *Agamemnon*'. Andrew Clements, in the programme booklet for 'Endless Parade', a festival of Birtwistle's music at London's Barbican Centre, 10–13 January 1988, pp. 48–9.

19 The texts for *Songs by Myself* and *Words Overheard* appear in *Contemporary Music Review*, 5 (1989), pp. 97–8.

20 *HB*, p. 157.

21 Birtwistle, on BBC Radio 3 broadcast of *Ring a Dumb Carillon*, 27 May 1991.

22 *Musica Britannica*, X–XII (London: Stainer and Bell, 1955–61).

23 John Potter, 'Reconstructing lost voices', in Tess Knighton and David Fallows, eds., *Companion to Medieval and Renaissance Music* (London: Dent, 1992), p. 313.

24 Ausonius' verse comes, once again, from Waddell's *Mediaeval Latin Lyrics*.

25 Kramer, *Music and Poetry*, p. 127.

26 Ibid., p. 169.

27 Hegel, in Wintle, 'Webern's lyric character', p. 231.

28 Schoenberg, in Kramer, *Music and Poetry*, p. 168.

29 Clements, 'Endless Parade', p. 44.

30 Michael Hamburger, 'Introduction', in Michael Hamburger, ed., *Poems of Paul Celan* (London: Anvil Press Poetry, 1988), pp. 17–18.

31 Kramer, *Music and Poetry*, p. 168.

32 Ibid.

33 See Anne C. Shreffler, *Webern and the Lyric Impulse: Songs and Fragments on Poems of Georg Trakl* (Oxford: Clarendon Press, 1994), pp. 202–3.

34 From a letter written by Dr J. I. Garstin, *Opera* (October 1991), p. 1137.

35 Andrew Clements, '*Gawain* – an opera about people', *Opera* (August 1991), p. 879.

36 Birtwistle, programme note to *Songs by Myself* (held by Universal Edition).

37 Whittall, review of *Meridian* and *Songs by Myself*, p. 450; *HBRY*, pp. 36–9.

38 Hamburger, 'Introduction', p. 22.

39 Ibid., p. 29.

40 Ibid., p. 28.

41 *HBRY*, pp. 138–9.

42 Hamburger, 'Introduction', p. 30.

43 Ibid., p. 18.

44 Ibid., p. 23.

45 Birtwistle himself mentioned this in an interview prior to the British premiere of *Pulse Shadows* at the Queen Elizabeth Hall, London, 29 April 1996.

46 *HBRY*, p. 88.

47 Clements, 'Endless Parade', p. 44.

48 Levy, 'Text setting', p. 734.

49 Anton Webern, *Letters to Hildegard Jone and Josef Humplik*, ed. Josef Polnauer, trans. Cornelius Cardew (London: Universal Edition, 1967), p. 43.

50 Pierre Boulez, *Stocktakings from an Apprenticeship*, trans. Stephen Walsh (Oxford: Clarendon Press, 1991), p. 42.

51 Célestin Deliège, 'The convergence of two poetic systems', in William Glock, ed., *Pierre Boulez: A Symposium* (London: Eulenberg, 1986), pp. 99–126.

52 Dai Griffiths, review of Anne C. Shreffler, *Webern and the Lyric Impulse*, *Music Analysis*, 16/1 (March 1997), p. 152.

53 Countering this position is the argument that the specific representational burden of pieces like *Erwartung*, *Pierrot Lunaire* or *Lulu* – pieces that are at once centrally concerned with women in states of mental derangement, *and* pivotal to the development and dissemination of modernist musical styles – remains sedimented in modernist musical language more generally. This proposal has been put forward by Susan McClary ('Terminal prestige', pp. 74–5). The prominence of hysterical women in Birtwistle's operas – Pretty Polly, Mrs Green, the Dark Sister in *Bow Down*, the Oracle, Morgan – can certainly make it difficult to hear his solo songs without these associations.

4 Times

1 Birtwistle, in *HB*, p. 74.

2 The positions of these and many other composers on this subject are documented in Jonathan D. Kramer, *The Time of Music: New Meanings, New Temporalities, New Listening Strategies* (New York: Schirmer Books, 1988).

3 Birtwistle, in *HB*, p. 22.

4 Stephen Pruslin, note to compact disc recording of *Précis*, Clarinet Classics CC0019.

5 Peter Zinovieff, note to LP recording of *Chronometer*, Argo ZRG 790.

6 *HB*, p. 105.

7 G. W. F. Hegel, *Phenomenology of Spirit*, trans. A. V. Miller (Oxford University Press, 1977), p. 27.

8 See R. Pattman, 'Commitments to time in Reformation Protestant theology, Hegelian Idealism, and Marxism', in B. Cullen, ed., *Hegel Today* (Aldershot: Avebury Press, 1988), pp. 102–15.

9 Adorno's writings on time are scattered throughout his work. For a more extended account of his views, and the problems that beset them, see Robert Adlington, 'Temporality in post-tonal music', D.Phil. thesis, University of Sussex (1997), pp. 160–95.

10 This is a rough and ready summary of Adorno's position. In actual fact, his dialectical philosophy simultaneously made necessary music's acknowledgement of clock time, as an ever-present cautionary reminder of that which must be resisted (see, for instance, Theodor Adorno, 'The schema of mass culture', trans. Nicholas Walker, in J. M. Bernstein, ed., *The Culture Industry: Selected Essays on Modern Culture* (London: Routledge, 1991) p. 64). It is the unchallenged hegemony of clock time that Adorno perceives in Stravinsky that is most dangerous.

11 See my own 'Musical temporality: perspectives from Adorno and de Man', *Repercussions*, 6/1 (1997); and Cross, *The Stravinsky Legacy*, pp. 81–8.

12 Nyman, 'Harrison Birtwistle', p. 122.

13 Isaac Newton, *Sir Isaac Newton's Mathematical Principles of Natural Philosophy and his System of the World*, trans. F. Cajori (Berkeley: University of California Press, 1962), pp. 6–8.

14 Birtwistle, in *HB*, p. 175.

15 *HB*, p. 84.

16 Birtwistle, in *HB*, p. 175.

17 Bowen, 'Harrison Birtwistle', p. 70.

18 *HB*, p. 11. See also Whittall, 'Modernist aesthetics', pp. 168 ff. In his second book Hall slightly alters his position (see *HBRY*, p. 6).

19 Birtwistle, in *HB*, p. 175.

20 This intriguing quotation is discussed further in Chapter 6.

21 Birtwistle, in *HB*, p. 144.

22 *HB*, p. 74.

23 Zinovieff 1986, p. 2.

24 The relationship of music and tense has been discussed by, amongst others, Carolyn Abbate and Robert Samuels. See Carolyn Abbate, *Unsung Voices: Opera and Musical Narrative in the Nineteenth Century* (Princeton University Press, 1991), and Robert Samuels, 'Music as text: Mahler, Schumann and issues in analysis', in Anthony Pople, ed., *Theory,*

Analysis and Meaning in Music (Cambridge University Press, 1994), pp. 152–63.

25 There is reason to believe that this 'Composer's Note' is not actually by Birtwistle, although it is attributed to him in the score of *Pulse Field*, and it presumably accurately represents his thoughts about the piece. The original typescript of the note, kept in the Rambert Dance Company's archive, cites the composer Glyn Perrin as the author. The 'Performance Notes', on the other hand, do appear to be by Birtwistle.

26 Birtwistle, in *The Harrison Birtwistle Site*, http://filament.illumin.co.uk/birtwistle/basics.html.

27 Birtwistle, in *HB*, p. 177.

28 Birtwistle includes the labyrinth in the score of *Silbury Air*; it is reproduced in full in Cross, *The Stravinsky Legacy*, p. 130.

29 William E. Benjamin, 'A theory of musical metre', *Music Perception*, 1/4 (1984), p. 373.

30 This argument underpins the anti-avant-garde polemic of George Rochberg, and the work on musical temporality of Barbara Barry (which is much influenced by Rochberg). See George Rochberg, 'The structure of time in music: traditional and contemporary ramifications and consequences', in J. T. Fraser and N. Lawrence, eds., *The Study of Time II* (Berlin: Springer-Verlag, 1975), pp. 136–49; and Barbara Barry, *Musical Time: The Sense of Order* (New York: Pendragon Press, 1990). David Epstein's wholesale omission of post-tonal repertoire from his mammoth study of time in music is a direct consequence of his belief that, 'To speak of time is virtually to speak of motion': see David Epstein, *Shaping Time: Music, the Brain, and Performance* (New York: Schirmer, 1995), p. 8.

31 This idea of temporal stratification receives further discussion in Chapter 6.

32 Stephen Pruslin, programme note to the first complete performance of *Harrison's Clocks* at the Pittville Pump Room, Cheltenham, 13 July 1998. See also Birtwistle, in *HBRY*, p. 149.

33 Ligeti in an interview with Péter Várnai; quoted in Jane Piper Clendinning, 'The pattern-meccanico compositions of György Ligeti', *Perspectives of New Music*, 31/1 (1993), p. 193.

34 For an elaboration of this point of view, see Barry, *Musical Time*, passim. For Barry, 'musical form orders and articulates time' (p. 66) and 'motion is characteristic of time articulation' (p. 259).

35 Birtwistle, in *HB*, p. 175.

36 Stephen Walsh, 'Harrison Birtwistle', in Sadie, ed., *New Grove*, vol. II, p. 738.

37 *HB*, p. 74.

38 Walsh, 'Harrison Birtwistle', p. 738.

39 Birtwistle, in Ford, *Composer to Composer*, p. 55.

40 *HBRY*, p. 96.

41 Birtwistle, in *HB*, p. 149.

42 Birtwistle, in *HB*, p. 175.

43 Birtwistle talks of the piece's 'modes of change'; see *HB*, p. 177.
44 See the discussion of 'the sanctity of the context' in the next chapter.
45 Birtwistle, in *HB*, p. 152.
46 Andrew Clements, in the programme booklet for 'Endless Parade', a festival of Birtwistle's music at London's Barbican Centre, 10–13 January 1988, p. 50.
47 The tendency of Birtwistle's new compositional concern for context to give rise to a form of continuity that highlights *the changing moment* over the route undertaken is a theme taken up in the next chapter.
48 Birtwistle, programme note to *Endless Parade* (held by Universal Edition).
49 The formal design of *Endless Parade* is described more fully in Chapter 5.
50 *HBRY*, p. 18.
51 Birtwistle, in *HBRY*, p. 143.
52 Birtwistle, in Boosey and Hawkes Press Release, 9 January 1998.
53 Birtwistle, in Lorraine, 'Territorial rites 2', p. 16.
54 Birtwistle, in Boosey and Hawkes Press Release, 9 January 1998. See also Birtwistle in *HBRY*, p. 145.
55 Birtwistle, in Boosey and Hawkes Press Release, 9 January 1998.
56 Ibid.

5 Sections

1 Walsh, 'Harrison Birtwistle', p. 737.
2 Jonathan Cross gives a comprehensive overview of 'block form' in *The Stravinsky Legacy* – see pp. 17–80.
3 Griffiths, *Modern Music*, p. 141.
4 Boulez, in Cross, *The Stravinsky Legacy*, p. 150.
5 Birtwistle, in *HB*, p. 173.
6 *HB*, p. 11.
7 Clements, programme note to *Refrains and Choruses*.
8 For a more detailed account of this section of the work, see Jonathan Cross, 'Music theory and the challenge of modern music: Birtwistle's *Refrains and Choruses*', in Pople, ed., *Theory, Analysis and Meaning in Music*, pp. 184–94.
9 David Lindley, *Lyric* (London: Methuen, 1985), p. 31.
10 This work is discussed in more detail in the next chapter.
11 This suggestion is made by Michael Hall in a programme note to *Three Movements with Fanfares*.
12 A fascinating analysis in Michael Hall's book shows how *all* the work's musical material is derived from Verse 1, so that each successive verse is essentially a reprise of the first (see *HB*, pp. 33–48). However, the musical surface more obviously presents the alternating verse scheme adumbrated in my description.
13 *HB*, p. 152.
14 Birtwistle's piece – a lusty setting of three ninth-century Latin verses, each separated by a 'Refrain' – appeared alongside songs by Peter Maxwell Davies, Colin Matthews, Dominic Muldowney and John Woolrich.

15 This work is discussed in more detail in Chapter 6.

16 Richard Middleton, writing in 1990, asserts that, in spite of the various formal innovations brought about by the advent of progressive rock, it remains the case that 'most rock songs are strophic' (Richard Middleton, *Studying Popular Music* (Milton Keynes: Open University Press, 1990), p. 48).

17 Birtwistle, in Hall, 'Composer and producer speak', in programme booklet for English National Opera production of *The Mask of Orpheus*, May 1986.

18 Birtwistle, in Griffiths, *New Sounds*, p. 191.

19 Nyman, 'Harrison Birtwistle', pp. 119–20.

20 Edgard Varèse, 'The liberation of sound', in Benjamin Boretz and Edward T. Cone, eds., *Perspectives on American Composers* (New York: Norton, 1971), p. 25.

21 *HB*, pp. 159–60.

22 These are described in Cross, 'Lines and circles'.

23 For a rather different account of the structure of *Verses for Ensembles*, see Cross, 'Birtwistle's secret theatres', pp. 210–12.

24 *HBRY*, p. 149.

25 See note to the score of *Verses for Ensembles*.

26 Birtwistle, in Lorraine, 'Territorial rites 1', p. 8.

27 The music contained in this manuscript is reprinted in *Musica Britannica*, XXXVI (London: Stainer and Bell, 1975).

28 Michael Nyman, 'Birtwistle's rituals', *The Listener* (27 August 1970), p. 285.

29 Edward T. Cone, 'Stravinsky: the progress of a method', in *Perspectives of New Music*, 1/1 (1962), pp. 18–26.

30 Cone, 'Stravinsky', p. 18.

31 Michael Nyman, 'Two New Works by Birtwistle', *Tempo*, 88 (1969), p. 47.

32 These are more fully discussed in Chapter 2.

33 Cone, 'Stravinsky', p. 19.

34 Taruskin, *Stravinsky*, vol. II, pp. 1486–93.

35 Taruskin, *Stravinsky*, vol. I, p. 965.

36 Michael Nyman, programme note to *An Imaginary Landscape*.

37 Birtwistle has described the *Symphonies of Winds* as 'one of the great masterpieces of this century . . . and certainly one of the most original, in that it's to do with the juxtaposition of material without any sense of development' (Birtwistle, in Cross, *The Stravinsky Legacy*, p. 70).

38 Ibid.

39 Cone, 'Stravinsky', p. 19.

40 See Cross, *The Stravinsky Legacy*, pp. 26–8 for a critique of this aspect of Cone's analysis, and an overview of other approaches to the *Symphonies of Winds*. An additional, recent article on the piece appeared too late to be included in Cross's discussion: Alexander Rehding, 'Towards a "logic of discontinuity" in Stravinsky's *Symphonies of Wind Instruments*: Hasty, Kramer and Straus reconsidered', *Music Analysis*, 17/1 (1998), pp. 39–65.

41 Birtwistle, in *HB*, p. 177.

42 Birtwistle, in *The Harrison Birtwistle Site*, http://filament.illumin.co.uk/
    birtwistle/carmen.html.

43 Taruskin, *Stravinsky*, I, p. 957.

44 A comprehensive account of the structure of this work is given in Brian
    Robison, '*Carmen arcadiae mechanicae perpetuum*: toward a methodology
    for analyzing Harrison Birtwistle's music since 1977', Doctor of Musical Arts
    thesis, Cornell University, 1999.

45 Cone, 'Stravinsky', p. 19.

46 See Alison Deadman, 'Mechanical arcady: the development of an aesthetic in
    Birtwistle's orchestral works written for the London Sinfonietta between
    1977 and 1984', M. Phil. thesis, University of Leeds (1990), pp. 56–69;
    Robison, '*Carmen arcadiae mechanicae perpetuum*', passim; and Cross, *The
    Stravinsky Legacy*, pp. 71–8. Deadman's analysis differs considerably from
    Cross's and Robison's, and the latter two disagree over the identity of the
    sections starting at b. 83, b. 96 and b. 131. Robison gives exhaustive accounts
    of Birtwistle's transformational methods.

47 Stockhausen, in Kramer, *The Time of Music*, p. 201.

48 G. W. Hopkins, 'Stockhausen', in Sadie, ed., *New Grove*, vol. XVIII, p. 152.

49 Cone, 'Stravinsky', p. 20.

50 Birtwistle, in *HB*, p. 147.

51 See Griffiths, *Modern Music*, p. 321.

52 However, the fact that there are fifteen sections does suggest a connection, at
    some level, with Birtwistle's eight original pieces and the seven links that join
    them together.

53 Michael Nyman, programme note to *An Imaginary Landscape*.

54 Birtwistle, in *HB*, p. 149.

55 Ibid., p. 145; p. 146.

56 Ibid., p. 133.

57 *Secret Theatre* is introduced in Chapter 2.

58 Cross, 'Birtwistle's secret theatres', p. 220.

59 See Chapter 2.

60 A broader pattern may be discerned in Birtwistle's choice of emphasised
    pitches. In the 1960s, as in the 1980s, it is D that appears to be favoured –
    Refrains and Choruses, *Monody for Corpus Christi* (especially the 'Fanfare'
    movement), *The World is Discovered*, *Tragœdia* and parts of *Punch and Judy*
    all endow it with a special function. In the 1970s, E becomes predominant, in
    works including *Meridian*, *The Fields of Sorrow*, *The Triumph of Time*,
    Melencolia I, *Silbury Air* and *...agm...*; and E once again appears to be more
    significant in important works of the 1990s, including *The Second Mrs Kong*,
    Panic, many of the Celan settings and *Exody*.

61 Birtwistle, in *HB*, pp. 148–9.

62 *HBRY*, p. 16; p. 92.

63 Jean-Jacques Nattiez, *Music and Discourse: Toward a Semiology of Music*,
    trans. Carolyn Abbate (Princeton University Press, 1990), p. 128.

64 Kirsty Kirkpatrick, 'Perceived structure in Debussy's *Jeux*: an empirical investigation', unpublished paper, Lancaster University (1994), p. 18.
65 Ibid.
66 Birtwistle, in *The Harrison Birtwistle Site*, http://filament.illumin.co.uk/ birtwistle/carmen.html.
67 Elma Sanders, 'Frieze', in Jane Turner, ed., *The Dictionary of Art*, vol. XI (London: Macmillan, 1996), p. 790.
68 Ibid., p. 791.
69 Stephen Pruslin, programme note for a performance by the Arditti String Quartet and Capricorn of *Pulse Shadows* at London's South Bank Centre, 29 April 1996.
70 Lorraine, 'Territorial rites 1', p. 8.
71 See the Chronological list of works at the end of this book.
72 Note in score of *Pulse Shadows*.

6 Layers

1 *HB*, p. 20.
2 *HB*, p. 8. Hall's more recent book generally sticks to the same argument – noting, for instance, the composer's open claim that even the lengthy and complex *Gawain* is built on a 'fundamental melodic line' (*HBRY*, p. 92).
3 Michael Hall devotes a section of his second book to 'Works Focusing on Melody' (see *HBRY*, pp. 81–9).
4 Julian Johnson offered this succinct description in the course of a research seminar at the University of Sussex in June 1998.
5 Lorraine, 'Territorial rites 1', p. 5.
6 Birtwistle, speaking at a Colloquium of the Institute of Advanced Musical Studies, King's College, London, 17 March 1998.
7 Birtwistle, in *The Harrison Birtwistle Site*, http://filament.illumin.co.uk/ birtwistle/basics.html.
8 *HB*, p. 95; p. 26.
9 Birtwistle, in *HB*, p. 177.
10 Klee, in Hajo Düchting, *Paul Klee: Painting and Music* (Munich: Prestel, 1997), pp. 66–7. See also Paul Klee, *Notebooks: The Thinking Eye*, ed. Jürg Spiller (London: Lund Humphries, 1961), pp. 369 ff.
11 Both of these works are reproduced in Düchting, *Paul Klee*, p. 42.
12 Klee, *The Thinking Eye*, p. 105; see also Paul Klee, *Pedagogical Sketchbook*, trans. Sibyl Moholy-Nagy (London: Faber, 1968), p. 16.
13 Klee, *Pedagogical Sketchbook*, p. 16.
14 Klee, *The Thinking Eye*, pp. 325–6.
15 Birtwistle, in *HB*, p. 173.
16 Peter Cooke, 'Heterophony', in Sadie, ed., *New Grove*, vol. VIII, p. 537.
17 Klee, *The Thinking Eye*, p. 107. See especially examples 11 and 13.
18 *HB*, p. 20.

19 *HBRY*, p. 34.

20 *HBRY*, p. 179.

21 Michael Hall identifies the chorale melody as 'Wer nur den lieben Gott lässt walten'.

22 See Michael Nyman, 'With reference to Birtwistle's "Medusa"', *The Listener* (13 November 1969), p. 676.

23 Webern, in Martin Zenck, 'Tradition as authority and provocation: Anton Webern's confrontation with Johann Sebastian Bach', in Don O. Franklin, ed., *Bach Studies* (Cambridge University Press, 1989), p. 316.

24 Zenck, 'Tradition', p. 318.

25 Birtwistle sets, respectively, BWV 637, 691, 620, 728 and 614.

26 Birtwistle sets BWV 599, 639, 617, 619, 628, 615, 622 and (once again) 637. This is the order in which they appear in the provisional Boosey and Hawkes score, although the first performance followed a slightly different sequence.

27 Nyman, 'Birtwistle's "Medusa"', p. 676.

28 Taruskin, *Stravinsky*, vol. II, p. 1317.

29 *Tempo*, 81 (Summer 1967).

30 See *HB*, p. 20; pp. 37–8; pp. 100–1; and Robison, '*Carmen arcadiae mechanicae perpetuum*', Chapter 4.

31 Robison, ibid.

32 Birtwistle, in Ford, *Composer to Composer*, pp. 54–5.

33 Birtwistle in *HB*, p. 148.

34 Philip Tagg, 'From refrain to rave: the decline of figure and the rise of ground', in *Popular Music*, 13/2 (March 1994), p. 216.

35 *HBRY*, p. x.

36 R. H. Hoppin, *Medieval Music* (New York: Norton, 1978), p. 420.

37 This was not Birtwistle's first arrangement of Machaut's piece. Birtwistle came across the piece in 1955 as a student in Manchester, where he made a transcription of it for two clarinets and bassoon (Birtwistle, programme note to *Les Hoquets du Gardien de la Lune*). This arrangement was later expanded for military band during Birtwistle's national service (Andrew Clements, programme note to *Machaut à ma manière*).

38 Ockeghem's piece is transcribed in Arnold Schering, ed., *Geschichte der Musik in Beispielen: Dreihundertfünfzig Tonsätze aus Neun Jahrhunderten* (Leipzig: Breitkopf und Härtel, 1931), pp. 44–8.

39 Leeman L. Perkins, 'Ockeghem, Johannes', in Sadie, ed., *New Grove*, vol. XIII, p. 493.

40 Birtwistle, programme note to *Les Hoquets du Gardien de la Lune*.

41 Birtwistle, programme note to *Mercure – poses plastiques*.

42 *HB*, pp. 9–10.

43 *HB*, Chapter 3.

44 Robison, '*Carmen arcadiae mechanicae perpetuum*'.

45 See, for instance, *HBRY*, *passim*; David Beard, 'An analysis and sketch study of Harrison Birtwistle's early instrumental music (c. 1957–77)', D.Phil.

thesis, University of Oxford (1999); Michael Taylor, 'Birtwistle's first *The Triumph of Time*', *Mitteilung der Paul Sacher Stiftung*, 8 (March 1995), pp. 17–21; Michael Taylor, 'Harrison Birtwistle: *Endless Parade* (1986–87)', in Felix Meyer, ed., *Settling New Scores: Music Manuscripts from the Paul Sacher Foundation* (Basel: Paul Sacher Foundation, 1998), pp. 41–3.

46 *HB*, p. 155.

47 Gustave Reese, *Music in the Renaissance*, revised edition (London: Dent and Sons Ltd, 1959), p. 643.

48 This aspect of Isaac's music was presumably significant for Webern, who prepared an edition of Isaac's *Choralis Constantinus* for his doctoral thesis.

49 Peter Dickinson, review of *The World is Discovered*, *Musical Times* (November 1963), p. 808.

50 *HB*, p. 23.

51 Stephen Pruslin, 'Second Taverner Fantasia', in Stephen Pruslin, ed., *Peter Maxwell Davies: Studies from Two Decades* (London: Boosey and Hawkes, 1979), p. 30.

52 Nyman, 'Harrison Birtwistle', p. 122.

53 Webern, *Letters*, p. 48. The English edition of these letters was published in 1967, and *Nomos* was begun at the very end of the same year, suggesting that Webern's comment may have provided the idea for the piece.

54 Roger Smalley, 'Birtwistle's *Nomos*', *Tempo*, 86 (1968), p. 7.

55 Note in the score.

56 Smalley, ibid.

57 Birtwistle, 'Notes made prior to composing *Secret Theatre*', reproduced in *HBRY*, pp. 26–8.

58 Ibid.

59 Klee, *The Thinking Eye*, pp. 285–7.

60 See, for instance, Jonathan W. Bernard, *The Music of Edgard Varèse* (New Haven: Yale University Press, 1987).

61 Klee, *The Thinking Eye*, p. 237.

62 Ibid., p. 299.

63 Ibid., p. 300.

64 Birtwistle comments on the connections between the two pieces in his interview with Paul Griffiths, which he gave while he was writing *Earth Dances* (Griffiths, *New Sounds*, pp. 188–9).

65 Hall, 'The sanctity of the context', p. 15.

66 Birtwistle, in an interview with Meirion Bowen, *The Guardian* (13 March 1986), p. 12.

67 See Cross, *The Stravinsky Legacy*, pp. 81–131.

68 The graphical methods used in Figure 6.2 are indebted to Jonathan Bernard's analytical method, as used in his book on Varèse.

69 See Taylor, 'Harrison Birtwistle: *Endless Parade*'.

70 Griffiths, *New Sounds*, p. 189.

71 Ibid., p. 188.

72 Hall, 'The sanctity of the context', p. 15.

73 *HB*, p. 77.

74 Clements, programme note for the first performance of *Slow Frieze* at London's South Bank Centre, 26 April 1996.

7 Audiences

1   Bowen, 'Harrison Birtwistle', p. 60. This description was later taken up by Michael Hall (*HB*, p. 12).

2   *HBRY*, p. 130.

3   *HBRY*, p. 1.

4   Jonathan Cross, 'Thoughts on first hearing Sir Harrison Birtwistle's "Panic"', *Tempo*, 195 (January 1996), pp. 195–6.

5   Robert Maycock, review of Last Night of the Proms, *The Independent*, Section 2 (18 September 1995), p. 10.

6   Birtwistle, in Cook, *Music*, p. 40.

7   Note in the score of *Panic*.

8   *HBRY*, p. 130.

9   David Bruce, 'Challenging the system', *Musical Times* (April 1996), pp. 11–16. Bruce notes the piece's interleaving of moments of structural clarity and obscurity, but argues that the latter are contained by being positioned within a set of orientational frames – and are in any case 'only moments . . . [that] *temporarily* threaten the work's structure' (p. 16; my emphasis). For Bruce, 'Most of the music may be wild and unruly in character, and may even come under such anarchic "attacks", but balance and context are still the primary organisational concerns' (p. 11). This reading is offered essentially as a recommended way of listening to the piece (there is little in Bruce's reading that could not be heard in another way), and as an interpretation it is driven by the belief that Birtwistle is a modernist composer, and that, 'for the "modernist" . . . there is still the need for some kind of overall integration . . . whose authority can then be challenged' (p. 11). My own preference is to remain open to the ways in which Birtwistle's music eludes integration – even integration of a modernistically 'challenged' sort.

10 See *HBRY*, p. 1.

11 Peter Conrad, 'A little knight music', *The Observer*, Magazine (May 1991), p. 54.

12 Birtwistle, in *HB*, pp. 147–8.

13 *HBRY*, p. x.

14 Birtwistle, in *HB*, p. 150.

15 Robison, '*Carmen arcadiae mechanicae perpetuum*'.

16 Francis Bacon, in Sylvester, *The Brutality of Fact*, p. 17; p. 54.

17 Dai Griffiths, 'Genre: grammar school boy music', *Critical Musicology Newsletter*, 3 (1995), p. 2.

18 Griffiths, 'The high analysis of low music'.

19 Theodor Adorno, 'Vers une musique informelle', in *Quasi una Fantasia*, p. 322.
20 Griffiths, 'Genre', p. 2.
21 Theodor Adorno, 'Music and new music', in *Quasi una Fantasia*, p. 255.
22 Adorno, 'Music and new music', p. 256; p. 260.
23 Bruce, 'Challenging the system', p. 16.

Chronological list of works

This list follows the numbering used in Michael Hall's two books, to allow easier comparison. In some instances Hall gives separate work numbers to pieces that are considered as part of a larger work in this book: cross-references are included beneath the relevant entries. My list provides basic instrumentation and date of completion only. Readers requiring fuller details are referred to the 'Catalogue of Works' in *HBRY* (pp. 154–91).

1 *Refrains and Choruses* for wind quintet.
1957

2 *Monody for Corpus Christi* for soprano, flute, horn and violin.
1959

3 *Three Sonatas for Nine Instruments.*
1960 (unpublished)

4 *Précis* for piano.
1960

5 *The World is Discovered.* Six instrumental movements after Heinrich Isaac (1450–1517), for two flutes, oboe, cor anglais, two clarinets (second doubling basset horn or bass clarinet), two horns, two bassoons, harp and guitar.
1961

6 *Entr'actes* for flute, viola and harp.
1962 (not published separately; discussed under 11)

7 *Chorales for Orchestra.*
1963

8 *Narration: A Description of the Passing of a Year* for a cappella chorus.
1963

9 *Music for Sleep.* A lullaby for children under eleven to perform, for children's voices, piano and percussion (at least three players).
1963

10 *Three Movements with Fanfares* for chamber orchestra.
1964

11 *Entr'actes and Sappho Fragments* for soprano, flute, oboe, violin, viola, harp and percussion.
1964

12 *Ring a Dumb Carillon* for soprano (doubling suspended cymbals), clarinet and percussion.
1965

13 *Carmen Paschale.* Motet for SATB with organ obligato.
1965

14 *Tragœdia* for flute, oboe, clarinet, horn and bassoon (all doubling claves), two violins, viola, cello and harp.
1965

15 *Verses* for clarinet and piano.
1965

16 *The Mark of the Goat.* Dramatic cantata for actors, singers, two choruses, three melody instruments, three players at one piano, large and small percussion ensemble.
1966

17 *The Visions of Francesco Petrarca.* Allegory for baritone, mime ensemble, chamber ensemble and school orchestra.
1966 (withdrawn)

18 *Punch and Judy*. A tragical comedy or comical tragedy in one act for singers, mime dancers and chamber ensemble.
1967

19 *Chorale from a Toy Shop*. First version for flute, oboe or clarinet, clarinet or cor anglais, horn or trombone, bassoon or tuba. Second version for two trumpets, horn, trombone and tuba.
1967 (first version); 1978 (second version)

20 *Monodrama* for soprano, speaker and chamber ensemble.
1967 (withdrawn)

21 *Three Lessons in a Frame* for piano solo, flute (doubling piccolo), clarinet, violin, cello and percussion.
1967 (withdrawn)

22 *Nomos* for four amplified instruments (flute, clarinet, horn, bassoon) and orchestra (without violins).
1968

23 *Linoi* for clarinet in A (with extension down to C) and piano.
1968

24 *Four Interludes for a Tragedy* for basset clarinet in A and tape.
1968

25 *Verses for Ensembles* for woodwind quintet, brass quintet and percussion.
1969

26 *Some Petals from my Twickenham Herbarium* for piccolo, clarinet, viola, cello, piano and bells.
1969

27 *Down by the Greenwood Side*. A dramatic pastoral for soprano, actors, mime and chamber ensemble.
1969

28 *Cantata* for soprano, flute (doubling piccolo), clarinet (doubling high-pitched B♭ clarinet), violin (doubling viola), cello, piano (doubling celesta) and glockenspiel (doubling small bongo).
1969

29 *Ut heremita solus*. An arrangement of the motet by Ockeghem (*c.* 1425–95) for flute (doubling piccolo and alto flute), clarinet (doubling bass clarinet), viola, cello, piano and glockenspiel.
1969

30 *Hoquetus David*. An arrangement of the motet by Machaut (*c.* 1300) for flute (doubling piccolo), clarinet in C, violin, cello, glockenspiel and bells.
1969

31 *Medusa*. First version for flute (doubling piccolo), clarinet (doubling A clarinet and soprano saxophone), viola, cello (all amplified), piano (doubling celesta), percussion, two electronic tapes and shozyg. Second version for the same, with viola doubling violin and synthesiser replacing shozyg.
1969 (first version; withdrawn); 1970 (second version; withdrawn)

32 *Eight Lessons for Keyboards*. Eight musical objects with instructions on how they might be realised.
1970 (withdrawn)

33 *Signals* for clarinet and electronic sounds.
1970 (not published)

34 *Nenia: the Death of Orpheus* for soprano, three bass clarinets (1st doubling B♭ clarinet), piano (doubling prepared piano) and crotales.
1970

35 *Dinah and Nick's Love Song* for three melody instruments and harp. 1970

36 *Meridian* for mezzo-soprano, horn, cello, two three-part choirs of sopranos, three oboes (doubling cors anglais), three clarinets (doubling bass clarinets), two harps, piano and percussion (two players). 1971

37 *Prologue* for tenor, bassoon, horn, two trumpets, trombone, violin and double-bass. 1971

38 *An Imaginary Landscape* for four trumpets, four horns, three trombones, tuba, eight double-basses and percussion (four players). 1971

39 *The Fields of Sorrow* for two sopranos, chorus, three flutes, three cors anglais, three bass clarinets, three bassoons, horn, vibraphone and two pianos. 1971

40 *Tombeau in Memoriam Igor Stravinsky* for flute, clarinet, harp and string quartet. 1971

41 *Chronometer* for two asynchronous four-track tapes. 1972

42 *Epilogue* for baritone, horn, four trombones and six tam-tams (two players). 1972

43 *The Triumph of Time* for orchestra. 1972

44 *La Plage: Eight Arias of Remembrance* for soprano, three clarinets, piano and marimba. 1972

45 *Grimethorpe Aria* for brass band. 1973

46 *Chanson de Geste* for amplified sustaining instrument and pre-recorded tape. 1973 (withdrawn)

47 Five Chorale Preludes. An arrangement of five chorale preludes by J. S. Bach for soprano, clarinet, basset horn and bass clarinet. 1975

48 *Melencolia I* for solo clarinet in A, harp and two string orchestras. 1976

49 *For O, for O, the Hobby-Horse is Forgot.* A ceremony for six percussionists. 1976

50 *Silbury Air* for chamber ensemble. 1977

51 *Pulse Field (Frames, Pulses and Interruptions).* Ballet in collaboration with Jaap Flier for six dancers and nine musicians (three bass trombones, two amplified double-basses and percussion (four players)). 1977

52 *Bow Down.* Music theatre for five actors and four musicians (bamboo flute, bamboo pipes, oboes, penny whistles and percussion). 1977

53 *Carmen Arcadiae Mechanicae Perpetuum* for chamber ensemble. 1977

54 *...agm...* Music for sixteen voices and three instrumental groups. 1979

55 *Choral Fragments from ...agm...* for sixteen voices. 1979 (not published separately; discussed under 54)

56 *Mercure – poses plastiques.* An arrangement of Satie's ballet for chamber ensemble. 1980

57 *On the Sheer Threshold of the Night*.
    Madrigal for four solo voices and
    twelve-part chorus.
    1980
58 Clarinet Quintet.
    1980
59 *Pulse Sampler* for oboe and
    claves.
    1981
59a *The Oresteia*. Incidental music for
    National Theatre production.
    1981 (not published)
60 *The Mask of Orpheus*. A lyric tragedy
    in three acts, for solo voices, mime
    troupe, twelve-part chorus,
    orchestra (without strings) and pre-
    recorded tape.
    1983
61 *Duets for Storab* for two flutes.
    1983
62 *Deowa* for soprano and clarinet.
    1983
63 *Yan Tan Tethera*. A 'mechanical
    pastoral' in one act for solo voices, a
    chorus of thirteen sheep and
    chamber ensemble.
    1984
64 *Still Movement* for thirteen solo
    strings.
    1984
65 *Secret Theatre* for chamber
    ensemble.
    1984
66 *Songs by Myself* for soprano, flute
    (doubling alto flute), piano,
    vibraphone, violin, viola, cello and
    double-bass.
    1984
67 *Berceuse de Jeanne* for piano.
    1985
68 *Words Overheard* for soprano and
    chamber orchestra.
    1985
69 *Earth Dances* for orchestra.
    1986

70 *Hector's Dawn* for piano.
    1987
71 *Endless Parade* for trumpet,
    vibraphone and string orchestra.
    1987
72 *Fanfare for Will* for three trumpets,
    four horns, three trombones and
    tuba.
    1987
73 *Les Hoquets du Gardien de la Lune*.
    An arrangement of Machaut's
    Hoquetus David for orchestra.
    1987 (not published; discussed
    under 76)
74 *Four Songs of Autumn* for soprano
    and string quartet.
    1988
75 *An die Musik* for soprano, flute
    (doubling piccolo), oboe, clarinet,
    bassoon, percussion, two violins,
    viola, cello and double-bass.
    1988
76 *Machaut à ma manière*. An
    arrangement of *Fons tocius/O livoris
    feritas/Fera pessima, Hoquetus David*
    and an 'Amen' from *La Messe de
    Nostre Dame* by Machaut for
    orchestra.
    1988
77 *Salford Toccata* for brass band.
    1989
78 *White and Light* for soprano, two
    clarinets, viola, cello and double-
    bass.
    1989 (discussed under 99 and
    101)
79 *The Wine Merchant Robin of Mere*
    for male voice and piano.
    1989 (not published)
80 *Ritual Fragment* for chamber
    ensemble.
    1990
81 *Gawain*. Opera in two acts for solo
    voices, chorus and orchestra.
    1991

Bibliography

Short programme notes, newspaper interviews and reviews, and sleeve notes to recordings are not listed here.

Abbate, Carolyn. *Unsung Voices: Opera and Musical Narrative in the Nineteenth Century*. Princeton University Press, 1991.

Adlington, Robert. 'Musical temporality: perspectives from Adorno and de Man', *Repercussions*, 6/1 (1997).

   'Temporality in post-tonal music', D.Phil. thesis, University of Sussex (1997).

Adorno, Theodor. *Philosophy of Modern Music*, trans. Anne G. Mitchell and Wesley V. Blomster. London: Sheed and Ward, 1973.

   'The schema of mass culture', trans. Nicholas Walker, in J. M. Bernstein (ed.), *The Culture Industry: Selected Essays on Mass Culture*. London: Routledge, 1991, pp. 53–84.

   'Music and new music', in *Quasi una Fantasia: Essays on Modern Music*, trans. Rodney Livingstone. London: Verso, 1992, pp. 249–68.

   'Stravinsky: a dialectical portrait', in *Quasi una Fantasia: Essays on Modern Music*, trans. Rodney Livingstone. London: Verso, 1992, pp. 145–75.

   'Vers une musique informelle', in *Quasi una Fantasia: Essays on Modern Music*, trans. Rodney Livingstone. London: Verso, 1992, pp. 269–322.

Anderson, Warren D. *Music and Musicians in Ancient Greece*. Ithaca: Cornell University Press, 1994.

Aristotle. 'On the art of poetry [Poetics]', trans. T. S. Dorsch, in T. S. Dorsch (ed.), *Classical Literary Criticism*. Harmondsworth: Penguin, 1965, pp. 31–75.

Arnott, Peter D. *Public and Performance in the Greek Theatre*. London: Routledge, 1989.

Astley, Neil (ed.). *Tony Harrison*. Newcastle upon Tyne: Bloodaxe Books, 1991.

   'The Wizard of [Uz]: preface', in Neil Astley (ed.), *Tony Harrison*. Newcastle upon Tyne: Bloodaxe Books, 1991, pp. 10–13.

Banham, Martin (ed.). *The Cambridge Guide to Theatre*. Cambridge University Press, 1992.

Barry, Barbara. *Musical Time: The Sense of Order*. New York: Pendragon Press, 1990.

Beard, David. 'Birtwistle and serialism: *Three Sonatas for Nine Instruments*', unpublished paper delivered at Theory and Analysis Graduate Study Day, University of Oxford, 21 May 1998.

   'An analysis and sketch study of Harrison Birtwistle's early instrumental music (*c.* 1957–77)', D.Phil. Thesis, University of Oxford (1999).

Bell, Catherine. *Ritual Theory, Ritual Practice*. New York: Oxford University Press, 1992.

Benjamin, William E. 'A theory of musical metre', *Music Perception*, 1/4 (1984), pp. 355–413.

Berio, Luciano. *Two Interviews with Rossana Dalmonte and Balint Andras Varga*, trans. David Osmond-Smith. London: Marion Boyars, 1985.

Bernard, Jonathan W. *The Music of Edgard Varèse*. New Haven: Yale University Press, 1987.

Boulez, Pierre. *Stocktakings from an Apprenticeship*, trans. Stephen Walsh. Oxford: Clarendon Press, 1991.

Bowen, Meirion. 'Harrison Birtwistle', in Lewis Foreman (ed.), *British Music Now: A Guide to the Work of Younger Composers*. London: Elek, 1975, pp. 60–70.

Brackett, David. *Interpreting Popular Music*. Cambridge University Press, 1995.

Brandon, James R. 'Nō', in Martin Banham (ed.), *The Cambridge Guide to Theatre*. Cambridge University Press, 1992, pp. 716–17.

Brown, Andrew. 'Greece, ancient', in Martin Banham (ed.), *The Cambridge Guide to Theatre*. Cambridge University Press, 1992, pp. 407–12.

Brown, E. B. *The Poetical Works of Elizabeth Barrett Browning*. London: Smith, Elder, and Co., 1897.

Bruce, David. 'Challenging the system', *Musical Times* (April 1996), pp. 11–16.

Bye, Antony. 'Birtwistle's *Gawain*', *Musical Times* (May 1991), pp. 231–3.

Clements, Andrew. '*Gawain* – an opera about people', in *Opera* (August 1991), pp. 874–9.

  'Music theatre', in Stanley Sadie (ed.), *The New Grove Dictionary of Opera*, vol. III. London: Macmillan, 1992, pp. 529–30.

Clendenning, Jane Piper. 'The pattern-meccanico compositions of György Ligeti', *Perspectives of New Music*, 31/1 (1993), pp. 192–234.

Collier, John Payne. *Punch and Judy, with Illustrations Drawn and Engraved by George Cruikshank...*, second edition. London: S. Prowett, 1828.

Cone, Edward T. 'Stravinsky: the progress of a method', *Perspectives of New Music*, 1/1 (1962), pp. 18–26.

Cook, Nicholas. *Music: A Very Short Introduction*. Oxford University Press, 1998.

Cooke, Peter. 'Heterophony', in Stanley Sadie (ed.), *The New Grove Dictionary of Music and Musicians*, vol. VIII. London: Macmillan, 1980, pp. 537–8.

Cross, Jonathan. 'Issues of analysis in Birtwistle's *Four Songs of Autumn*', in Michael Finnissy and Roger Wright (eds.), *New Music '89*. Oxford University Press, 1989, pp. 16–23.

  'Lines and circles: on Birtwistle's *Punch and Judy* and *Secret Theatre*', *Music Analysis*, 13/2–3 (July–October 1994), pp. 203–25.

  'Music theory and the challenge of modern music: Birtwistle's *Refrains and Choruses*', in Anthony Pople (ed.), *Theory, Analysis and Meaning in Music*. Cambridge University Press, 1994, pp. 184–94.

  'From opera house to concert hall', *Tempo*, 192 (April 1995), p. 37.

  'Thoughts on first hearing Sir Harrison Birtwistle's *Panic*', *Tempo*, 195 (January 1996), pp. 34–5.

  'Birtwistle's secret theatres', in Craig Ayrey and Mark Everist (eds.), *Analytical*

Strategies and Musical Interpretation: Essays on Nineteenth- and Twentieth-Century Music. Cambridge University Press, 1996, pp. 207–25.

The Stravinsky Legacy. Cambridge University Press, 1998.

Crosse, Gordon. 'Birtwistle's *Punch and Judy*', *Tempo*, 85 (Summer 1968), pp. 24–6.

Cuddon, J. A. *The Penguin Dictionary of Literary Terms and Literary Theory*, third edition. London: Penguin, 1992.

Davidson, Michael. Review of Netherlands Opera Production of *Punch and Judy*, *Opera* (April 1993), pp. 465–6.

Deadman, Alison. 'Mechanical arcady: the development of an aesthetic in Birtwistle's orchestral works written for the London Sinfonietta between 1977 and 1984', M.Phil thesis, University of Leeds (1990).

Deliège, Célestin. 'The convergence of two poetic systems', in William Glock (ed.), *Pierre Boulez: A Symposium.* London: Eulenberg, 1986, pp. 99–126.

Dickinson, Peter. Review of *The World is Discovered, Musical Times* (November 1963), p. 808.

Drain, Richard (ed.). *Twentieth-Century Theatre: A Sourcebook.* London: Routledge, 1995.

Düchting, Hajo. *Paul Klee: Painting and Music.* Munich: Prestel, 1997.

Epstein, David. *Shaping Time: Music, the Brain, and Performance.* New York: Schirmer, 1995.

Fay, Stephen and Philip Oakes. 'Mystery behind the mask', in Neil Astley (ed.), *Tony Harrison.* Newcastle upon Tyne: Bloodaxe Books, 1991, pp. 287–90.

Ford, Andrew. *Composer to Composer: Conversations about Contemporary Music.* London: Quartet Books, 1993.

Gaskell, Ronald. *Drama and Reality: The European Theatre since Ibsen.* London: Routledge and Kegan Paul, 1972.

Grass, Günter. *From the Diary of a Snail*, trans. Ralph Manheim. London: Picador, 1989.

Graves, Robert. *Collected Poems 1975.* London: Cassell, 1975.

Green, A. E. 'Ritual', in Martin Banham (ed.), *The Cambridge Guide to Theatre.* Cambridge University Press, 1992, pp. 828–31.

Griffiths, Dai. 'Genre: grammar school boy music', *Critical Musicology Newsletter*, 3 (1995).

Review of Anne C. Shreffler, *Webern and the Lyric Impulse, Music Analysis*, 16/1 (1997), pp. 144–54.

'The high analysis of low music', *Music Analysis*, 18/3 (October 1999).

Griffiths, Paul. *Modern Music and After: Directions Since 1945.* Oxford University Press, 1995.

New Sounds, New Personalities: British Composers of the 1980s. London: Faber, 1985.

'The twentieth century: 1945 to the present day', in Roger Parker (ed.), *The Oxford History of Opera.* Oxford University Press, 1996, pp. 212–34.

Haffenden, John. 'Interview with Tony Harrison', in Neil Astley (ed.), *Tony Harrison.* Newcastle upon Tyne: Bloodaxe Books, 1991, pp. 227–46.

Hall, Michael. *Harrison Birtwistle*. London: Robson Books, 1984.
'Composer and producer speak', in programme booklet for English National Opera production of *The Mask of Orpheus*, May 1986.
'The sanctity of the context: Birtwistle's recent music', *Musical Times* (January 1988), pp. 14–16.
Harrison Birtwistle in Recent Years. London: Robson Books, 1998.

Halliwell, Stephen. *The* Poetics *of Aristotle: Translation and Commentary*. London: Duckworth, 1987.

Hamburger, Michael. 'Introduction', in Michael Hamburger (ed.), *Poems of Paul Celan*. London: Anvil Press Poetry, 1988, pp. 17–32.

Harrison, Tony. *Theatre Works 1973–1985*. Harmondsworth: Penguin, 1986.
'*The Oresteia* in the making: letters to Peter Hall', in Neil Astley (ed.), *Tony Harrison*. Newcastle upon Tyne: Bloodaxe Books, 1991, pp. 275–80.

Hartnoll, Phyllis (ed.). *The Oxford Companion to the Theatre*, third edition. Oxford University Press, 1967.

Hegel, G. W. F. *Phenomenology of Spirit*, trans. A. V. Miller. Oxford University Press, 1977.

Herbert, Jocelyn. 'Filling the space: working with Tony Harrison on *The Oresteia* and *The Trackers of Oxyrhynchus*', in Neil Astley (ed.), *Tony Harrison*. Newcastle upon Tyne: Bloodaxe Books, 1991, pp. 281–6.

Hewett, Ivan. 'The second coming', *Musical Times* (January 1995), pp. 46–7.

Hoban, Russell. *The Second Mrs Kong: an Original Opera Text*. London: Universal Edition, 1994.

Hoggart, Richard. 'In conversation with Tony Harrison', in Neil Astley (ed.), *Tony Harrison*. Newcastle upon Tyne: Bloodaxe Books, 1991, pp. 36–45.

Holden, Amanda (ed.). *The Penguin Opera Guide*. Harmondsworth: Viking, 1995.
'Harrison Birtwistle: *The Second Mrs Kong*', in Holden (ed.), *The Penguin Opera Guide*. Harmondsworth: Viking, 1995, p. 42.

Hopkins, G. W. 'Stockhausen', in Stanley Sadie (ed.), *The New Grove Dictionary of Music and Musicians*, vol. XVIII. London: Macmillan, 1980, pp. 151–9.

Hoppin, R. H. *Medieval Music*. New York: Norton, 1978.

Josipovici, Gabriel. *The Lessons of Modernism and Other Essays*. London: Macmillan, 1977.

Keller, Hans. 'Metrical rhythms', *The Listener* (3 September 1981), pp. 251–2.

Kirkpatrick, Kirsty. 'Perceived structure in Debussy's *Jeux*: an empirical investigation', unpublished paper, Lancaster University (1994).

Klee, Paul. *Notebooks: The Thinking Eye,* ed. Jürg Spiller. London: Lund Humphries, 1961.
Pedagogical Sketchbook, trans. Sibyl Moholy-Nagy. London: Faber and Faber, 1968.

Kramer, Jonathan D. *The Time of Music: New Meanings, New Temporalities, New Listening Strategies*. New York: Schirmer Books, 1988.

Kramer, Lawrence. *Music and Poetry: The Nineteenth Century and After*. Berkeley: University of California Press, 1984.

Classical Music and Postmodern Knowledge. Berkeley: University of California Press, 1995.

Lebrecht, Norman. 'Music that makes a stand: Norman Lebrecht talks to Harrison Birtwistle', *ENO and Friends*, 10 (Summer 1986), pp. 8–10.

Levi, Peter. 'Tony Harrison's dramatic verse', in Neil Astley (ed.), *Tony Harrison.* Newcastle upon Tyne: Bloodaxe Books, 1991, pp. 158–66.

Levy, Edward. 'Text setting and usage', in John Vinton (ed.), *Dictionary of Twentieth-Century Music.* London: Thames and Hudson, 1974.

Lewis, Peter. *The National: A Dream Made Concrete.* London: Methuen, 1990.

Ley, Graham. *A Short Introduction to the Ancient Greek Theater.* University of Chicago Press, 1991.

Lindley, David. *Lyric.* London: Methuen, 1985.

Lorraine, Ross. 'Territorial rites 1', *Musical Times* (October 1997), pp. 4–8.
  'Territorial rites 2', *Musical Times* (November 1997), pp. 12–16.

Magee, Bryan. *Aspects of Wagner.* London: Panther, 1972.

Maus, Fred Everett. 'Music as drama', *Music Theory Spectrum*, 10 (1988), pp. 56–73.

McClary, Susan. 'Terminal prestige: the case of avant-garde music composition', *Cultural Critique*, 12 (Spring 1989), pp. 57–81.

Middleton, Richard. *Studying Popular Music.* Milton Keynes: Open University Press, 1990.

Murray, Oswyn. 'Tony Harrison: Poetry and the Theatre', in Neil Astley (ed.), *Tony Harrison.* Newcastle upon Tyne: Bloodaxe Books, 1991, pp. 262–74.

Nattiez, Jean-Jacques. *Music and Discourse: Toward a Semiology of Music*, trans. Carolyn Abbate. Princeton University Press, 1990.

Newton, Isaac. *Sir Isaac Newton's Mathematical Principles of Natural Philosophy and his System of the World*, trans. F. Cajori. Berkeley: University of California Press, 1962.

Nyman, Michael. 'Harrison Birtwistle's "Punch and Judy"', *The Listener* (10 October 1968), p. 481.
  'Two new works by Birtwistle', *Tempo*, 88 (1969), pp. 47–50.
  'Mr Birtwistle is out', *Music and Musicians* (November 1969), pp. 27, 78.
  'With reference to Birtwistle's "Medusa"', *The Listener* (13 November 1969), p. 676.
  'Birtwistle's rituals', *The Listener* (27 August 1970), p. 285.
  'Harrison Birtwistle', *London Magazine*, 11/4 (October–November 1971), pp. 118–22.

Osmond-Smith, David. *Berio.* Oxford University Press, 1991.

Ovid. *Metamorphoses I–IV*, trans. D. E. Hill. Warminster: Aris and Phillips, 1985.

Pattman, R. 'Commitments to time in Reformation Protestant theology, Hegelian Idealism, and Marxism', in B. Cullen (ed.), *Hegel Today.* Aldershot: Avebury Press, 1988, pp. 102–15.

Perkins, Leeman L. 'Ockeghem, Johannes', in Stanley Sadie (ed.), *The New Grove Dictionary of Music and Musicians*, vol. XIII. London: Macmillan, 1980, pp. 489–96.

Porter, Andrew. 'Another Orpheus sings', *New Yorker* (23 June 1986), pp. 84–8.

Potter, John. 'Reconstructing lost voices', in Tess Knighton and David Fallows (eds.), *Companion to Medieval and Renaissance Music*. London: Dent, 1992, pp. 311–16.

Pruslin, Stephen. 'Second Taverner Fantasia', in Stephen Pruslin (ed.), *Peter Maxwell Davies: Studies from Two Decades*. London: Boosey and Hawkes, 1979, pp. 26–35.

Reese, Gustave. *Music in the Renaissance*, revised edition. London: Dent and Sons Ltd, 1959.

Rehding, Alexander. 'Towards a "logic of discontinuity" in Stravinsky's *Symphonies of Wind Instruments*: Hasty, Kramer and Straus reconsidered', *Music Analysis*, 17/1 (1998), pp. 39–65.

Robbe-Grillet, Alain. 'La Plage', in *Instantanés*. Paris: Les Editions de Minuit, 1962, pp. 61–73.

Robison, Brian. '*Carmen arcadiae mechanicae perpetuum*: toward a methodology for analyzing Harrison Birtwistle's music since 1977', Doctor of Musical Arts thesis, Cornell University (1999).

Rochberg, George. 'The structure of time in music: traditional and contemporary ramifications and consequences', in J. T. Fraser and N. Lawrence (eds.), *The Study of Time II*. Berlin: Springer-Verlag, 1975, pp. 136–49.

Sadie, Stanley (ed.). *The New Grove Dictionary of Opera*, four volumes. London: Macmillan, 1992.

Samuel, Rhian. 'Gawain's musical journey', in programme boklet for Royal Opera House production of *Gawain* (April 1994), pp. 21–5.

Samuels, Robert. 'Music as text: Mahler, Schumann and issues in analysis', in Anthony Pople (ed.), *Theory, Analysis and Meaning in Music*. Cambridge University Press, 1994, pp. 152–63.

Sanders, Elma. 'Frieze', in Jane Turner (ed.), *The Dictionary of Art*, vol. XI. London: Macmillan, 1996, pp. 790–2.

Schechner, Richard. *The Future of Ritual: Writings on Culture and Performance*. London: Routledge, 1993.

Schering, Arnold (ed.). *Geschichte der Musik in Beispielen: Dreihundertfünfzig Tonsätze aus Neun Jahrhunderten*. Leipzig: Breitkopf und Härtel, 1931.

Schiff, David. *The Music of Elliott Carter*. London: Eulenberg Books, 1983.

Shreffler, Anne C. *Webern and the Lyric Impulse: Songs and Fragments on Poems of Georg Trakl*. Oxford: Clarendon Press, 1994.

Small, Christopher. 'Performance as ritual: sketch for an enquiry into the true nature of a symphony concert', in Avron Levine White (ed.), *Lost in Music: Culture, Style and the Musical Event*. London: Routledge, 1987, pp. 6–32.

Smalley, Roger. 'Birtwistle's *Nomos*', *Tempo*, 86 (1968), pp. 7–10.

Sturrock, John. 'Introduction', in John Sturrock (ed.), *Structuralism and Since: From Levi-Strauss to Derrida*. Oxford University Press, 1979, p. 10.

Sutcliffe, Tom. Review of Glyndebourne production of *The Second Mrs Kong*, *Musical Times* (July 1995), pp. 373–5.

Sylvester, David. *The Brutality of Fact: Interviews with Francis Bacon,* third, enlarged, edition. London: Thames and Hudson, 1987.

Tagg, Philip. *Kojak – 50 Seconds of Television Music: Towards the Analysis of Affect in Popular Music.* University of Gothenburg, 1979.

'From refrain to rave: the decline of figure and the rise of ground', in *Popular Music,* 13/2 (March 1994), pp. 209–22.

Taruskin, Richard. *Stravinsky and the Russian Traditions: A Biography of the Works Throuth Mavra,* two volumes. Oxford University Press, 1996.

Taylor, Michael. 'Birtwistle's first *The Triumph of Time'*, *Mitteilung der Paul Sacher Stiftung,* 8 (March 1995), pp. 17–21.

'Harrison Birtwistle: *Endless Parade* (1986–87)', in Felix Meyer (ed.), *Settling New Scores: Music Manuscripts from the Paul Sacher Foundation.* Basel: Paul Sacher Foundation, 1998, pp. 41–3.

Varèse, Edgard. 'The liberation of sound', in Benjamin Boretz and Edward T. Cone (eds.), *Perspectives on American Composers.* New York: Norton, 1971, pp. 25–33.

Waddell, Helen. *Mediaeval Latin Lyrics,* fifth edition. London: Constable, 1948.

Walsh, Stephen. 'Harrison Birtwistle', in Stanley Sadie (ed.), *The New Grove Dictionary of Music and Musicians,* vol. II. London: Macmillan, 1980, pp. 737–9.

Webern, Anton. *Letters to Hildegard Jone and Josef Humplik,* ed. Josef Polnauer, trans. Cornelius Cardew. London: Universal, 1967.

Westrup, Jack, et al. 'Aria', in Stanley Sadie (ed.), *The New Grove Dictionary of Music and Musicians,* vol. I. London: Macmillan, 1980, pp. 573–9.

Whittall, Arnold. Review of *Melencolia I, Music and Letters,* 59/1 (1978), pp. 110–11.

Review of *Meridian* and *Songs by Myself, Music and Letters,* 69/3 (1988), pp. 449–50.

Music Since the First World War, second edition. London: Dent, 1988.

'Comparatively complex: Birtwistle, Maxwell Davies and modernist analysis', *Music Analysis,* 13/2–3 (1994), pp. 139–59.

'Modernist aesthetics, modernist music: some analytical perspectives', in James M. Baker et al. (eds.), *Music Theory in Concept and Practice.* Rochester, New York: University of Rochester Press, 1997, pp. 157–80.

Wintle, Christopher. 'Webern's lyric character', in Kathryn Bailey (ed.), *Webern Studies.* Cambridge University Press, 1996, pp. 229–63.

'A fine and private place', *Musical Times* (November 1996), pp. 5–8.

Zenck, Martin. 'Tradition as authority and provocation: Anton Webern's confrontation with Johann Sebastian Bach', in Don O. Franklin, ed., *Bach Studies.* Cambridge University Press, 1989, pp. 297–322.

Zinovieff, Peter. *The Mask of Orpheus: An Opera in Three Acts.* London: Universal Edition, 1986.

The Mask of Orpheus: Libretto. Included with compact-disc recording of *The Mask of Orpheus* (1997), NMC Recordings: NMC D050.

Index of works

The main discussions of each piece are indicated in bold type. Numbers in brackets refer to the 'Chronological list of works'.

General index

academia 2–3
Adorno, Theodor W. 195–6
  on instruments 40
  on primitivism 32, 203 n. 118
  on time 99, 210 n. 9, 210 n. 10
  on violence 8
  Philosophy of Modern Music 32
Aeschylus
  Agamemnon 83
  The Oresteia 13, 23–4
agency 39, 62
  ambiguity of 48, 53–7, 59, 60
  in Klee 158
  melody as symbolic of 158, 161–3
  in narrative 146
aleatoricism 57, 186–8
Anderson, Barry 20
Andriessen, Louis
  De Staat 87
  De Tijd 87
aria (*see* 'recitative')
Aristophanes 11
Aristotle 8
  on 'catharsis' 10
  on character 56
  on music 38
  on tragedy 41–2, 126
  on tragedy and comedy 11
  Poetics 11, 38, 41
Artaud, Antonin 31
audiences 3, 152, 189, 190–7
Ausonius 81
avant-garde music 38, 97, 122, 127, 164
  and communication 195–6
  and expression 6–7
  and time 211 n. 30

Babbitt, Milton 68, 73
Bach, J. S. 164–8
  chorale harmonisations 165, 166–7
  chorale preludes 166–7

Klee analysis of Sonata for Violin and
  Harpsichord, BWV 1019 178–9
'Meine Seele erhebt den Herren'
  165
Orgel-Büchlein 166
'Ricercar' from *The Musical Offering*
  165–6
Bacon, Francis
  on chance 195
  on realism 37
  on violence 9
Ballet Rambert 51, 105
Barbican Centre (London) 191
Barnes, Djuna 56
Beard, David 57
Bedford, David 33
Bell, Catherine 33
Berg, Alban
  Lulu 209 n. 53
  Wozzeck 11
Berio, Luciano 68
  on syllabicism 69
  Circles 48, 73
  O King 80
Berlin Philharmonic Orchestra 190
Berlioz, Hector 5
Bernard, Jonathan 178, 217 n. 68
Berners, Lord 33
Blake, William 186
block form 30, 121–55, 212 n. 2
  and continuity 142–55
  and interruption 133–42
  and repetition 122–33
Boethius 72–3
Boulez, Pierre 175
  on text-setting 94
  Domaines 48
  Improvisation sur Mallarmé I 94
  Le marteau sans maître 74, 132
  Rituel: in memoriam Bruno Maderna 32,
  122